"Bridging the existing and often wide gap between high quality, relevant research and public policy development and implementation is more critical today than ever before. Jenni W. Owen and Anita M. Larson have shown us the way in this book. The insightful, clear case studies coupled with Owen's and Larson's thoughtful, creative recommendations for and approaches to informing policymaking with research are extremely valuable. Their coherent and beneficial treatment of this topic adds significantly to the fast-emerging world of researcher–policymaker partnerships."

Thomas W. Ross, *President of the Volcker Alliance and President Emeritus of the University of North Carolina, USA*

"In a time when researcher–policymaker partnerships are essential, this book provides helpful insights into strategies that are successfully addressing the struggles that current collaborators are experiencing. The examples illustrate dynamic relationships and the potential opportunities for successful collaborative practices. Jenni W. Owen and Anita M. Larson capture the reality that policymakers need data to inform decisions, ultimately providing a solution through broad value to federal, state, and local partnerships. This is a critical read for any researcher–policymaker collaboration."

Missy Coffey, *Applied Engineering and Management Corporation, USA*

Researcher–Policymaker Partnerships

Gone are the days when researchers, policymakers and practitioners each worked in isolation. In recent years, a few interrelated issues have emphasized the need for greater collaboration among these groups: the increased emphasis on results and accountability (particularly where public funds are at stake), the need to improve services and the growing use of technology. This book is about these all-important partnerships, specifically the relationships between those searching for evidence and those putting evidence to use, designing and implementing policy at the federal, state, or local level.

Yet the science or art of how to create partnerships and how to make them work has just begun. This book offers the reader a toolkit for effective researcher–policymaker collaborations by exploring innovations underway around the country and developing an analytic framework to describe the process. It asks questions such as: What can we learn from these examples? How can and should partners communicate? Where should partners plan together, and where is it best to leave some separation to respect the differences in our roles? Through carefully chosen and organized case studies, this book demonstrates the motivations that lead to partnerships, the core elements of successful implementation and the lessons to be learned about sustaining these relationships. It further examines the use of research once the research phase has concluded, as well as the ever-important consideration of investing in collaboration by both nonprofit and public-sector funders.

For policymakers, this book offers a greater appreciation of the role of research in the policy process and new insights into different types of research. For researchers, the book provides insights into how best to formulate questions, how to work closely with those most affected and how to communicate findings in ways that can be more easily understood by those who are depending on clear answers. Students of public policy, public administration, social work and education will find much to inform future roles in research, policy, or practice.

Jenni W. Owen is Policy Director for North Carolina Governor Roy Cooper. She is on leave from Duke University's Sanford School of Public Policy where she is a senior lecturer and the Director of Policy Engagement.

Anita M. Larson teaches in the Public Administration program at Hamline University in Saint Paul, Minnesota, USA.

American Society for Public Administration
Series in Public Administration & Public Policy
David H. Rosenbloom, Ph.D.
Editor-in-Chief

Mission: Throughout its history, ASPA has sought to be true to its founding principles of promoting scholarship and professionalism within the public service. The ASPA Book Series on Public Administration and Public Policy publishes books that increase national and international interest for public administration and which discuss practical or cutting edge topics in engaging ways of interest to practitioners, policy makers, and those concerned with bringing scholarship to the practice of public administration.

Recent Publications

The Handbook of Federal Government Leadership and Administration
Transforming, Performing, and Innovating in a Complex World
Edited by David H. Rosenbloom, Patrick S. Malone, and Bill Valdez

Managing Digital Governance
Issues, Challenges, and Solutions
Yu-Che Chen

The Future of Disaster Management in the US
Rethinking Legislation, Policy, and Finance
Edited by Amy LePore

Case Studies in Disaster Response and Emergency Management, Second Edition
Nicolas A. Valcik and Paul E. Tracy

Researcher–Policymaker Partnerships
Strategies for Launching and Sustaining Successful Collaborations
Edited by Jenni W. Owen and Anita M. Larson

Advances in E-Governance
Theory and Application of Technological Initiatives
Anthony Trotta

Researcher–Policymaker Partnerships

Strategies for Launching and Sustaining Successful Collaborations

Edited by
Jenni W. Owen and Anita M. Larson

Routledge
Taylor & Francis Group

LONDON AND NEW YORK

First published 2017 by Routledge
2 Park Square, Milton Park, Abingdon, Oxon OX14 4RN
605 Third Avenue, New York, NY 10017

First issued in paperback 2021

Routledge is an imprint of the Taylor & Francis Group, an informa business

© 2017 Taylor & Francis

Publisher's Note
The publisher has gone to great lengths to ensure the quality of this reprint but points out that some imperfections in the original copies may be apparent.

Library of Congress Cataloging-in-Publication Data
Names: Owen, Jenni W., editor. | Larson, Anita M., 1965- editor.
Title: Researcher-policymaker partnerships : strategies for launching and sustaining successful collaborations / edited by Jenni W. Owen and Anita M. Larson.
Description: New York : Routledge, [2017] | Includes bibliographical references and index.
Identifiers: LCCN 2016048451 | ISBN 9781498735216 (hbk : alk. paper) | ISBN 9781315212722 (ebk)
Subjects: LCSH: Policy sciences—Research. | Political planning—Research.
Classification: LCC H97 .R482 2017 | DDC 320.6072—dc23
LC record available at https://lccn.loc.gov/2016048451

ISBN 13: 978-1-03-209671-1 (pbk)
ISBN 13: 978-1-4987-3521-6 (hbk)

Typeset in Sabon
by Apex CoVantage, LLC

We dedicate this book to the policymakers and researchers who are partnering today, to those who are considering forming partnerships and to students across disciplines—may they bring the spirit and practice of partnership with them into all of their future roles.

Contents

Illustrations and Tables

Figures

Tables

About the Editors

Jenni W. Owen is Policy Director for North Carolina Governor Roy Cooper on leave from Duke University's Sanford School of Public Policy where she is a Senior Lecturer and the Director of Policy Engagement. She has held prior roles in the executive and legislative branches of government at the state and federal levels, respectively. She has a longtime passion for cross-sector interaction and partnership and has served on multiple public and non-profit boards, including the North Carolina Indigent Defense Services Commission and the Association for Public Policy Analysis and Management Policy Council.

Anita M. Larson teaches in the Public Administration program at Hamline University in Saint Paul, Minnesota, USA, and has worked over 25 years in a variety of direct service, planning and evaluation and data and measurement positions in local and state government. Her recent work has included the implementation of two federal grants: Race to the Top and Institute of Education Sciences (IES).

About the Case Authors

Jon Baron is the Vice President of Evidence-Based Policy at the Laura and John Arnold Foundation—a nonprofit philanthropic foundation. He leads the foundation's strategic investments in rigorous research aimed at growing the body of evidence-based social programs and scaling those shown to produce meaningful improvements in people's lives. Mr. Baron is the founder and former president of the Coalition for Evidence-Based Policy, a nonprofit, nonpartisan organization that worked with federal policy officials from 2001 to 2015 to advance important evidence-based reforms, many of which were enacted into law and policy. He was twice nominated by the president and confirmed by the Senate to serve on the National Board for Education Sciences (2004–2011), and was the board's chairman during the last year of his term. He has also served on the National Academy of Sciences' Committee on Capitalizing on Science, Technology, and Innovation, and is a Fellow of the National Academy of Public Administration, an Honorary Fellow of the Academy of Experimental Criminology and a recipient of the Society for Prevention Research's Public Service Award. Mr. Baron's earlier positions include executive director of the Presidential Commission on Offsets in International Trade, Program Manager for the Defense Department's Small Business Innovation Research program and Counsel to the House of Representatives Committee on Small Business. Mr. Baron holds a law degree from Yale Law School, a master's degree in Public Affairs from Princeton University and a bachelor of arts degree from Rice University. His case study with Kathy Stack is based on an interview.

Peter Bell is the director of San Diego Unified School District's Data Analysis and Reporting Department, overseeing a large array of data gathering, statistical analysis and reporting for the district, including extensive large-scale mandated federal and state reporting. For years he directed district review of proposals to conduct research within the district by outside researchers and coordinated efforts to provide approved researchers needed district data, as well as for a broad range of ad hoc and recurring data for requests and reporting needs within and outside the district. Prior to working in the district, he conducted ethnographic research on collective farming in rural Communist Hungary and published a book and articles on that work. He holds a PhD in Cultural Anthropology from the University of California, San Diego.

Julian R. Betts is a professor and former chair of economics at the University of California, San Diego, where he is executive director of the San Diego Education Research Alliance (sandera.ucsd.edu). He is also an adjunct fellow at the Public Policy Institute of California (PPIC) and a research associate at the National Bureau of Economic Research. He has written extensively on the link between student outcomes and measures of school spending and has studied the role that educational standards, accountability, teacher qualifications and school choice play in student achievement. He has served on three National Academy of Sciences panels, the Consensus Panel of the National Charter School Research Project and various advisory groups for the U.S. Department of Education. He is also co-principal investigator for the federal evaluation of the D.C. Opportunity Scholarship Program. He holds a PhD in economics from Queen's University, Kingston, Ontario, Canada.

Karen Bogenschneider is a Rothermel-Bascom Professor of Human Ecology at the University of Wisconsin-Madison. Since its inception in 1992 through 2016, Dr. Bogenschneider served as director of the Wisconsin Family Impact Seminars—a series of presentations, briefing reports and discussion sessions that communicate research-based, family-focused information to state policymakers on timely topics they identify. From 1999 to 2014, she served as Executive Director and is currently Research Director of the Family Impact Institute that provides training and technical assistance to about two dozen states that have conducted over 200 Family Impact Seminars. Prof. Bogenschneider's book, *Family Policy Matters: How Policymaking Affects Families and What Professionals Can Do*, is in its third edition. A second edition has been requested of her book co-authored with Thomas Corbett, *Evidence-Based Policymaking: Insights from Policy-Minded Researchers and Research-Minded Policymakers*. Dr. Bogenschneider was invited to write the family policy decade reviews in 2000 and 2010 for the leading family science journal. In 2014, she gave invited addresses at the United Nations in Geneva and New York on using research to build better public policy for families. She holds a named professorship at the University of Wisconsin-Madison. She has received several awards for her research and outreach, including being named a fellow and receiving the President's Award from the National Council on Family Relations. She received the Engagement Award from the Board of Human Sciences of the Association of Public and Land-Grant Universities. She currently serves on a National Academy of Science Panel on the application of social and behavioral science research.

Randal Brown is a doctoral candidate in interdisciplinary social psychology at the University of Nevada, Reno. He enjoys working with the Washoe County School District developing and testing social and emotional learning (SEL) measurement tools. Randal's research projects center around the development and maintenance of healthy relationships. As such, he serves as a liaison to the advisory board for the sexual health education program in the local school district. Additionally, Randal specializes in human sexuality and communication within romantic relationships. His research has been presented at the International Association for Relationship Research and the Society for the Scientific Study of Sexuality, among others.

Ann McKay Bryson is a social and emotional learning (SEL) professional development specialist for the Collaborative for Academic, Social and Emotional Learning (CASEL). In her CASEL role, Ann works with the Oakland Unified School District in California, the Anchorage School District in Alaska and the Washoe County School District in Nevada to build their capacity to systematically implement SEL for adults and P–12 students. She has been a member of research teams at CASEL, focusing on SEL competence assessment and integration of SEL into academic instruction.

Ann is the co-author of the Devereux Student Strength Assessment (DESSA) Strategy Guide. Her professional learning focus areas include strengthening adult SEL skills; building and supporting trauma-informed educational communities; expanding SEL development in classrooms, school sites and at the district level; and leveraging formative and summative assessments for developing student capacity.

In her thirty-two years with the Anchorage School District, Ann followed two decades as a classroom and special education teacher at both the elementary and secondary levels with twelve years of facilitating SEL professional development for teachers, administrators and school staffs.

Ann served as an Adjunct at University of Alaska, Anchorage, with courses including SEL Professional Inquiry, SEL-Based Principal Leadership, Mentoring and Induction and Trauma-Aware Effective Teaching Practices. She served two terms as National Writing Project Board Chair for the Alaska State Writing Consortium. Ann develops and facilitates SEL professional learning for schools and youth-serving agencies across the country and has presented at national conferences, including AERA (2008, 2010, 2014) and Learning Forward (2014, 2015, 2016).

Karen Cadigan is an education innovator focused on improving the lives and outcomes of young children and their families, especially those at risk. She is known for bringing together disparate people and ideas to improve systems to this end and currently works as an early childhood coordinator for the Bloomington-Richfield Public Schools. Dr. Cadigan is a nationally certified school psychologist and worked from 1995–2002 in public schools in Virginia and Minnesota. From 2002–2011 she served as a research assistant, lecturer and policy director at the University of Minnesota, Twin Cities. During this time she directed the Family Impact Seminars, connecting state legislators to research, and was the idea originator and co-principal investigator of the National Science Foundation–funded *Wonder Years: The Science of Early Development* exhibition at the Science Museum of Minnesota. In 2011 Dr. Cadigan was appointed the founding director of the Minnesota state Office of Early Learning where she, along with counterparts in other state agencies, led the cross-agency team that wrote, earned and implemented Minnesota's $45 million Race to the Top Early Learning Challenge grant. In addition to earning a PhD from the University of Minnesota, Cadigan is a 1973 graduate of Arrowhead Head Start.

Heidi Carter was elected to the Durham Board of County Commissioners and will begin her term in December 2016. Previously, she has been a member of the Durham Public Schools (DPS) Board of Education from 2004–2012, where she served as Board Chair for four years. She has also been active on numerous community committees, including the Durham County Board of Health, Student U Board of Directors, Youth Council of the Workforce Development Board, Partnership for a Healthy Durham, YMCA Board of Directors, Mayor's Poverty Reduction Initiative Health Task Force, Gang Reduction Steering Committee, DPS School Health Advisory Council and Friends of the DPS Hub Farm. Heidi has worked as a research scientist, medical assistant and substitute teacher. While her children were in school, she was a steady volunteer for DPS, including PTA president and School Improvement Team leadership. Heidi holds an MPH from the UNC Gillings School of Global Public Health, an MS in Medicinal Chemistry from UNC and a BS in Biology from Duke University. She is married to Scott Carter, an electrical engineer at Lenovo. She and Scott have lived in Durham since 1979, and they have four children, all graduates of DPS. For fun, Heidi likes to read, cook, bike and run.

Gabriella Celeste, JD, is Policy Director at Case Western Reserve University's Schubert Center for Child Studies. She works with fellow staff to identify and implement strategies that bridge child-related research, education, policy and practice, and to enhance community partnerships that promote effective public policy and practice for the well-being of children. She also teaches child policy curriculum and supervises Schubert's child policy externship program. Celeste has worked extensively with vulnerable children in various nonprofit and administrative roles, both directly and conducting applied research, evaluation and technical assistance for foundations, nonprofit and government agencies. She co-founded the Juvenile Justice Project of Louisiana in 1997, a nonprofit law practice that became a premier statewide legal reform organization, and currently sits on the Ohio Public Defender Commission, Cuyahoga County "Defending Childhood" Governing Board and on the Board of Directors for Magnolia Clubhouse. She received her BS from Northwestern University and JD from the University of Michigan Law School.

Carrie Conaway is the chief strategy and planning officer for the Massachusetts Department of Elementary and Secondary Education. She manages a team of analysts responsible for providing analysis, research, planning and implementation support and tools so that the agency and the field can implement effective programs and improve educational outcomes. She has served as the agency's lead or principal investigator on numerous evaluations of state education programs and policy and has published two peer-reviewed articles on connecting research to practice. Her team also led the development of the state's top-scoring, $250 million Race to the Top proposal and managed its implementation. Previously she was the deputy director of the New England Public Policy Center at the Federal Reserve Bank of Boston and an associate editor of the bank's flagship publication, *Regional Review*. She holds a bachelor's degree in sociology from Oberlin College; a master's degree in policy analysis and labor policy from the Humphrey Institute of Public Affairs, University of Minnesota; and a master's degree in sociology and social policy from Harvard University.

Marisa Crowder is presently a doctoral candidate in the Interdisciplinary Social Psychology PhD Program at the University of Nevada, Reno. Her research interests include examining cultural differences in emotions, particularly the self-conscious emotions, and their consequences. More specifically, she is interested in the factors that lead individuals to overcome the shame of failure when quite often this experience leads individuals to withdraw or disengage. Eventually, she would like to investigate how students' social and emotional skills moderate the impact of certain academic setbacks and allow them to persist in the face of intrapersonal and interpersonal obstacles.

Laura Davidson is the Director of Research and Evaluation for the Washoe County School District (WCSD). She coordinates the major research and evaluation efforts of the district, including WCSD's annual Staff, Parent, and Student School Climate Surveys, and supporting and designing evaluations for a wide range of district projects, including Social and Emotional Learning, Special Education Services, Multi-Tiered Systems of Support (MTSS), and Common Core State Standards implementation, among other district initiatives. Prior to her current position,

Laura worked as an independent evaluator while completing her PhD in Social Psychology at the University of Nevada, Reno. Dr. Davidson's research interests primarily focus on factors that promote adolescent resilience, including (1) identifying core competencies of staff that promote positive youth development in out-of-school-time program settings, (2) examining the interaction of risk and protective factors for recidivism among youth in juvenile detention settings and (3) evaluating intervention programs designed to increase youth's help-seeking behavior during emotional crises.

Celene E. Domitrovich is an Associate Research Professor in the Department of Psychiatry at Georgetown University and a member of the research faculty at the Prevention Research Center at Penn State University. Most recently, before coming to Georgetown, Dr. Domitrovich was the Vice President for Research at the Collaborative for Academic, Social, and Emotional Learning (CASEL) and now serves as a Senior Research Scientist with that organization. Dr. Domitrovich is the developer of the preschool version of the Promoting Alternative Thinking Strategies (PATHS) Curriculum. She has conducted randomized trials of this and several other SEL programs that are designed for students from preschool through middle school. Dr. Domitrovich is interested in the development of integrated intervention models and understanding the factors that promote high-quality implementation of evidence-based interventions. She has published numerous articles in peer-reviewed journal articles and written several federal reports on evidence-based interventions and implementation. Dr. Domitrovich served two terms on the board of the Society for Prevention Research and received the CASEL Joseph E. Zins award in 2011 for Action Research in Social Emotional Learning.

Kathie Doty directs the Hennepin-University Partnership, an innovative program created to build bridges and on-going connections between Minnesota's largest unit of local government, Hennepin County, and Minnesota's premier public research institution, the University of Minnesota. In this capacity, Ms. Doty led the launch of the partnership in 2005 and subsequently has overseen the development of this program into an award-winning model for collaboration between local government and academia. Ms. Doty's previous experience includes advancing through progressively responsible management positions at Hennepin County in the areas of financial and strategic planning and program design. She subsequently gained significant experience in the private sector when recruited to join a Twin Cities public policy consulting firm as a senior associate. She holds a master's of Business Administration from the University of St. Thomas and a bachelor of arts from the University of Minnesota. In addition, she has advanced training in project management and risk analysis from the University of Minnesota Carlson School of Management, and Charrette System training from the Harvard Graduate School of Design. In addition to her leadership role with the Hennepin-University Partnership, she continues to provide project management services for communications and public outreach projects/programs, policy analysis for intergovernmental and agency collaborations and strategic planning services to clients involved in public works, environmental and transportation projects.

Stephanie Eddy received her BA in Psychology from Wheaton College (1999) and MA in Ecological-Community Psychology from Michigan State University (2002). She has worked in the Wisconsin state legislature and contributed significantly to both the Michigan and Wisconsin Family Impact Seminar programs, filling multiples roles including coordinator, evaluator and consultant. She has consulted with the Family Impact Institute, participated in training more than twelve states to begin their own seminars and provided on-site consulting assistance to three of those states.

Annalee Good (PhD, University of Wisconsin-Madison) is a researcher at the Wisconsin Center for Education Research and co-director of the Wisconsin Evaluation Collaborative. Her current projects include studies of digital tools in K–12 supplemental education, academic tutoring partnerships and the challenges of instruction and assessment for advanced learners. She has published and presented numerous papers on topics including public contracting for digital instructional tools, the nature of the instructional landscape in out-of-school-time tutoring, the role of tutoring in school reform and the role of K–12 teachers in the creation of public policy. She was a classroom teacher before earning her master's and doctoral degrees in Educational Policy Studies from UW-Madison, and continues to teach online courses for middle school students in Wisconsin.

Rachel A. Gordon is Professor in the Department of Sociology and Institute of Government and Public Affairs at the University of Illinois at Chicago. Gordon's research broadly aims to measure and model the contexts of children's and families' lives, often using longitudinal data sets. She has examined numerous contextual and social factors that affect children and families, including the use of child care and preschool quality measures for high-stakes policy purposes, the health outcomes of child care and maternal employment, the implications of teenagers' looks for their social and academic achievement, the association between community context and child well-being, the relationships between youth gang participation and delinquency, the causes and consequences of grandmother co-residential support for young mothers and the evaluation of an innovative job program for young couples. She is the author of two textbooks (*Regression Analysis for the Social*

Sciences and *Applied Statistics for the Social and Health Sciences*) and has published her research in leading academic journals, including the *American Journal of Evaluation, Child Development, Criminology, Demography, Developmental Psychology, Early Childhood Research Quarterly, Journal of Marriage and Family,* and *Journal of Research on Adolescence.* Throughout her career, Gordon has worked at the intersection of academic research and social policy, including a decade spent directing the Illinois Family Impact Seminars. She has been the principal investigator on multiple grants from the National Institutes of Health (NIH) and Institute of Education Sciences (IES), including for her recent research examining the psychometric properties of widely used measures of preschool and child care quality such as the ECERS-R and CLASS.

Ben Hayes Washoe County School District's Chief Accountability Officer Ben Hayes has been working with public schools for sixteen years, since completing his graduate degree in experimental psychology from the University of Nevada, Reno. In 2009, Ben Hayes helped create the district's first Research and Evaluation Department dedicated to providing schools, the district and the broader education community with data products, research and support needed to make effective decisions based on high-quality, user-friendly data. He oversees all research and evaluation, accountability, data products and school performance planning for the district. Mr. Hayes is recognized as a state and national leader in accountability and data literacy. He leads and serves on a variety of state committees that inform accountability policy and practice, and has been invited to talks on the limits of test scores in teacher evaluation for the Education Writers' Association, the Regional Education Laboratories in the West and Northeast and the Nevada State Legislature.

A recurring theme across Mr. Hayes' research interests is the translation of complex data into tools that can be used by educators to improve the educational outcomes of students. In pursuit of this effort, Ben has led dozens of Data Summits for students, staff and community members and has developed a system of data dashboards and school profiles, including a live data warehouse, all tools that enable schools to more effectively monitor student achievement and help schools share their data stories.

Carolyn J. Heinrich (PhD, University of Chicago) is a Professor of Public Policy and Education in the Department of Leadership, Policy, and Organizations at the Peabody College and a Professor of Economics in the College of Arts and Sciences at Vanderbilt University. Heinrich's research focuses on education, workforce development, social welfare policy, program evaluation and public management and performance management. She works directly with federal, state and local governments in her research to improve policy design and program effectiveness and also collaborates with nongovernmental organizations (such as the World Bank, UNICEF and others) to improve the impacts of economic and social investments in middle-income and developing countries. She received the David N. Kershaw Award for distinguished contributions to the field of public policy analysis and management in 2004 and was elected to the National Academy of Public Administration in 2011. Prior to her appointment at Vanderbilt University, she was the Sid Richardson Professor of Public Affairs, affiliated Professor of Economics and Director of the Center for Health and Social Policy at the University of Texas at Austin, and formerly the Director of the La Follette School of Public Affairs at the University of Wisconsin-Madison.

Joan Lombardi, PhD, is an international expert on child development and social policy. She currently serves as Senior Advisor to the Bernard van Leer Foundation on global child development strategies and to the Buffett Early Childhood Fund on national initiatives. She also directs Early Opportunities LLC, focusing on innovation, policy and philanthropy. In 2016, she is serving as a Senior Fellow at the Center for American Progress and a Senior Advisor to the Center for the Study of Social Policy.

Over the past forty years, Dr. Lombardi has made significant contributions in the areas of child and family policy as an innovative leader and policy advisor to national and international organizations and foundations and as a public servant. She served in the U.S. Department of Health and Human Services as the first Deputy Assistant Secretary for Early Childhood Development (2009–2011) in the Obama administration and as the Deputy Assistant Secretary for Policy and External Affairs in Administration for Children and Families and the first Commissioner of the Child Care Bureau, among other positions (1993–1998), during the Clinton administration. Outside of public service, she served as the founding chair of the Birth to Five Policy Alliance (now the Alliance for Early Success) and as the founder of Global Leaders for Young Children.

Joan is the author of numerous publications, including *Time to Care: Redesigning Child Care to Promote Education, Support Families and Build Communities*, and co-author of *Beacon of Hope: The Promise of Early Head Start for America's Youngest Children*. She serves as the president of the board of *1000 Days*, a member of the board of trustees of *Save the Children* and as a member of Investing in Young Children Globally, a project of the Institute of Medicine and the National Research Council.

Olivia Little is an Assistant Researcher at the University of Wisconsin Population Health Institute, where she works to administer the RWJF

Culture of Health Prize, a program to recognize, promote and support local communities that are making great strides in improving the health and well-being of their populations. While earning her doctoral degree at the University of Wisconsin-Madison, Olivia helped implement and evaluate the Wisconsin Family Impact Seminars, a series of presentations and briefing reports for state policymakers covering a range of social policy topics. She also supported the Family Impact Institute, a national network providing technical assistance to over twenty states replicating the Family Impact Seminar model, and has participated in national presentations on advancing evidence-based policymaking and bringing a family lens to policy. Her dissertation focused on effective strategies for communicating about poverty issues, racial disparities and family economic security to policy audiences. Her previous work has included interdisciplinary research on poverty and safety net programs, early childhood development and education policy. Olivia holds a PhD in Human Development and Family Studies from the University of Wisconsin and a BS in Psychology from the University of California, Davis.

Mary Nienow is a PhD candidate in social work at the University of Minnesota and an adjunct instructor in the School of Social Work at St. Thomas University. She has over fifteen years of macro social work practice, including policy consulting, health and human services researcher in the Minnesota Senate, executive director of a child care advocacy organization and founder of a nonprofit lobbying group. Her research interests include professional socialization of macro practice social workers, interprofessional collaborations, early childhood policy, economic policy, work and family life and indigenous research methods.

Dina Policar is the director of San Diego Unified School District's (SDUSD's) Instructional Data Support Department and is responsible for internal program and policy evaluation for SDUSD. She oversees the district's web-based assessment management system, Illuminate, which gives school staff access to a broad range of student data, and she works closely with school sites to examine student data to target intervention and improvement efforts and to evaluate the effectiveness of existing policies. She holds an M.Ed degree in educational psychology with an emphasis in research methods and statistics from the University of Washington, Seattle.

Ronald G. Rode is the director of San Diego Unified School District's (SDUSD's) Office of Research and Development. With nearly twenty-five years of experience in program evaluation, monitoring and accountability work at SDUSD, Rode has worked closely with Julian R. Betts and his team at UCSD since the creation of the UCSD–SDUSD partnership in 2000. As chair of SDUSD's Research Proposal Review

Panel, Rode works cooperatively and extensively with many outside researchers to provide and clarify data and district workings and ensure that research is done well and meets district needs. He also works on data reporting requirements associated with the district's Local Control and Accountability Plan, a California requirement with metrics associated with eight state priority areas, as well as others selected by the district.

Trish Shaffer is the Coordinator for Multi-Tiered System of Supports (MTSS) and Social and Emotional Learning (SEL) for the Washoe County School District (WCSD). Prior to her role in MTSS, Trish was involved in special education at the university, district and classroom levels. She has teaching experience in both special and general education; has provided professional development and technical assistance for pre-K–12; has consulted for school districts across the nation; and has presented at the local, state and national level.

Trish is a passionate leader of SEL in the Nevada community and most recently received the Mary Utne O'Brien Award for Excellence in Expanding the Evidence-Based Practice of Social and Emotional Learning (SEL) from the CASEL/NoVo Collaborating Districts at the 2013 CASEL Forum in Chicago.

Trish was raised in Lake Tahoe and attended the University of Nevada, Reno, and is still proud to call northern Nevada home. Her greatest joy is spending time with her two sons, Quin and Grant. She also likes to spend time with extended family and friends, as well as participate in triathlons, marathons, ski, read, and listen to music.

Hilary Shager is the Associate Director of the Robert M. La Follette School of Public Affairs at the University of Wisconsin-Madison, where she provides programmatic leadership and teaches courses in evidence-based policymaking, program evaluation and professional development. In July 2016 she became the director of the Wisconsin Family Impact Seminars—a series of presentations, briefing reports and discussion sessions that communicate research-based, family-focused information to state policymakers on timely topics they identify. Formerly, Dr. Shager was a research analyst at the Wisconsin Department of Children and Families, where she designed and conducted evaluations of the state's early care and education, child welfare, Temporary Assistance for Needy Families and child support programs, and was a lead grant writer and evaluation specialist for several federal awards to Wisconsin, including the Race to the Top Early Learning Challenge; the National Child Support Noncustodial Parent Employment Demonstration Project; the Federal Title IV-E Waiver Demonstration Project; and the Maternal, Infant, and Early Childhood Home Visiting competitive expansion grant. More broadly, her research interests include early childhood education, poverty, the intersection of education and social welfare policy and program evaluation. Dr. Shager is a graduate of the University of Wisconsin-Madison, where she received her PhD in public policy in 2012. She is also a La Follette School of Public Affairs alumna who received her Master of Public Affairs in 2005.

Robert (Rob) Schamberg is a senior district advisor for the Collaborative for Academic, Social and Emotional Learning (CASEL). In his CASEL role, Rob works with large and small districts throughout the country to build their capacity to systematically and systemically implement social and emotional learning for all K–12 students. He has also been a member of research teams at CASEL, focusing on SEL competence assessment and integration of SEL into academic instruction. He was the primary researcher and developer of the CASEL SEL Financial Sustainability project and website.

Prior to joining CASEL, Rob was Executive Vice President, Chief Administrative Officer and Superintendent in Residence at the Forum for Youth Investment in Washington, DC. In these roles, Rob worked with forum staff and community, state and federal constituents to build capacity to ensure that all young people they serve are Ready by 21: ready for college, work and life.

Rob has thirty years of experience as an educational leader in California, serving as a superintendent in two school districts, as an assistant superintendent for instruction, a high school teacher and administrator, an elementary school principal and a district educational technology coordinator.

Rob earned a bachelor's degree in applied physics and information sciences at the University of California, San Diego, along with a teaching credential from the University of California, Berkeley. He obtained a master's degree in educational leadership from California State University, East Bay.

Nora Slawik works as Project Manager for the Health Living as You Age Initiative for the Metropolitan Agency on Aging and she is serving her first term as mayor of Maplewood. She served seven terms in the Minnesota House of Representatives, serving two terms as the chair of the Early Learning Finance Committee. Nora has an MPA from the Humphrey School, University of Minnesota, and a BS from Arizona State University.

She serves as chair of the Rush Line Task Force Policy Advisory Committee, is a member of the Ramsey County Family Collaborative and serves as fourth vice president of the Minnesota Mayor's Association. She has two adult children.

Kathy Stack is Vice President of Evidence-Based Innovation at the Laura and John Arnold Foundation. She joined the Laura and John Arnold Foundation after a distinguished career in the federal government, including twenty-seven years at the White House Office of Management and Budget (OMB), where she served under five presidents. Under the George W. Bush and Barack Obama administrations, Kathy helped federal agencies design innovative grant-making models that allocate funding based on evidence and evaluation. While at OMB, she oversaw budget, policy, legislation, regulations and management issues for the departments of Education and Labor, the Social Security Administration, the Corporation for National and Community Service and major human services programs, including Head Start, Temporary Assistance for Needy Families, child welfare and food and nutritional assistance. She co-led a review of science and mathematics education programs across fourteen federal agencies, which spurred the development and adoption of common evidence guidelines for evaluating a broad range of other programs. In addition, she devised strategies for sharing data—while preserving privacy protections—among federal agencies. She built a network of partners at the state and local level and in the academic, nonprofit and philanthropic communities that collaborate to improve the impact of social programs by using evidence and innovation. Kathy is a graduate of Cornell University and is a Fellow of the National Academy of Public Administration. Her case study with Jon Baron is based on an interview.

Gary VanLandingham is the Reubin O'D. Askew Senior Practitioner in Residence at Florida State University's Askew School of Public Administration and Policy. Prior to joining the Askew School, Dr. VanLandingham was director of the Pew-MacArthur Results First Initiative with The Pew Charitable Trusts, a national initiative that supports evidence-based policymaking in state and local governments. He also previously led the Florida Legislature's Office of Program Policy Analysis and Government Accountability. He has over thirty years of experience in program evaluation and policy analysis at the state and local government levels. He has served in leadership positions with the National Conference of State Legislatures, the National Legislative Program Evaluation Society, the Southeast Evaluation Association, and the North Florida Chapter of the American Society for Public Administration. Dr. VanLandingham has a Ph.D. in Public Administration and Policy and has published on performance budgeting, policy research utilization, and public management.

Karen Volz Bachofer is the director of the San Diego Education Research Alliance (SanDERA) in the Department of Economics at the University of California, San Diego. Previously, she was the executive director of the San Diego Unified School District's Research and Evaluation Division, where her responsibilities included oversight of national, state and district assessment and accountability processes and reporting; internal, external and commissioned research and evaluation activities;

and the development and rollout of the district's data management tool. She served as a member of California's Academic Performance Index Technical Design Group and the Advisory Committee for the national evaluation of Title I Accountability Systems and School Improvement Efforts. She holds a PhD in education from the Claremont Graduate School and San Diego State University.

Roger P. Weissberg is Chief Knowledge Officer of the Collaborative for Academic, Social, and Emotional Learning (CASEL), an organization committed to making evidence-based social and emotional academic learning an essential part of education. He is also University/LAS Distinguished Professor of Psychology and Education and NoVo Foundation Endowed Chair in Social and Emotional Learning and at the University of Illinois at Chicago. For the past thirty-five years, he has trained scholars and practitioners about innovative ways to design, implement and evaluate family, school and community interventions. Weissberg has authored 250 publications focusing on preventive interventions with children. He has received several awards, including the American Psychological Association's Distinguished Contribution Award for Applications of Psychology to Education and Training, the Society for Community Research and Action's Distinguished Contribution to Theory and Research Award and the "Daring Dozen" award from the George Lucas Educational Foundation for being one of twelve people who are reshaping the future of education. He is also a member of the National Academy of Education for contributions to education research and policy.

Darcy White is an officer of the Pew-MacArthur Results First Initiative with The Pew Charitable Trusts. In this capacity, Ms. White manages research projects to promote evidence-based policymaking in state and county governments. Prior to joining Pew, Ms. White worked at the Public International Policy Group, where she conducted research and policy analysis on good governance, and served as a Peace Corps Volunteer in Kenya's Deaf Education sector. She has a master's degree from American University's School of International Service and has published on government performance.

Andrew C. Zau is a senior statistician for the San Diego Education Research Alliance (SanDERA) in the Department of Economics at the University of California, San Diego. Previously, he was a research associate at the Public Policy Institute of California (PPIC). Before joining PPIC, he was an SAS programmer and research assistant at the Naval Health Research Center in San Diego, where he investigated the health consequences of military service in Operations Desert Shield and Desert Storm. He holds a BS in bioengineering from the University of California, San Diego, and an MPH in epidemiology from San Diego State University.

Foreword

The world is a series of connections. Gone are the days when people worked in isolation—researchers, policymakers, practitioners. Just as we know the domains of child development are integrated—physical, social, emotional, cognitive, calling for sector coordination—we now have an ever-growing awareness about the importance of connecting research with policy and practice.

This book is about these connections; specifically the partnerships taking place between those searching for evidence and those who are putting evidence to use through designing and implementing policy at the federal, state or local level or striving to improve practice at the program level. This is not a new topic, but one that is evolving at a rapid pace. Although connections between research and policy may be more evident in areas such as medicine, the study of human development, broadly defined, has an increasing influence on policy development in the United States and around the world. Today, "evidence" requirements are built into legislation, reviews of evidence have become central to program implementation, policy briefs based on emerging research are commonplace and conferences for public administrators are research rich. All of these realities point to the increasing interplay between research and policy.

In recent years, three interrelated issues have come to bear on the need for greater collaboration among researchers, policymakers and practitioners:

- The increased emphasis on results and accountability to assure effectiveness, particularly where public funds are at stake
- The need to scale and improve services with more of a focus on examining and understanding implementation rather than just thinking about impact as if it existed in a black box
- The growing use of technology for data collection and a greater sophistication in how to actually use information for planning rather than reporting it only for compliance

Putting this multicomponent picture together, there is now a revolution in thinking about how policymakers and researchers can work together.

During the more than forty years that I have spent in and out of public service, I have lived more on the policy side than on the research side. Yet I always believed that research was critical to good planning, and I became a fellow traveler in efforts to bring these worlds together. On a practical level, this meant a range of ongoing activities, including bringing in researchers to talk with the policy team, encouraging state administrators to work with local universities to take a creative look at administrative data and being open to research with different types of methodologies (and trying to understand how different methodologies affected results), as well as appreciating the richness of qualitative data that can provide a deeper understanding of family and community dynamics and cultural context. It also meant encouraging research that looked at implementation issues, not just impact alone, so we could better understand the core elements that led to the impact in order to inform what we do "Monday morning."

What I have found over the years, and what the examples in this book illustrate so well, is that whether researcher, practitioner or policymaker, we need each other. Although we have different and unique roles, they can complement each other. As a public official, I needed to plan for program monitoring and support by using data to inform decisions. At the same time, I needed to set an example to managers at the program level that we can actually gather information and make evidence-based choices to improve effectiveness and to learn what works for which children, families and communities

Yet the *science* or *art* of how to create partnerships and how to make them work has just begun. It is this picture that Jenni Owen and Anita Larson have painted; it is the knowledge and understanding of effective collaborations that they document by highlighting innovations underway around the country and developing an analytic framework to describe the process. The editors have thoughtfully organized the case studies to best document the process of partnership development: the *motivations* that lead to partnerships, the core elements of successful *implementation* and the lessons learned about *sustainability*. They also have included a critical component that used to go almost unmentioned: the *use of research* once the research phase has concluded. Finally, they attend to the ever-important consideration of *investing* in these partnerships and how the investments have simultaneously grown and become more thoughtful by both nonprofit and public-sector funders.

Like any relationship, the success of a partnership depends on having a common goal and ongoing trust. There is a mutuality that motivates the collaboration. What is common across the case studies featured in this book is that both researchers and policymakers recognized a window of opportunity. For the policymaker, it was an opportunity that could help inform and guide policy formation and implementation. For the researcher, the partnership often presented an opportunity to answer key questions in a way that would lead, not just to a publication, but that also could help address pressing education or social policy issues.

We know a successful partnership depends on more than the initial motivation. It also depends on the ongoing work to keep collaboration going, to check in during the process, to continually look at data, to adjust assumptions. It is important that this process extends to those being studied—that practitioners and families are brought into the process so they can contribute to it and understand the benefits of participation. This ongoing process of dialogue, this give and take, is often different from the classic research approach, which may put more distance between those asking for the information and those gathering it. There is room for both, and both have greater chances of success with the other's input and involvement.

The sustainability of researcher–policymaker partnerships is more complex. As the editors indicate, the most lasting legacy of the partnership may be the attitudes and knowledge that each partner gains. This deeper understanding of each other's roles may be more important than sustaining any one particular partnership. For policymakers, this may lead to a greater appreciation of the role of research in the policy process and new insights into different types of research and how best to use them. For researchers, the partnership may lead to insights into how best to formulate questions, how to work more closely with those most affected and how to communicate findings in ways that can be more easily understood by those who are depending on clear answers. Although naturally each role in the process is very different, understanding the other's perspective is always useful.

So if you are reading this book, either as a public official or a researcher, you are probably either considering such a partnership or are already deeply involved in such collaboration and eager for insights about how others have approached such partnerships. Before you get started, and during the process, consider reading through the examples and asking yourself and your team: What can we learn from these examples? What motivates our own partnership? How will it work? How will we communicate among the partners? Where should we plan together, and where is it best to leave some separation to respect the differences in our roles? You may also be reading this as a student of public policy, public administration, social work, education or any number of other disciplines or degrees. If so, take advantage of the experiences and lessons shared throughout this book to inform whatever future roles you hold in research, policy or practice.

More than anything, we all need to keep in mind that the end goal is not the partnership itself; collaboration is only a means to an end. The goal is the creation of new knowledge and policies that can improve and enhance the lives of children, families and communities. This is what the examples in this book demonstrate, and this is the challenge to be addressed as we move forward together.

Joan Lombardi, PhD
Washington, DC

Acknowledgements

This all started on a conference call. At least that's what we say in Chapter 1 about our approach to this book and why we structured it as we did. But that's not exactly right. In fact, between the two of us, we have talked for decades with our researcher and policymaker colleagues about the importance of partnerships between the two, what makes them strong and why they falter. And for almost as long, we have been perplexed as to why there seemed to be no resource that shared these researcher–policymaker insights in an organized, accessible way. To the extent that we have accomplished that here, we are grateful to a host of policymakers, researchers and some simply wise people with good guidance. With regard to the researcher–policymaker partnership cases featured in this book, we remain humbled that "yes" was the response we received to the first ten potential contributors whom we asked. To a person, they have been tremendous partners to us. Not only did that make this book project enjoyable, but it further highlighted the need for the book. As with the experts we consulted before we committed to this project, not one of the contributing partners told us that the book was unnecessary. This is unfortunate, perhaps, as we believe there is a need for multiple such resources, but it is also fortunate, as it reinforced that we had set out on a meaningful pursuit. We are grateful to Joan Lombardi for her foreword. Joan has a remarkable history of policy and research, rigor and relevance—and partnerships—which she continues to bring to her ongoing work and to her insightful comments that open this book. We could not be more appreciative of the professionalism, responsiveness and support from everyone we interacted with at Routledge and Taylor & Francis. Finally, we thank the future partners, including Duke University students Jenn Acosta, who provided invaluable assistance with the initial literature review; Anna Alcaro for her help with transforming our interviews with Jon Baron and Kathy Stack into a full-fledged case; and Brandi Thomas, a staff assistant at Duke who provided copy editing support for this book on top of her day job.

We also thank each other. This effort has been a true and immense partnership. At various times, we shared with each other how struck we were by our own partnership. One of us has recently resided mostly in the public sphere, the other mostly in academia. At other times, our roles have been the reverse. Perhaps the researcher–policymaker–practitioner conference call during which we first "met" and the theme of this book are what situated us so well for our partnership that produced this book.

1   Approach and Structure

Who We Are

We are two people who believe in the value of research. We also care deeply about providing the best possible public policy and public service. For the most effective policies and practices to exist, researchers and policymakers often must collect and test evidence to show effects in multiple jurisdictions or over an extended period. Effective practices frequently begin in what is referred to as "the field"—the places where public service takes place each day, and particularly where new problems become apparent and require attention quickly. Rigorous research can generate new knowledge that, when applied to the field or through public policy change, can improve lives and communities, as well as use scarce public resources more effectively.

Applying research to test and implement established, evidence-based practice, or to qualitatively explore an emerging promising practice, usually requires the expertise of researchers. Although some public agencies employ staff who possess research skills, they are often unable to undertake research projects in-house either because of limitations of time, job descriptions or legitimacy in terms of their expertise. Some public agencies have never employed individuals with research skills. At the same time, researchers who care deeply about applying their work in practice seek out opportunities to support public agencies' efforts to make the use of research happen. With the need for rigorous forms of inquiry to improve public work and the desire by researchers to make their work more broadly relevant, partnerships between research and policy take place with varying degrees of success in meeting both sets of needs.

We are also two individuals who have worked on both sides of these types of partnerships. Jenni Owen is the Policy Director for North Carolina Governor Roy Cooper, on leave from her role as the Director of Policy Engagement and Senior Lecturer at the Sanford School of Public Policy at Duke University. In this role she engaged in multiple efforts to enhance the interactions among research, policy and practice, including developing and implementing strategies for supporting policy engagement by researchers and research informed by policymakers. In addition to teaching and advising undergraduates and graduate students, she directed the North Carolina Family Impact Seminar, a legislative education initiative that responds to legislators' demands for research and provides that research when and how legislators need it. Before coming to Duke, she served as a senior policy advisor to North Carolina Governor James B. Hunt, Jr. and many years before that was staff to a congressional subcommittee of the U.S. Senate.

Anita Larson currently works at Minnesota's state Department of Education implementing two federal grants focused on creating and enhancing access to data to support public policy and local practice in the area of early learning. She teaches for Hamline University's Public Administration program in Saint Paul from which she was conferred her doctorate. Anita also worked as a research fellow at the University of Minnesota for five years, leading family and policy research projects. Her previous local government work has been in a variety of service areas, including poverty programs, children's mental health, public health, and juvenile corrections.

Throughout our careers, we have experienced the excitement and promise of dynamic researcher–policymaker partnerships. We have also experienced partnerships that threaten to fall apart at nearly every point along the way. In some cases, opportunities dissolve quickly and the partnership never takes shape. Other times, partnerships end abruptly before or after work is finished, leaving no potential for sustainability and at times even bad feelings in their wake. Stemming from our experiences, we each have developed clear perspectives about what makes for a great strong and successful partnership. Therefore, when we see a partnership that is struggling or even failing, we are eager to get it back on track, as we know that the costs of failed partnerships to both the research and policy sectors can ripple far beyond one negative experience.

Even before we met, we had each begun to form ideas of what characteristics define healthy, robust researcher–policymaker partnerships, what they need and what they do not need. These mental models began to take shape, and we were both refining and solidifying them. However, we were forming ideas that we were not documenting, both of us certain that *someone else must have written about this.* Yet each time we looked for a book of insight and guidance on forming and sustaining researcher–policymaker partnerships, we came up with nothing that discussed such partnerships in ways we believe both the research and policy realms need, nor with anything that focused on social and education policy, areas about which we care most deeply.

Why We Invited the Cases and Synthesized Their Implications

We met on a conference call in 2013 that was about, of all things, possibilities for partnership between policymakers and researchers in the social policy realm. The call was for a national project involving researchers, policymakers and practitioners. We were discussing the utilization of research in practices focused on families and children. One topic of discussion was the benefits of cross-sector partnerships, and Anita commented that "it would be wonderful if there were a book focused on helping people do this work well." Jenni agreed and said she had looked for the book—as it turned out, so had Anita—but it did not seem to exist. We decided to talk about it again.

In our first follow-up conversation about this idea, we shared a number of observations about the lack of such a resource. Several of these observations bear mentioning here to help readers understand our motivations for pursuing the book project. We had both recognized that guidance is lacking. It is difficult, if not impossible, to know where to go for insight either to start a partnership or how to fix one that is not going well. This was vexing to us because we both understood the great promise and mutual benefits that exist when these partnerships work well. In addition to the important cross-sector learning that occurs, such as the career benefits of publication for researchers and legitimizing practices for public agencies, meaningful long-term relationships may develop as well. These relationships support ongoing and future work and exploration. Sometimes these relationships are mainly practical, simply supporting information exchange by having someone to call "at the university" when a public agency has a question about "what the research says." Other times the relationships lay the foundation for the award of large federal grants or broad initiatives that inform policy and practice well beyond the county or state initially involved.

On multiple occasions, we reflected that universities and policymakers, including public agencies, need one another. These sentiments were affirmed further when we served on a roundtable panel together at the Association for Public Policy Analysis and Management conference in fall 2014 titled *The (Critical) Next Level of Evidence-Based Policy-making: Case studies of successful policymaker-researcher collaboration at the state level*. The case studies featured in the session highlighted the importance of cross-sector partnerships to the adoption of evidence-based practices. The partnerships did not ensure successful integration of evidence-based practices, but they helped provide a solid foundation. The panelists also highlighted some of the motivations for these partnerships, which resonated with our personal and professional experiences.

Partnership Drivers

Our chapters on motivations for and investing in partnerships go into much more detail about the factors that drive researcher–policymaker partnerships. At the outset, however, it is important to acknowledge that multiple private, nonprofit foundations have taken to funding these partnerships in recent years. Among the most active in the partnership realm are the W. T. Grant and Spencer foundations. At the federal government level, the Institute of Education Sciences at the Department of Education and the departments of Health and Human Services and Justice also have demonstrated increased investment in cross-sector partnerships. Partnerships often form as a condition of funding. As we discuss later in the book, mandates and the associated funding can be essential to these partnerships. But it is equally important to address other ways that partnerships get started and the organic conditions for their formation.

"More with Less"

Researchers and policymakers share other experiences and challenges that make partnerships supportive of both sectors in multiple ways. First, at the time of this writing, most public universities have weathered decades of annual decreases in state revenue contributions. This budget trend has hit land grant universities particularly hard to the point that a significant number now receive such a low percentage of their funding from state revenues that they may be in danger of losing their land grant status if those contributions decrease any further (The Economist, 2001).

The ripple effects of these cutbacks do not stop at the doors of the university. Gwynne (2010) suggested that the loss of research funding to public universities will have dramatic effects on specific industries such as technology and medicine because public institutions produce far more graduates than do private institutions. The Center on Budget and Policy Priorities (CBPP, 2013) noted that since the Great Recession, all states but two (North Dakota and Wyoming) have cut public funding, with an overall cut of 28 percent nationwide (p. 3). The center associates these cuts directly with subsequent increases in tuition and spending cuts that damage the quality of education. Further, loss of public support to public universities has dampened university salaries. In 2010 public university faculty salaries were 80 percent of their private university faculty counterparts (Gwynne, 2010). Although public universities may be particularly driven by the financial challenges they share with state and local governments, private universities also have faced budget-related constraints, as well as constraints related to the often-conflicting incentives of the research and policy realms. With regard to researcher–policymaker partnerships, both public and private universities figure prominently in this book's case studies.

Simultaneous with universities' challenges, local and state governments have been experiencing reductions in revenue since the 1990s in response to negative public sentiment about taxes, public services, and government in general. This trend accelerated during the Great *Recession*, in contrast to the fiscal policies employed during the Great *Depression* when federal funding increased for a variety of work and welfare programs. The Center on Budget and Policy Priorities' (2011) report on state funding cuts showed that forty-six states cut services to vulnerable populations over the Recession period of 2008 and 2009 (CBPP, 2011). There is some evidence of variation in cuts by specific sector, with education receiving additional property tax revenues over this period in some parts of the country as local school districts sought simply to keep current services stable (Dye & Reschovsky, 2008). Economic challenges are aggravated by an aging workforce, and like universities and the impact of cuts on salaries, local governments struggle with pension and health care costs. This confluence of economic circumstances sets in motion the need for careful juggling acts as governments attempt to maintain some level of pension benefit, managing costs while at the same time dealing with an aging public workforce (Barkin, 2014).

As revenues decrease, government agencies are also under pressure to measure the effectiveness of their work and prove to their constituents and elected officials that they use public dollars wisely for good results. Having "proof" of effectiveness has become essential. Arguments for informing the public of the contribution of public organizations such as local governments and universities contend that if the public had a better understanding of results, they would be less likely to vote for tax reductions (Delli Carpini & Keeter, 1996). Regardless of what might reverse this disinvestment trend, universities and governments are dealing with similar funding challenges.

Education and Social Policy

This book offers a set of structured descriptions and discussions of the factors that seem to matter most when organizations and individuals undertake and sustain successful researcher–policymaker partnerships focused on education and social policy. The factors we have chosen emerge from the literature, our own experiences, and the experiences of others. We focus on education and social policy in part because they are what we know, but also because they are areas of public policy that are integral to individual, family, and community well-being. Whether trying to tackle economic or education disparities, public health, public safety or political engagement, education and social policy have important roles.

Education and social policy are also important because they require broad and varied approaches to inquiry. This is less true in areas of study that have enjoyed longer histories of partnership with nonresearch partners such as medicine, agriculture, pharmaceuticals, aerospace and medical devices. These fields often rely upon the "hard" sciences, laboratory-based research and development and control–trial models of testing for efficacy. Hard science partnerships can involve commercialization, patenting and profit—in contrast to education and social policy research, which produces new knowledge that may eventually become part of the public good through evidence-based practice and policy change.

Wicked Problems

Social changes always affect families and children. There is no question that with each new major change in technology, economic crisis, means of production, rapid spread of a lethal disease, globalization, displacement or the effects of large disparities in income, social problems affecting children and families can be complex and result in part from these broader changes. The term "wicked problems" (Rittel & Webber, 1973) has come to describe complex social challenges that individuals, families and communities face and which are not solvable with known formulaic approaches. Wicked problems are particularly challenging when previous strategies for addressing them no longer work. In addition, solutions to these problems may involve measurements of success that are extremely difficult for policymakers—or anyone—to access. When it comes to wicked problems, researchers may need to focus on improving the situation but not solving it and usually need to take into account multiple unique points of view. Examples of such problems include persistent racial disparities in academic performance, gun violence and global climate change. Each of these problems involves multiple systems, policies, scientific disciplines and ideologies in terms of both causes and potential solutions. With such complexity, it is difficult to know if the problem is ever "fixed." Furthermore, confusion over what constitutes "success" may leave researchers and policy analysts feeling embedded in a sense of chaos.

In fact, applying chaos theory to social problems acknowledges the challenges of traditional approaches to complex problems and how many of those methods typically no longer work (Overman, 1996). What is encouraging about this theoretical acknowledgement of complex modern problems is that there is agreement around approaches that are likely to produce effective solutions. In particular, research and public sectors are encouraged to work together: Individuals who do the work as well as those who study the work must align their problem-solving efforts. In Wilson's (1998) book *Consilience*, he pointed out that cross-disciplinary approaches to complex problems would become a necessity in the twenty-first century. Researchers and policymakers who are experts in day-to-day work are perfectly positioned to join forces to find solutions to persistent social challenges. They are increasingly working across programs and departments to do so. At the same time, students across a wide range of university programs ask for real-world experience as part of their academic training. Partnerships can occur across academic disciplines, across state departments and between policymakers and researchers.

We Have No Specific Recipe, But We Know Good Ingredients

We believe there are factors associated with effective partnerships between researchers and policymakers, but we do not have all the answers. In this way, researcher–policymaker partnerships are like cooking a dish that requires certain high-quality ingredients to make sure the dish tastes good. In the case of cross-sector partnerships, we are suggesting those high-quality ingredients but the exact proportions, timing and combinations almost certainly vary by factors including institution, geographic location, local politics, history and others. Yet although the attributes of partnerships vary in ways such as location and timing, we believe that some elements are simply necessary.

We have not undertaken causal research, utilizing controls to measure the effectiveness of pursuing one type of partnership model versus another. There may be consensus that randomized controlled trials (RCTs) are the gold standard, but in the context of researcher–policymaker partnerships, there is too much variation based on human relationships and other factors to make RCTs the optimal approach. Moreover, this book is not about interventions, evidence-based practices, or experimental models intended to prove a specific theory.

Before moving into a description of how we approached the topic of researcher–policymaker partnership, we will share our perspective about the public roles of our two sectors of focus: research and policy. We encourage anyone engaged in partnerships across these sectors to be mindful throughout the partnership of the respective roles of the sectors, as well as of public perception of those roles.

Public Roles

The public role of government agencies and policymakers is fairly clear. Elected officials pass laws, allocate funding and task public agencies with implementing those laws, often in the form of programs or services. Across multiple levels and branches of government, public servants "serve the public." In the context of policy implementation, however, the role of the civil service in the evolution of the U.S. public sector and the importance of professional, competent implementation (e.g., Lipsky's street-level bureaucrat) include the expectation that the public sector is expected to implement the public will expressed through legislative action. Whether these civil servants have the time, staff or skills to perform analysis of program performance or engage in other forms of inquiry is less certain and varies by agency. That the individuals working in these public systems must be publicly engaged is a given.

The public engagement work of the research community is often less clear though it is gaining increased attention. Although both public and privately funded universities are at times publicly engaged in meaningful ways, it was the publicly funded land grant university from which service to the community was expected and written into the Morrill Act of 1862, establishing the land grant system. In spite of massive cuts over past decades to state universities, Curris's (2006) opinion piece argued that the work of the land grant university needs to be based on purpose, not funding source. The purposes of access, affordability, economic advancement, public education, homeland security, scientific research and citizenship education are at the core of what public universities do. In spite of these objectives, academic systems often reward publishing, bringing in grant dollars and teaching. These priorities often do not align well with the goals of public engagement. As demonstrated throughout this book, through cross-sector partnerships, research partners are sometimes able to deftly combine the publishing, funding and teaching objectives to which they are held with the higher-order engagement purposes of their university.

Our Approach

Because we have a good idea of the ingredients that go in to successful researcher–policymaker partnerships, we approached each of the case authors with a set of focused questions about these ingredients, while encouraging them to expand upon and add nuances to what we asked. We then held follow-up conversations, during which we asked additional questions of case authors when a new issue arose in our conversations. In this way, we adopted a loose constructivist approach to the case studies, leaving ample room for contributors to elaborate and expound on their experiences. Although our approach was fluid, we created a conceptual framework to guide our thinking and the feedback provided by contributors. The following diagram describes the *Design Map* (Maxwell, 2013) of our approach.

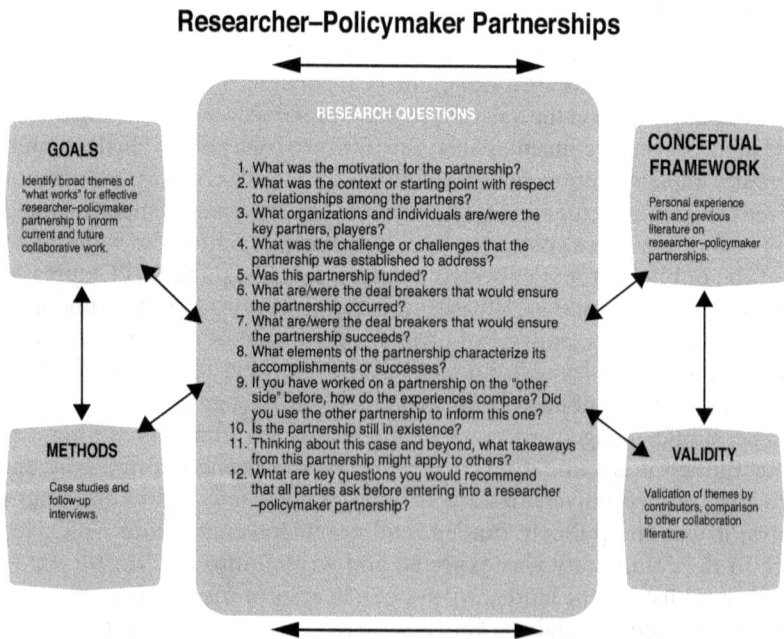

Researcher–Policymaker Partnerships

RESEARCH QUESTIONS

GOALS

Identify broad themes of "what works" for effective researcher–policymaker partnership to inrorm current and future collaborative work.

CONCEPTUAL FRAMEWORK

Personal experience with and previous literature on researcher–policymaker partnerships.

1. What was the motivation for the partnership?
2. What was the context or starting point with respect to relationships among the partners?
3. What organizations and individuals are/were the key partners, players?
4. What was the challenge or challenges that the partnership was established to address?
5. Was this partnership funded?
6. What are/were the deal breakers that would ensure the partnership occurred?
7. What are/were the deal breakers that would ensure the partnership succeeds?
8. What elements of the partnership characterize its accomplishments or successes?
9. If you have worked on a partnership on the "other side" before, how do the experiences compare? Did you use the other partnership to inform this one?
10. Is the partnership still in existence?
11. Thinking about this case and beyond, what takeaways from this partnership might apply to others?
12. Whtat are key questions you would recommend that all parties ask before entering into a researcher –policymaker partnership?

METHODS

Case studies and follow-up interviews.

VALIDITY

Validation of themes by contributors, comparison to other collaboration literature.

Figure 1.1 Concept Map, Researcher–Policymaker Collaboration

The twelve questions we asked each contributor conveyed our primary areas of interest and provided cues to facilitate contributors sharing their experiences in ways that would be of interest to readers and, in particular, those who intend to pursue cross-sector partnerships. As a result, the case studies vary in terms of what questions resonated most with each contributor and on which topical area they expounded. We communicated with most contributors multiple times over several months. After receiving the authors' cases we held numerous conversations and exchanges to ensure that we had the clearest understanding of the partnerships the contributors were sharing as we integrated them into the broader sections of the book. We then placed each case study in the chapter where it fits best in terms of illustrating a given concept. However, as would be expected, every case study is multifaceted and many could be situated in multiple sections of the book.

Structure

Each chapter of the book focuses on a theme. Within each chapter are one or more cases that reflect the chapter's focus. We have woven case studies together by introducing the key concept that we believe each case exemplifies based on the literature and our knowledge and experiences. In this way, we frame each case study for the reader and situate it within the broader context of the book. We then "get out of the way" and allow the case authors their own voice to describe their experiences with researcher–policymaker partnerships. Wherever possible, we end each chapter with examples of tools, processes or other resources that relate to the theme and case studies shared. In several instances, those resources are incorporated within a case. For some cases, we also include appendices of examples and tools such as forms, agreements and frameworks that contributors have generously made available for others to learn from and use.

Language and Definitions

Language and definitions are important to successful partnerships, and we want readers to be clear about our use of certain terms. We know that terminology about academia and government, for example, can vary by level of organization as well as by region of the country. We use the following throughout the book:

Academic. Member of a university or college who teaches and may also conduct research.

Academic researcher. Member of a university or college who conducts research but does not teach.

Collaboration. Interaction between two or more parties stemming from the desire or need to accomplish a particular goal or set of outcomes. Often a subset of a partnership formed to address a shared interest in generating new information about a problem or challenge.

Education and social policy. Areas of public policy that involve a wide array of issues of critical importance to children, families and communities, broadly defined. Addressed by researchers and policymakers in multiple disciplines, including but not limited, to pre-K–16 education, child development, juvenile and criminal justice, public safety, public health and public assistance.

Partnership. An arrangement between at least two individuals or entities with specified roles and responsibilities and who are working together. Includes collaboration but (in the context of this book) is deeper and more sustained than is often the case with collaboration.

Policymaker. Anyone in the public sector—government—who has an influence on the outcome or implementation of a public policy decision. These individuals may be elected officials (governors, legislative representatives, county commissioners), executive branch leaders (politically appointed agency heads, program directors, program managers) or public-sector staff (supervisors and direct service providers).

Practitioner. An individual, usually employed by a public agency or nonprofit, engaged in providing services to the public or subset of the public.

Research. Professional social inquiry, policy analysis or research around a problem or challenge.

Researcher. Individual engaged in professional social inquiry, policy analysis or research. Researchers may be affiliated with an academic institution or another entity, just as a think tank or research consulting firm is a member of a professional research group.

What Is at Stake?

Although the prospect of researchers and policymakers continuing to work separately on their disparate objectives within their distinct systems may not cause immediate alarm, it is the lost opportunities when partnerships fail or are not sought out that are concerning and come at a cost to society. Specifically, when researchers and policymakers join together around a problem, they are productive and dynamic, greater than the sum of their parts. They have the potential to help public policy be more responsive and impactful by using scarce resources wisely and effectively. When they reveal the results of good work, they affirm the tireless efforts of public employees who may not know whether their work is making a positive difference. Having evidence that a policy or program is making a positive difference can provide a significant boost to morale in public agencies. Knowing that a policy, program or practice is not effective can free up resources to be applied where they are needed more.

For researchers wanting to make a real-world impact, researcher–policymaker partnerships provide opportunities to share their skills and knowledge beyond the walls of the university and outside the pages of academic journals. For students under the tutelage of faculty members, having real-world experience in public policy is an invaluable opportunity to tie what is happening in the classroom to what happens in practice. For some, it can lead to inspiration for career paths and employment. These partnerships can lead to long-term working relationships and the cultivation of understanding and mutual respect among professionals who can benefit from one another's expertise and as a result benefit countless others as well.

When partnerships fail, the effects can extend well beyond attempts at collaborative work. In addition to the perpetuation of the gaps, suspicion and sometimes outright hostility between the two sectors, a failed attempt can prevent consideration and pursuit of future partnerships. An openness and vulnerability must be present when embarking upon a partnership that can be violated when things go badly. Preconceived notions and biases about the "other side" behaving badly are reinforced, leading to deterioration in trust. Professionals in both sectors who leave failed partnerships are unlikely to expend the time and take the risk to try another anytime soon. Lost is the possibility of making a positive difference in education and social policy that can improve the lives of individuals, families and communities. This is an unfortunate and unnecessary loss that can be prevented with information, planning and learning from those who have done it well. Each partnership case in this book reinforces the value of these partnerships in ways that can inform those who are currently involved in partnerships and those who are considering them.

References

Barkin, R. (2014). Blowing up the benefits package. *American City and County*, *129*(2), 18–24.

Center on Budget and Policy Priorities. (2011). *At least 46 states have imposed cuts that hurt vulnerable residents and the economy*. Washington, D.C. Retrieved from: http://www.cbpp.org/research/an-update-on-state-budget-cuts.

Center on Budget and Policy Priorities. (2013). *Recent deep state higher education cuts may harm students and economy for years to come*. Washington, D.C. Retrieved from: http://www.cbpp.org/research/recent-deep-state-higher-education-cuts-may-harm-students-and-the-economy-for-years-to-come.

Curris, C.W. (2006). The public purpose of public colleges. *Chronicle of Higher Education*, *52*(31), 2–5.

Delli Carpini, M.X., & Keeter, S. (1996). *What Americans know about politics and why it matters*. New Haven, CT: Yale University Press.

Dye, R.F., & Reschovsky, A. (2008). Property tax responses to state aid cuts in the recent fiscal crisis. *Public Budgeting and Finance*, *28*(2), 87–111.

The Economist. (2001). *An old dream in trouble: A very American institution tries to survive in the Information Age.* Retrieved from: http://www.economist.com/node/638824.

Gwynne, C. (2010). Public universities face funding crisis. *Research Technology Management, 53*(5), 4–5.

Maxwell, J.A. (2013). *Qualitative research design: An interactive approach* (3rd ed.). Thousand Oaks, CA: Sage.

Overman, S. (1996). The new science of management: Chaos and quantum theory method. *Journal of Public Administration Research and Theory, 6*(1), 75–89.

Rittel, H. W., and Webber, M. (1973) Dilemmas in a general theory of planning. *Policy Science, 4,* 155–169.

Wilson, E.O. (1998). *Consilience: The unity of knowledge.* New York, NY: Alfred A. Knopf.

2   Motivations for Collaboration

Why Partner?

A university researcher approaches a school district superintendent seeking data for cutting-edge research and offers to "partner." A federal agency's request for proposals requires university researchers and public agency officials to sign a joint letter expressing a commitment to partner on a project. A private foundation invites proposals that must include collaboration among "partners."

These examples reflect a few of the motivations for which researchers and policymakers create so-called partnerships. They are characterized by requirements related to receipt of funding or a need for data in order to conduct research. They also are characterized by a decision to partner that may not have occurred absent the motivating factors of funds and data. Such partnerships may be valuable. Despite being somewhat forced due to an initial motivator, they may lead to future, voluntary partnering. Yet when partnerships start as a requirement, absent mutual interest, they are less likely to last beyond the requirement either in terms of substance or longevity (Cousins & Simon, 1996).

Other types of motivations bode better for more meaningful and impactful interaction between researchers and policymakers, the impacts that are likely to result from the partnerships and how long the partnerships are likely to last. These motivations include the current climate of support for bridging research and policy. The iron is hot thanks in part to a multisector focus on evidence-based policy, which is strong and getting stronger. Policymakers, practitioners and funders, all more than ever, face expectations that they will know what research says about what works in their field. They thus face related expectations that they will collaborate in some form with producers of research. The evidence-based policy movement has become increasingly important when it comes to initiating, developing and sustaining researcher–policymaker partnerships.

Unlike the funding and data motivations, partnerships established as an offshoot of a desire for evidence-based policy are likely to have greater chances at lasting beyond a particular research project or policy initiative. There are multiple possible explanations for this. First, given the well-documented differences between the timeframes that researchers and policymakers require to carry out their work, it behooves both to develop foundational relationships that each can leverage beyond a one-time need (Choi et al., 2005).

Second, as they are increasingly asking for evidence of "what works," policymakers benefit from having colleagues in the research realm. The policymakers behind evidence-based policy need a source for the evidence they are holding up to explain and defend their decisions (Lindblom & Cohen, 1979).

Third is essentially the second explanation in reverse—namely a growing recognition among researchers that they must be better connected with policymakers to ensure that their research is responsive to policymakers' requests for research evidence. Researchers are becoming more willing to consider policymaker partnerships as part of their scholarship, instead of considering such partnerships only as fulfilling obligations or as nothing more than sources of data (Brownson, Royer, Ewing, & McBride, 2006). Academics who may typically have thought of interacting with policymakers as pro bono work now recognize the interaction for the value it brings to all phases of research endeavors. More specifically, engaging policymakers during the formulation of research questions, throughout the research process and in the knowledge sharing and application phases not only improves the research, but also increases the likelihood that it will reach real-world users. Related, research entities often carry out dissemination efforts with a weak understanding of how policymakers prefer to receive information. This is a strong example of where established partnerships can help, in that they are likely to involve ongoing, two-way interaction (Gooden, Graham, & Martin, 2014).

Two-way interaction between researchers and policymakers is important for research utilization, which is a goal of many partnerships and the theme of Chapter 5 of this book. With partnerships in place in advance of when research efforts are complete, policymakers can guide the process of knowledge sharing in a way that works best for eventual users in the policy realm. Although some institutions such as research-focused think tanks have been sharing research with policymakers for many years, the research–policy interaction in these instances is often quite different from the interaction exemplified by the partnerships featured in this book. A key distinction is that many institutions typically do not involve policymakers in the research process. Such involvement is an attribute of each of the partnerships that we feature.

Still another explanation for policymakers' more frequent demand for research is the ease of access to new science. Policymakers are better positioned to proactively access scientific sources and knowledge than they were just a few decades ago. This is thanks in no small part to technological developments. It also reflects the importance of skills development within policymaking contexts, some of which have been facilitated by researcher–policymaker partnerships themselves, as the Results First case in Chapter 5 illustrates. In Chapter 5, we discuss the role of research utilization in the context of researcher–policymaker partnerships and, in particular, strategies for mitigating common barriers to use.

Finally, feedback from those involved in researcher–policymaker partnerships highlights that cross-sector engagement is enjoyable and stimulating. Although the reasons for this may be different depending on the partner's sector and role, the enjoyment of partnership work is important.

What the Research Says

Before delving into specific partnership cases, it is important and useful to consider the relevant literature. Research on the motivations for partnerships reinforces what we learn from the experiences of the partners in each of this book's cases. Researcher–policymaker partnerships are often motivated by one partner's desire to move a policy agenda forward or to achieve social change (Gatta & McCabe, 2008). By collaborating with researchers, policymakers benefit from a diversity of perspectives that researchers can provide across a range of disciplines and topic areas. Researchers can benefit government by "gleaning best practices," "providing technical assistance," "convening forums and conferences" and by bringing their "sophisticated research and economic modeling" skills to the table (Gatta & McCabe, 2008, p. 129). Gerardi and Wolff (2008) describe the specialized knowledge and skills researchers can bring to policymakers; namely, their ability to "design research," "collect and analyze data," "contextualize their findings within the broader academic and policy literature" and "write grant applications, reports, and articles" (p. 151). Researchers also come with the resources needed to conduct quality research, such as software for entering and analyzing data, high-speed computers and research assistants (Gerardi & Wolff, 2008, p. 151). Likewise, policymakers provide valuable assets to the relationship. Specifically, they can provide researchers with an environment conducive to performing research, management information systems and connections to administrators and public-sector leaders (Gerardi & Wolff, 2008).

Gerardi and Wolff (2008) also bring up a valuable, albeit often overlooked, opportunity for researcher–policymaker partnerships: the potential to expand their organizations' respective infrastructures to better achieve their missions (p. 148). By working together, research-policymaker partnerships can produce "peer-reviewed publications informing their fields" and obtain "external funding that expands the base of services and training available within practice settings and academe," as well as learn how to "improve the efficiency and effectiveness of practice" (Gerardi &

Wolff, 2008, p. 148). Finally, examinations of research utilization in the health sciences have much to share about effective "researcher-decision maker" partnerships. Of particular relevance is the finding that "[o]ur analyses suggest that partnerships are most effective when researchers see the value of contextualising their work and decision-makers see how this work can help them accomplish their purpose at hand" (Golden-Biddle et al., 2003).

It is telling that the partners in each of the three cases we feature here were motivated beyond the original impetus for partnering. In accomplishing what they set out to do, they established processes for future partnerships. We would characterize this as an "important side effect," to use a phrase stated by Carrie Conaway, a partner in one of the cases.

Speaking from Experience—Partners' Perspectives

In addition to reviewing relevant literature about motivations for researcher–policymaker partnerships, an important part of our process for developing this book involved interviews with researchers and policymakers who have experience with successful and unsuccessful partnerships. As described in the previous chapter, we conducted this direct outreach in part to supplement the theoretical basis for attributes of successful partnerships. It was also to learn about the motivations, beyond our experiences, for which researchers and policymakers from across sectors had pursued partnerships with one another.

Their responses were distinct but complementary. Perhaps the most common refrain was the recognition of mutual needs and benefits, though those needs and benefits were not necessarily the same for each partner. Researchers need real-world problems to study and ideally to solve. To do so, they need access to subjects and data to test hypotheses. Policymakers and public entities need the external legitimacy that comes with experts' analysis of programs and services. For maximum credibility, they need that analysis to be about their context and conditions, not about abstract scenarios that may appear inapplicable to their circumstances. Policymakers also may need support for internal capacity building and skills transfer, particularly when adopting, implementing and monitoring evidence-based practices. When successful, these different but complementary motivations for partnering yield a "partnership model that emphasizes shared learning objectives," making it "possible for the agency to receive their evaluation or analysis while the researchers are able to also publish their paper" (T. Zuel, personal communication, October 10, 2015). Doing so also serves to move away from what is often "ego-centered" work (Zuel, 2015).

As research and direct experience demonstrate, every partnership has motivating factors. The three partnerships we feature are most effective when considered in tandem as they illustrate that although motivations may differ, certain conditions increase the partnerships' chances of success.

The Partnerships and Their Motivations

This chapter features three researcher–policymaker partnerships that differ with regard to their motivations, factors that led to the formation of each partnership. The motivations range from needing the answer to a research question for informing policy decisions, to addressing an existing challenge between research and policy institutions, to pursuing legislative reform. Another difference is the level of government involved. Two are state-level partnerships, and one is a local-level partnership. A third distinction among the partnerships featured here is the array of stakeholders engaged in the partnership. In the first, a small number of individuals representing one policymaking and two research institutions form the crux of the partnership. The second partnership stemmed from the formation of an institutional-level research–policy partnership that has led to a range of individual researcher–policymaker partnerships. The third example is a partnership led by researchers and policy experts, inclusive of stakeholders from multiple other institutions.

There are also similarities among the partnerships. Each illustrates common and feasible reasons for building partnerships, recognizes a window of opportunity for establishing a partnership and acknowledges challenges to overcome and strategies for doing so.

The first of the three cases is that of the Massachusetts Charter School Research Partnership, a partnership of the Massachusetts Department of Elementary and Secondary Education, the Massachusetts Institute of Technology and Harvard University. As the case reveals, initial motivation for this partnership came from the policymaker. The Department of Elementary and Secondary Education desired an "unbiased answer to a research question." That motivation, stemming from the policymaker realm, was bolstered by the researchers' recognition that the partnership had the potential to yield findings that were both relevant for policymaking and worthy of publication in top peer-reviewed journals. Strengthening the motivations for each partner was a preexisting relationship between some of the leading individuals involved, a testament to the value of relationship building in advance of pursuing a partnership.

Other cases in this book offer insights about motivations for researcher–policymaker partnerships, just as the three cases we feature here have much to offer about other themes that the book addresses. For this chapter, we have selected cases that fit particularly well with the motivations theme. Together they portray an array of possible motivations and underscore the importance of key conditions aligning with the motivations.

The Massachusetts Charter School Research Partnership

Carrie Conaway

Background

I arrived to the Massachusetts Department of Elementary and Secondary Education in March 2007 as the agency's first research director. On my first day, Deputy Commissioner Jeff Nellhaus handed me a list of a dozen tasks that had been awaiting my arrival. Most of these were straightforward: research how other states calculated their graduation rates, meet with representatives of the federal Regional Education Laboratory program and so forth. And then there was one more: "Study the impact of Massachusetts charter schools on student outcomes." Little did I know that answering this question would create one of the agency's most enduring, innovative research partnerships—one that persists to this day and has helped answer numerous important policy questions for our state.

In the Beginning

Our initial work on the impact of charter schools was born from a marriage between the policy environment and data availability. Charter schools—independent public schools that operate under five-year charters from the state, with increased flexibility and accountability—were established in Massachusetts in 1993 as part of the landmark Massachusetts Education Reform Act. By the 2006–2007 school year, the state had sixty-one charter schools, enrolling about 23,000 students statewide (2.3 percent of student enrollment overall). Charter schools were controversial from the start. As elsewhere nationally, supporters argued that charter schools provided more choices and opportunities for families and greater competition in the educational arena. Detractors argued that charters drew public resources away from traditional public schools and "creamed" the strongest students, particularly in urban areas, leaving the traditional schools to serve the most challenging students.

A key policy question in the debate was whether the students in charter schools performed better than those in traditional public schools. Although the state statute did not specifically identify higher student outcomes as one of the goals of establishing charters, it stood to reason that if charter students outperformed those in traditional schools, it would make sense to continue to support or even expand charter schools; if they did not, then it would make more sense to stay steady or retract over time. Similarly, decisions on whether to close charter schools or put them on probation were made in part on the basis of student performance data. Understanding how best to compare student performance between charter and traditional schools was therefore of keen interest.

The state had made some initial attempts to analyze this question by comparing the average performance of charter schools to the schools those students would otherwise have enrolled in. But these analyses couldn't account for self-selection: that is, students who chose charters might be systematically different from those who stayed in traditional schools and different in ways that couldn't be readily measured and controlled for with available data. The studies also didn't use longitudinal data to track individual students over time, instead simply comparing performance at the school level at a point in time. A more rigorous research design was needed—one that could account for self-selection and longitudinal trends and thereby compare charters to traditional public schools on equal footing.

Fortunately, state law in Massachusetts requires that when a charter school has more applicants than it has spaces available, students must be admitted by lottery (with some exceptions, such as admitting siblings of currently enrolled students first). If the lottery is fair, then the students from the waitlist are being admitted at random. Examining the longitudinal outcomes of waitlisted students who did and did not gain admission to charters would provide a fair comparison, because the only factor that differed between the two groups is whether they had been randomly offered the opportunity to enroll in a charter school. Tracking these two groups' outcomes over time would provide a much more convincing analysis, one that promised to shed light on the empirical reality of charter school performance in our state.

Although we knew that we needed this more rigorous analysis in order to thoroughly answer our question, three factors had prevented us from pursuing it in the past. First, the state had only begun to collect individual, student-level data on student demographics, program participation and state assessment results in the 2001–2002 school year. It was only by the time of my arrival at the agency that sufficient time had elapsed for students who had won and lost the lottery to have progressed through enough years of school to examine their outcomes. Second, the state did not have access to the lottery data, as these were collected at the individual charter schools but not systematically statewide. And third, the statistical techniques required were beyond the skills and familiarity of most of the analysts at the state, nor did those with the skill to do it have the time to embark on this large a project on top of their other duties.

But by the time I arrived at the state, the agency was poised to embark on such a project. The policy environment was right, and we finally had enough years of data available to allow a deeper look at this question. We wanted a study that would take advantage of charter school lottery data where available, but also would include a traditional regression analysis simply controlling for observable factors, which we called the "observational analysis." In doing so, we could compare the results across the two methodologies and in the observational analysis could use data from all schools, not just those that had more applicants than available spaces. For the initial study we focused specifically on charter schools within the city of Boston to keep the scope manageable and to allow us to examine a third type of schools, pilot schools, which have similar autonomies as charter schools but run within the Boston public schools rather than being chartered by the state. We obtained funding to support the initial research from the Boston Foundation, a local funder with an interest in school choice policy.

To answer this question rigorously in a politicized environment, we needed a research group that would use the most sophisticated analytical techniques possible and couldn't be accused of having their thumb on the scale. We found that group in the Center for Education Policy Research (CEPR) at Harvard University, paired with researchers at the Massachusetts Institute of Technology. The research team included nationally known researchers to guide the work and exceptionally capable graduate students to gather and clean data and run analyses. The researchers had deep expertise on school choice policy and program evaluation and were familiar with the policy environment because they were based locally. Further, I had worked with several of the researchers while in graduate school and in previous positions, so I could be confident that we would be able to communicate effectively with the team.

The First Report

As it turned out, identifying the right research group was the easy part. Getting from there to our first published report took us a year and a half and a lot of sweat and shoe leather. The biggest challenge for the agency was establishing a memorandum of understanding that allowed the researchers to have access to the state's confidential student data for the analysis. My agency had never released data for this purpose before, so we had no preexisting practices or documentation to rely on—and we needed to establish these terms before we could sign a contract with the research team to commence the project. I spent hours with our and Harvard's attorneys hammering out the terms and conditions under which the data could be released. The biggest stumbling block was around the review and publication process. As university-based researchers who valued academic freedom, the Harvard team wanted to ensure that they would be able to publish whatever they found and that we wouldn't rescind the right to publish at the last minute if the results turned out to shine a poor light on the state. On our side, we wanted a right to review and comment on the findings before they were published. This was in part to ensure that no confidential data were inadvertently released in the final publication, but more importantly, we wanted to ensure that the policy context was described accurately and that results were interpreted in light of the state's detailed knowledge about the charter sector and the individual schools involved. Although the agency's leadership wanted an unbiased answer to the research question, we knew that the findings were likely to be widely distributed because of the strong interest statewide in the research question. We wanted to be cautious about when and how findings were released, because we were taking a risk that we would end up with a rigorously designed, highly visible study that might not support our current policy direction. What convinced our leadership to agree to this was my prior relationship with the research team, which created a preexisting basis of faith in the team that they wouldn't leave us unprepared to manage the fallout from the findings, whether positive or negative. From initial bidding until signing the contract, getting through this process took us six months, from initial bidding until contract signature; we finally signed a contract and data-sharing agreement in late 2007.

Then the challenges began for the research team—first and foremost of which was collecting the lottery data from the charter schools. The budget for this project was $100,000, but I'm certain the CEPR team spent much more than that in sending their research assistants all over the city of Boston to gather these data. My agency does not require the schools to submit their lottery data to the state or to maintain it in any particular way, so the staff encountered everything from well-organized Excel spreadsheets that clearly indicated which students applied each year, were admitted in the initial lottery, were admitted at a later time, accepted and declined their offers, and so forth, all the way to boxes filled with reams of paper records, or worse yet, no records at all. Once the data were organized electronically, the researchers had to find the state-assigned identifier for each student who had applied to a charter school lottery so that their lottery data could be merged with the state's student longitudinal data system. In addition, not all charter schools were oversubscribed; some never fill all their seats each year and do not need to conduct a lottery. This further limited the sample of schools for which we could conduct lottery analyses. In the end, lottery data were available for eight Boston charter schools, all serving middle or high school grades. Data for the observational analysis were available for all twenty-nine charters in the city at that time, including schools at the elementary, middle and high school levels.

Once the lottery data were collected, the research team began conducting their analyses. This, too, was challenging. This was the first time these researchers had worked with our state data, so they needed to become familiar with how it was organized and to test their statistical modeling. We checked in with them frequently to provide support on using our data, as well as on understanding state charter school policy because some of the rules around how lotteries operated affected their analytical work. After about six months of data collection and analysis, in summer 2008 we began receiving tantalizing hints that the results were going to be provocative—so provocative, in fact, that the researchers wanted extra time on internal review to pressure-test the results. When we finally got the initial findings that fall, we were stunned. Students enrolled in charter schools in the city of Boston were performing between 0.09 and 0.5 standard deviations higher on state assessments than their peers who attended the traditional Boston public schools, depending on the grade and subject area of English language arts or mathematics (Abdulkadiroglu, Angrist, Dynarski, Kane, & Pathak, 2011). These are among the largest impacts I have seen for a school-level intervention, and they are all the more astonishing because they are measured annually. Students who enrolled in Boston's charter schools for multiple years were benefiting from that acceleration of their achievement each and every year. Further, we saw substantively similar findings in both the lottery and observational designs, reducing the likelihood that the lottery results were being driven by a self-selection mechanism in which only the most effective charters were oversubscribed (and therefore had lottery data available).

The policy community could not help but notice such unambiguous findings. The Boston Foundation, which had funded the initial study, held a well-attended public forum in January 2009 releasing the findings and including a discussion with a panel of policymakers and district personnel. The study was also mentioned in several *Boston Globe* editorials that year as evidence for why the state should expand charter schools. But the biggest impact came the following year, when the state legislature passed and Governor Deval Patrick signed the Achievement Gap Act of 2010. A key feature of the act was to double the limit on the number of charter school seats available in the state's lowest-performing districts, increasing the cap to 18 percent of student enrollment from 9 percent. Although the study's results were not the only factor that increased momentum for this policy change, having credible evidence that students in Boston's charter schools were far outperforming their peers in the Boston public schools certainly made it harder to argue against a cap lift.

An Evolving Partnership

Establishing any research partnership is challenging. It is hard to know at the beginning of a project whether the researchers and agency program experts will be able to work effectively together, whether a particular line of research will yield any notable findings and whether the findings will come in time to be useful for policymaking and programmatic decisions. As a result, my agency cast the net widely at first by providing data for many projects of potential value and then investing more deeply in the most beneficial, productive relationships. In this case, the benefits of the partnership have gone far beyond what we could initially have imagined and have been well worth our investment of time and resources in the work.

The initial charter school study represented an uncommon confluence of the policy and research spheres: a topic that was of great relevance to our state and of great interest to researchers working on the impact of school choice. Since the initial report, our partnership has evolved to examine a much broader array of issues related to charter school and school choice policy in Massachusetts. The research team, now centered at the School Effectiveness and Inequality Initiative (SEII) at the Massachusetts Institute for Technology, has examined the impact of charters in our urban districts and statewide, not just in Boston (e.g., Angrist, Pathak, & Walters, 2013). As additional longitudinal data have become available, researchers have studied charter school outcomes beyond student assessment data, such as AP and SAT results, on-time graduation and college enrollment (Angrist, Cohodes, Dynarski, Pathak, & Walters, forthcoming). Some of the papers the partnership has generated have been fairly academic; for example, one examined the demand for Boston charter schools using a structural approach involving both an optimal choice model and a correction for self-selection (Walters, 2014); others have examined technical aspects of market design and school choice mechanisms (Abdulkadiroglu, Angrist, Narita, & Pathak, 2015). But over time, our research agenda has become increasingly driven by current policy and implementation questions. The research team has gone beyond merely measuring program impacts to digging into the potential reasons why charters might be more effective, in particular examining the influence of the "No Excuses" instructional and behavioral model commonly used in Massachusetts' urban charter schools (Angrist et al., 2013). Other work has focused on special cases that are particularly informative for the state's current policy priorities. One recent paper examined the impact of charters on student outcomes in cases where they are used as turnaround partners in district schools—a situation in which some students enter the school by lottery and others by grandfathering (Abdulkadiroglu, Angrist, Hull, & Pathak, 2015). Findings show that students who are grandfathered in perform equally as well, if not better, as those who enter by lottery. This is crucial information that our program office has used to consider how a charter model might help support the state in turning around other low-performing district schools. Another recent study (Setren, 2015) found that over the last five years, the Boston-based charter schools have closed the gap in enrollment for special education and English language learner ("special needs") students and now enroll similar shares of these groups as the traditional Boston schools. Further, using lottery-based evidence, the results show that enrolling in a charter reduces the likelihood of a student being designated as special needs in the first place, increases the chance of the student being served in an inclusive classroom, and substantially improves their academic outcomes. Our program office has used this evidence to rebut a common misperception that charter schools serve fewer special needs students and/or are serving only the academically strongest among them. The findings will also inform a statewide initiative on access and equity in all charter schools so that other charters can learn from the work in Boston and expand their own efforts to include more special needs students.

The projects that we have collaborated on have generated research findings that are both relevant for policymaking and worthy of publication in top peer-reviewed journals. More recently we have also begun producing short, two-page summaries of the findings for our state's district and school leaders so that they can learn from the work as well (e.g., Abdulkadiroglu, Angrist, Hull, & Pathak, 2014). Several graduate students who have worked on these projects have gone on to receive approval to conduct other studies using our state data, on charter schools and on other policy-relevant topics. This benefits the state enormously because we can work with researchers who already know our data systems and can answer additional questions with minimal additional investment of our time.

A particularly important side effect of the partnership is the improvement it has generated in our state data systems and policies. By dint of the initial study, the agency developed data-sharing policies that have been used to facilitate dozens of other research projects on topics ranging from the impact of the state's merit scholarship on college enrollment and completion to the implementation and early outcomes of our state's School Redesign Grant program for turnaround schools. The charter school partnership also helped the state work out many thorny issues related to using our data systems for research. This team was among the first to tackle the issue surrounding the use of National Student Clearinghouse (NSC) data to track Massachusetts public high school graduates into college for research purposes, which helped us understand the advantages and limitations of these data. On the basis of what we have learned from the NSC data, we have just embarked on a joint research partnership with SEII and the Massachusetts Department of Higher Education. This will allow us for the first time to understand what happens to charter school students once they reach higher education institutions in terms of remediation, course enrollments and completion, declared major, time to degree and so forth.

But here is my favorite evidence of the long-run effects of the partnership: The SEII team recently organized a conference on leveraging research and policy to improve K–12 education in Massachusetts. This included a full day of research presentations with policymakers serving as discussants, and it attracted a broad mix of attendees from school districts, nonprofits, government agencies and research organizations. The fact that sufficient research on Massachusetts education policy issues is available to merit a full-day conference, that the research team rather than the state agency led the charge to organize the event and that policymakers valued the research enough to take time to participate is testimony to this partnership's broad impact in our state.

What Has Enabled Our Success?

Several factors allowed the partnership to launch in the first place. First, and in my view most important, my agency was willing to invest time and effort into answering a policy question of interest in a rigorous way, allowing the researchers to come to an independent conclusion on the impact of charter schools in Boston. Here I think the state's history as a leader in education reform was helpful. We could hardly say no to credible independent research on a state policy initiative when we were asking our schools and districts to examine their own evidence of impact and adjust course accordingly. Our senior leadership has consistently emphasized that we need to know whether our policies are working, and if so, why and how so that over time we can do more of what is effective and less of what is not. Their openness to independent analysis allowed the researchers to flourish, which in turn gave the agency much more valuable information about charter schools than it ever had before.

Second, we could not have conducted any of this work without a multimillion-dollar state and federal investment in the longitudinal data system mentioned earlier, which allowed us to track individual students over time through the Massachusetts public school system. Examining impacts for cohorts of students or for schools as a whole, as some of the state's earlier studies had done, left too many unanswered questions and opportunities for criticisms of the findings. The question of interest simply could not be answered well without student-level longitudinal data. Third, the initial funding of $100,000 by the Boston Foundation for the first study was instrumental. Without that seed money, the state probably would not have had the resources to support such a rigorous study on our own, nor would the Center for Education Policy Research have been likely to invest the time and staffing in a project with such intensive data collection requirements.

Once the partnership was established, several additional factors contributed to its success. First, the fact that we were able to study the impact of charter schools with such a rigorous design helped establish the value for policymaking of research of this kind. We were able to substantively advance the debate in the state about charter schools by providing the best possible evidence on their impact, and through a team of researchers whose credentials were unassailable. Looking back, this was a high-risk strategy; it might be more advisable to start a partnership with a study where the stakes were a little lower. But on the other hand, we immediately saw the influence of the work on state policy, and this initial and visible success made us all eager to continue to partner together and learn more. Another factor was my prior working relationship with two members of the research team. This meant we didn't have to build relationships entirely from the ground up and smoothed the way when we encountered challenges, such as the data-sharing negotiations mentioned earlier. Over time that initial trust in those two researchers expanded to the entire team, and now we all work together as peers and valued colleagues. Again, funding was also helpful, as the research team has successfully competed for funding from the Institute for Education Sciences, National Science Foundation, Arnold Foundation, and other grant makers on the basis of the strength and quality of the initial project and subsequent course of study.

Lessons for Other Partnerships

As I reflect on this and other research partnerships with my agency, a few lessons learned come to mind. First, study a question that matters. Our most successful partnerships have focused on areas of state policy where stakeholders inside and outside the agency were keenly interested in the findings—charter schools, educator evaluation, school and district turnaround and so forth. This creates an appetite for evidence that can generate fruitful discussions about the right questions to ask and the implications of research findings for policy, something that is much harder to do when a research project focuses on a topic that isn't high on the policy agenda at the moment.

Second, as a topic gets more politicized, rigor matters more. Opponents are much more critical of the methodology of research projects attempting to measure the impact of a controversial policy. It is hard to think of an education policy in Massachusetts that was more controversial in 2007 than charter schools. They have been a lightning rod ever since their creation because districts directly feel the impact of the losses in enrollment (and associated funding) if students exit to charters. Straightforward descriptive comparisons showing that students in charters outperformed students in traditional schools could not fully address the objections of critics about the influence of selection bias on the findings. A more rigorous methodology was needed in this case to ensure that we had fully accounted for other potential explanations of why those differences might exist.

That being said, in many cases, descriptive statistics are sufficient and shed useful insight on policy questions of interest. For example, in a different research partnership we conducted a survey on a representative sample of educators to find out more about their opinions on the implementation of the state's new educator evaluation framework. We learned that although many educators had concerns that the system overall was unfair, nearly 90 percent of those evaluated felt that their own evaluation had been fair. This simple descriptive statistic helped us begin to change the dialogue about the system, as educators began to realize that most of their peers were having good experiences and that perhaps their concerns about the fairness of the overall system might be unfounded.

Similarly, the deliverables associated with the project matter greatly. The charter school research described in this chapter has tended to focus more on producing academic research papers, in part because of the particularly technical nature of the research methodology and in part because of the interest and skills of the researchers. But even on this relatively academic project, we have asked the researchers to conduct briefings of state agency and district staff and to produce shorter, general-audience versions of their papers. On other partnerships, we have avoided technical papers altogether and produced only shorter, nontechnical reports intended to share actionable findings and examples from practice for district audiences. The point of doing the research is not just to learn for the sake of learning, but to help the agency and school districts improve their work, so we have worked hard to ensure that the products of our partnerships support that goal. (For more on this point, see Conaway, 2013.)

But far more important than defining the research question, methodology or deliverables is building the personal relationships that keep the work moving forward and help weather the rough patches that inevitably come up. In establishing a partnership, both the policymaking agency and the researchers are putting faith in one another. The agency must have faith that the researchers won't misuse their data or blindside them with unexpected findings, and the researchers must have faith that the agency will allow them enough freedom to conduct their research unencumbered. That kind of faith can only be built on trust accumulated through time and shared experiences. The trust stemmed from communicating with each other about our priorities and needs, and then following through on our commitments. We were fortunate with the charter school work that my preexisting relationships with two of the researchers could accelerate this process; others might need more time. But it is that faith in one another that has sustained our partnership for nearly a decade and yielded so many benefits for the agency and the researchers alike.

The Massachusetts Charter School Research Partnership case reveals a range of insights about motivations for researcher–policymaker partnerships. Key among them is its demonstration of how the needs of one partner—in this case, the policymakers—serve the needs of the other partner, the researchers. Acknowledging the foundational motivation, which was to answer a policy-relevant research question, other motivations became apparent throughout the partnership's processes of conception, development and implementation. These motivations include the potential for research and policy impact beyond the specific partnership and the initial question it sought to answer. Supporting the motivations are what we call key conditions. In the context of the Massachusetts case, these conditions included preexisting relationships and increasing clarity during the partnership about the positive returns on investment of human and other resources with respect to the knowledge and deliverables that the partnership was generating. In sum, the original motivations of each partner have led to long-term collaboration and sustained mutual benefits for the partners and their respective stakeholders.

Durham Public Schools and Duke University Research Partnership

Our second featured partnership case on motivations stems from a different context than the first. In contrast to the Massachusetts case, which was driven by the need for external experts to conduct research relevant to a specific policy challenge that policymakers faced, the Durham Public Schools case came about as the result of an institutional challenge involving the different cultures and needs of the policy-sector entity and the research entity. This partnership demonstrates the possibility of moving from a lack of knowledge and understanding between partners to shared and mutually beneficial purposes and processes for achieving them.

As with the Massachusetts case, the Durham School Research Partnership has led to a set of systems, processes and people that continue to adapt and evolve as conditions change and needs emerge, while keeping the core partnership principles intact.

Durham Public Schools and Duke University Research Partnership

Heidi Carter

Background

Durham Public Schools (DPS) is fortunate to share its hometown with excellent university partners, and Duke University is a stalwart partner. A strong component of Duke's town-grown relationship is the myriad support the university provides to Durham's public school system, and a significant case in point is the relationship between Duke researchers and DPS leadership. An important infrastructure that makes this relationship successful is the Sanford School of Public Policy's School Research Partnership (SRP).

Durham Public Schools is one of 115 school districts in North Carolina. Its size, history, demographic makeup, geographic location and other characteristics make it a much-sought-after laboratory for study by researchers. Data privacy concerns combined with limited financial and human resources for research support have made district leaders reticent to be eager research partners. Moreover, the proposed research typically came in terms of what the researcher needed, not what might benefit the district.

SRP provides a model for collaboration between the researchers at Sanford and DPS. DPS administrators and members of the DPS Board of Education have taken advantage of the partnership opportunities that the SRP helps facilitate. The SRP has evolved and strengthened over time to align with the needs of both the researchers and policymakers. The result is a symbiotic relationship that helps translate the empirical evidence that researchers uncover into best practices and policy decisions in the real-world setting.

Now over a decade into the formalized partnership, the SRP has matured and expanded to include several different mechanisms for collaboration: a process for introducing research into the school setting, a process for connecting Duke students who want research experience with DPS policymakers who want evidence-based solutions to challenges related to public education and a mechanism for the establishment of important relationships between members of the university community and the DPS community.

Motivation and Mutual Benefit

One motivation for the SRP was to create a structured process that Duke researchers could apply to conduct their research on students and educators in DPS. More than a decade ago, and prior to the establishment of the SRP, Duke researchers were experiencing frustration around the difficulties they perceived in working with DPS. Gaining access to students and educators for their research was very complicated. Having identified problems they believed were relevant to school success, the Duke researchers were naturally seeking subjects and settings to conduct their studies. They believed the research outcomes could in turn help DPS reach its district goals.

Meanwhile, school district leaders were faced with increasingly burdensome federal and state requirements for educating children. The accountability and school reform movements were conspiring to create a district culture that was highly focused on improving test scores, which were a national proxy for student learning. Part of this was driven by the testing regime of No Child Left Behind and the ever-important, high-stakes standardized test scores. School district leaders were consumed by their imperative to lift the test scores of the children in DPS, and this drive decreased the system's flexibility needed for successful collaboration.

Conversely, the district leaders maintained that the percentage of research proposals that they approved was actually rather high and that they were as open as possible for research in the schools. However, researchers who had relationships with school board members or administrators continued to complain that DPS was closed to researchers and was driving them into other school systems that were more welcoming and accommodating. They asserted that it was a shame that a research–district collaboration on problems of mutual benefit was not happening right here in our own hometown, but instead in other surrounding, less restrictive school districts.

Key Ingredients

Cross-sector collaborations of any type can be daunting, as all players have fully loaded responsibilities within their individual arenas. But faith in the power of working together is a motivating force that can drive success, especially when relationships are strong between two sectors. Success can often seem serendipitously tied to the existence of already established relationships between a researcher and a school district leader. Such a relationship helped turn the tide in bolstering the SRP.

When there are preexisting connections between researchers and school board members or school staff, partnerships may be more encouraged or facilitated because of that connection. Partnerships had been successfully formed between researchers and principals who were particularly open to collaborative problem-solving. Additionally, despite the difference in perceptions of the access to DPS for research purposes, partnerships had been successfully formed by way of a district-level portal of entry, but the process seemed disjointed and lacking a clear structure.

Although local decision-making may be the most effective in many situations, there are times when top-down decisions make good sense. Regarding the formation of collaborative relationships between DPS and Duke researchers, the top-down push seemed to be a key approach to making partnerships more successful. Pressure from the top can come through a superintendent or from the board of education.

Three contextual ingredients helped bolster the SRP over time. The first key element involved relationships. An elected member of the board of education (BOE) was a close associate with a faculty member who happened to be managing the SRP at the time. The faculty member had already partnered, in a way, with this school board member by serving as a policy advisor during her board of education election campaign. This relationship during the campaign helped strengthen the candidate's platform on the key issues because the university researcher could share evidence of what works to solve specific policy problems. This campaign relationship provided a firmer foundation for future collaborations within the realm of the SRP, as well as a point of contact for the university's SRP facilitator, should challenges arise.

The second key element for a successful partnership is linked to this researcher–board member policy connection. The newly elected BOE member believed in the importance of evidence-based policymaking and school reform and was willing to help troubleshoot challenges to improve functioning of the SRP. The orientation in favor of evidence-based policy was not only consistent with national trends among policymakers, but also was enhanced by the educational and professional backgrounds and experiences of some of the new board members. The willingness to address challenges was bolstered even further by discussions with other school board colleagues that reinforced the belief in the importance of using empirical evidence in policy decisions. Public schools were struggling to eliminate achievement gaps and lift student learning, and the national obsession with testing and accountability did not seem to be working. Board members were eager to know what the research was showing about other school reform approaches that might be tried in DPS. This led to a commitment to using research to inform policy decisions.

Third, because of this commitment to research-based policymaking, the BOE members were willing to gently encourage more full participation by the district in the SRP. There was a strong working relationship between the school board and the administration and a healthy respect for appropriate roles and responsibilities of each. Although board members were careful to maintain their role of overseers of administration and avoid micromanagement, they were inclined to make a good case with the administration for fuller participation in the SRP in order to expand access to data on which to base policy decisions. Board members were advocates for evidence-based practice by the administration, as well as evidence-based policymaking at the board level. In sum, there were at least three contextual ingredients that motivated this partnership: relationships, a commitment to evidence-based policy and a willingness to advocate for change that would benefit both institutions and ultimately the students across the district.

The thread tying all of this together was the tenacity of the Duke researchers over the long term. Having someone at the university level continuing to work with DPS to refine the process for collaboration seemed essential to maintaining momentum. This process of refinement and improvement occurred on two levels—one where the university met with the district to discuss ways to enhance their working relationship, and the second where the faculty member responsible for the SRP joined forces with a member of the school board to discuss potential mechanisms for improving the process. These types of discussions need to be ongoing for the partnership to flourish and flex with the changing needs of the university, school system and policymakers.

Research in schools and research to inform upcoming policy decisions are two major aspects of the SRP. The process for getting research projects into the schools was better defined and greatly enhanced for all parties. The district's Office of Data and Accountability developed a timeline and flow chart to be used by researchers to apply for access to the schools. The district also explained that it was imperative that the research be on topics of interest to DPS, that it be something that would directly benefit DPS students and that it not take time away from instruction. Grant-supported funding, secured by university researchers, seemed to enable the collaboration, either in the way of resources for schools that researchers needed and schools wanted, or for remuneration for school staff time. At this point in the partnership, funding continues to help and catalyze ongoing work, but the partnership will continue to develop and strengthen even without funding directed to it.

Connecting students with real-world research problems has been very successful for both the students and the policymakers. Durham leaders are very willing to work with students on research projects that help inform their policy or program development. It is important that the policymaker be accessible to the student, and it is equally important that the time required of the policymaker be limited. Finding the right balance is essential.

Elements of Success

Duke students tend to be very capable, conscientious and hard working; the Duke faculty members who sponsor the students' research also provide outstanding ongoing support to the student. These are fundamental elements for a successful outcome of this type of collaboration. The policymaker must be equally committed to working with a student for the partnership to benefit both parties. University professors and faculty advisors identify policymakers at the local and state level who have a desire to participate and a clear problem or research question for students to pursue. This process is fruitful when the faculty advisors have a network of community leaders they can contact about working with students on a project. Ideally, the network includes partners with whom the faculty have established relationships. As noted elsewhere, having existing relationships in place yields a range of benefits for the researcher, the policy partner and ultimately for students as well. In this instance, one of the Duke co-directors of the partnership has built a vast network of contacts within the community, many of whom are interested in working with students.

At the initiation of the partnership, the student, faculty advisor and policymaker must meet and confer in order to narrow the research topic and define the product that will be of use to the policymaker. This must happen in order to meet the goals of both parties. Usually, several additional meetings take place to give progress updates to the policymaker, provide clarity on student questions that may have arisen during the course of research and troubleshoot any areas of challenge. When the research projects are complete, usually at the end of the semester, all parties convene for a presentation of the results and a celebratory dinner. This provides the students with an opportunity to hone their presentation skills and a venue for continued relationship building among all parties. Finally, policymakers have solid information, in the form of an agreed-upon deliverable, to support better decision-making.

Once the basic features of the SRP process are in place, it is up to the student and policymaker to glean as much from the relationship as possible and to take full, mutual advantage of the opportunity. The best-case scenario is one where the policymaker is deeply interested in an issue with real-time relevance and the student is excited to be engaged and eager to work. There is an authentic problem to be solved, and each member of the SRP team is energetic and optimistic about the possibilities for addressing a complex social problem. One example of a very successful collaboration is the partnership around research and policy solutions to alternatives to suspension. Out-of-school suspension, and its subsequent loss of instructional time for the student, is an ongoing top issue of concern in Durham Public Schools. The school district and the school board remain committed to fair and effective discipline policies, decreasing overall suspensions, and eliminating potential biases that might exist in the assignment of student discipline. A student performed research on best practices using alternatives to the use of suspension from school that would help promote positive student behavior, decrease removal of students from the learning environment and keep students on track academically. Additional elements of this particular partnership included invitations to legislative updates in the North Carolina General Assembly around this topic and collaborative opinion editorials in local newspapers.

An SRP project will be fatally flawed if a student is unable to follow through on her assignment, and this is an ever-present possibility when working with students who may have busy schedules or be overcommitted elsewhere. The experience can be a negative one if the student fails to meet appointments with the policymaker or misses periodic deadlines in the research project timeline. This lack of follow-through can ultimately result in a weak deliverable for the policymaker (in my decade or more of experiences with SRP, this has only happened once). The policymaker must also be accountable for timeliness and scheduled meetings with the student in order to ensure a positive experience for the student-researcher as well. In turn, the faculty advisor must have a process for monitoring the student's work and follow-through. Each semester since its inception, the SRP process became more clearly defined as far as the roles of each partner (policymaker, student, faculty advisor) and what was expected of each to ensure the projects' success.

The relationships formed as part of the SRP have broadened opportunities for further collaboration. BOE members and other district and community leaders are invited to the Sanford lecture series, where highly regarded guest speakers from around the world are invited to present their research findings. Extremely relevant topics are explored that can help mold the judgments of decision-makers over time and can serve as the foundation for future policies and programs in the community. BOE members and community leaders or activists have also been invited to attend sessions where the Duke researchers brief the members of the North Carolina General Assembly on pertinent policy topics.

The relationships formed through the SRP have opened up occasions for policymakers to be guest speakers in Duke classes at the Sanford School. The school district has solicited advice and evidence from Duke researchers to support efforts to improve school outcomes. Sometimes this comes in the form of data analysis, reports and program evaluations. Other times there has been Duke participation on district ad hoc committees or task forces and presentations to the BOE or other community bodies. Sometimes these services are gratuitous, and other times the district contracts with Duke for the researchers' expertise.

Toward the Future

For the SRP to remain strong, it is critical that the university continue to invest in relationships with school board members, the superintendent, educators and staff. As school board members turn over, new relationships must be formed so that new board members understand the value added through this partnership with the university. In the same way that school board membership changes, superintendents and administrators also come and go. The SRP needs a driver from the university end to sustain ongoing relationships with the school district. Ideally, DPS would also have a point of contact for the SRP that is built into the job description of a particular administrative position. Care must be given to identify all of the important aspects of a well-oiled SRP so as to better institutionalize or codify the effective operations of the partnership to ensure its longevity.

The partnership is ongoing and has been professionally valuable for those who work in the world of policy development. Over the years, as major topics have been addressed, the collaboration with Duke has buttressed the district's approach to solving problems. The SRP and its derivative partnerships have provided invaluable input on topics such as out-of-school suspension, universal preschool, collaborations with charter schools, school bell schedules, school nutrition, effects of test-based accountability and many more. Relationships established through the SRP serve as a foundation for more widespread community collaborations, such as the Durham Children's Data Center. The SRP collaborations have helped policymakers be more effective in developing successful strategies and advancing positive change in Durham.

The likelihood of long-term sustainability for the SRP rests in large part on strong relationships between the university and the public school system. In order for the SRP to remain strong, it is critical that the university continue to invest in relationships with school board members, the superintendent, educators and staff.

This could provide the foundation for a formal agreement or memorandum of understanding between the university and the school system that would help the partnership withstand the turnover of individual board members, superintendents and university professionals

Unlike the Massachusetts partnership, which was motivated by the need for answers to a policy-relevant research question, the Durham Public Schools–Duke University partnership stemmed from the need for two institutions to develop strategies to address a gap in understanding. That gap was preventing each institution from receiving maximum benefit from working with the other and as a result limited the positive impact each could have more broadly. Although there were many preexisting relationships between DPS and Duke at both the individual and organizational level, none appeared to provide enough of the requisite conditions for successful researcher–policymaker partnerships of the sort featured throughout this book.

School board member Carter's reflections highlight how incremental and seemingly minor changes to the working relationships between Duke and DPS generated systematized, sustainable processes that are now mutually beneficial to both partners. Importantly, a key tenet of the Duke–DPS partnership is its replicability. The partners agree that the elements of success are not unique to DPS or to Duke and can inform existing and emerging partnerships between school districts and universities nationwide.

The Bridge to Somewhere: The Ohio Juvenile Justice Partnership

The third partnership featured in this chapter highlights yet another source of motivations for researcher–policymaker partnerships: pursuit of public policy reform. In the case of the Ohio juvenile justice reform, a multisector (research, policy practice), multidisciplinary (legal, research, policy, practice, advocacy/lobbying) team capitalized on the context and timing that made it possible to pursue a specific set of juvenile justice policy goals. As with many of the other cases, the team capitalized on key conditions that played a role in facilitating the partnership's success. These conditions included timeliness with regard to political context and new private funding targeting juvenile justice reform. Perhaps the most important condition, however, was "collective agreement on the nature of the social problem requiring action" in the words of the case author, Gabriella Celeste.

The Bridge to Somewhere

Gabriella Celeste

In January 2011 Ohio faced a looming budget crisis, which presented a window of opportunity for policymakers to consider significant legislative reforms to juvenile justice with budget savings or cost-neutral implications. In addition, political leadership had just shifted from a Democratic governor and politically divided state legislature to both Republican-controlled executive and legislative branches. The election of a conservative Republican governor who embraced a "smart on crime" approach to adult correctional reform proved critical and had implications for juvenile correctional reforms as well. At the same time, there was a new pool of dollars from national funders aimed at juvenile justice reform coupled with targeted local funding explicitly dedicated to substantive juvenile justice legislative reform in the current budget cycle. All of these factors facilitated the creation of a rigorous core campaign team that strategically coordinated expertise in research, policy content and political lobbying, with access to critical state leadership and influences. This core team included representatives from the following organizations: the Schubert Center for Child Studies; the R Strategies Group; M & R Strategic Services; Van Meter, Ashbrook & Associates, Inc.; Center for Innovative Practices at the Case Western Reserve University Begun Center for Violence Prevention, Research & Evaluation; the Office of the Ohio Public Defender; the George Gund Foundation; a former state legislator lobbyist; and a former Ohio Supreme Court justice. This work resulted in the passage of House Bill (HB) 86, a groundbreaking piece of legislation aimed at improving Ohio's juvenile justice system (see Appendix A for a summary of HB 86 provisions related to juveniles).

In addition to the political and fiscal landscape, a series of significant juvenile justice–related activities occurred that collectively made Ohio ripe for reform. These included ongoing litigation and monitoring of a settlement agreement stemming from a federal class-action lawsuit based on conditions of juvenile confinement, closure of several state juvenile institutions, strengthened juvenile appellate advocacy and policy efforts, capacity building for effective community-based options, the development of targeted approaches for incentivizing local courts to reduce state juvenile admissions and coalition building for policy reform among juvenile justice advocates. Behavioral and brain research concerning teens began to take hold in juvenile case law and in the public conscience, while political attention had begun to focus on adult criminal justice reforms, which provided an opening for highlighting issues related to children in the juvenile justice system. Although legislative and budgetary policy changes had not been a part of any recent successful juvenile justice–related reform efforts, the combination of these activities created the necessary foundation for legislative reform.

The federal litigation around unconstitutional confinement of children in state juvenile justice facilities (*S.H. v. Stickrath, 2008; J.P. v. Taft, 2007*) created the sense of urgency around reform that propelled change around the treatment of juveniles in Ohio. In fact, since the original filing of the conditions lawsuit in 2004, ODYS (Ohio Department of Youth Services) closed four juvenile correctional facilities and reduced facility average daily populations significantly. Additional reforms enacted were intended to hold the state accountable for the outcomes of these changes, and evidence and outcomes-based practices were becoming increasingly utilized through programs such as RECLAIM (Reasoned and Equitable Community and Local Alternatives to Incarceration of Minors), Targeted RECLAIM and the Behavioral Health Juvenile Justice (BHJJ) initiative. Evaluation of these efforts was undertaken through ODYS partnerships with the University of Cincinnati and the Begun Center for Violence Prevention at Case Western Reserve University. These efforts demonstrated Ohio's capacity to more cost effectively address the needs of the young people in the juvenile justice system and the opportunity for building on this success by increasing investments in quality, outcomes-based programming.

Other changes in the juvenile justice environment were creating increased awareness of the developmental needs of adolescents that further supported reform. The new knowledge about adolescent brain development was prompting the legal system and other youth-serving systems to rethink their approaches to serving this demographic. This research was revealing that teens' brains are significantly different from adults, particularly in the areas of executive functioning and the neurological capacities needed to understand the consequences of actions. Neurological research as well as behavioral science and ecological models of child development supported the notion that adolescents required different approaches in addressing juvenile crime.

Public policy change requires collective agreement on the nature of the social problem requiring action. In this case, the social problem (requiring a policy solution) was identified as the challenge of holding young people in the juvenile justice system accountable in developmentally appropriate and cost-effective ways so that they can be more successful, positively contributing community members in the future. Creating a shared understanding of this social problem involved understanding the intersection between the developmental life stage of adolescence and juvenile justice policy. Research and relevant data help illuminate the scope of a social problem as well as identify potential leverages for action. This latter aspect of policy research is paramount. Identifying what is "relevant" in the context of a policy change effort can be a daunting task. It is important for both accuracy and credibility to present as complete a picture as possible. In this case, relevant findings were presented using a variety of juvenile justice–related data on budget expenditures and projections, juvenile arrest and other crime statistics, juvenile correctional population, demographics, recidivism, community program service and evaluation and cost–benefit analyses. A literature review of social science articles on adolescent development and the juvenile justice population was conducted, as well as on best practices and developmentally appropriate strategies for meeting the needs of this population. Other sources included legal briefings, administrative and statutory research, state budgets and program documents, government publications and other reports by experts or interest groups and public opinion surveys. Creating this information landscape was key. Further, conducting secondary research to identify relevant data is only part of the process. Assembling, analyzing and translating the data are equally important to the task of social problem definition.

In addition to data, it was critical to identify potential solutions that were ambitious but achievable. Political scientist John Kingdon (2011) talks about the role of the policy "entrepreneur" in creating "frames" as categories for how one looks at the social problems. In this instance, Ohio's budget crisis required a fiscal cost–benefit focus; however, as noted previously, there were several important related frames, including child well-being, community safety, accountability and developmentally appropriate evidence-based practices (EBPs). Describing the social problems in this multifarious way (rather than exclusively as a problem of youth crime and recidivism, costly juvenile court and correctional systems and lack of funding, etc.) enabled the policy working group to design a set of policy solutions that integrated a broad view of "accountability"— fiscal, system, youth and public safety—with a similarly broad view of "success" as part of the policy change agenda. The proposed policy reforms in the agenda were also intentionally aligned with guiding principles based on the MacArthur Foundation's Models for Change (MfC) core principles that incorporate an understanding of child development and adolescent research. The policy agenda relied heavily on the research and data presented in the social problem, in the context of the state's current fiscal and political climate, thus providing a strong rationale for the system reform.

In this context, "research" has special meaning. Because the core team considered a wide range of information sources, including empirical research, case studies, rules and regulations, feedback from practitioners and families and so on, this mix was aligned with Vivian Tseng's (2012) description of a "broad conceptualization" of research needed to inform policy and help with interpretation. This conceptualization has everything to do with use. That is, there are times when information serves an "enlightenment function," influencing how policymakers think about an issue or problem, which Tseng calls "conceptual use."

The importance of effectively communicating information cannot be overstated and may be one of the primary reasons for the eventual passage of this bill. In an effort to present the facts that would be the most compelling to a policymaker, key data points from the policy research were gleaned and presented in a concise summary of facts that could provide a foundation for a policy change agenda in the briefing entitled *Rightsizing Juvenile Justice in Ohio: FY2012–2013 Budget—Why Ohio Needs to 'Get Smart' on Juvenile Justice Reform*. In light of the state budget crisis, this summary was framed as a budget reform opportunity in part by identifying some of the biggest cost drivers in the system and the fiscal impacts of certain policies and practices. Rightsizing Juvenile Justice, or Rightsizing JJ, also highlighted key findings to demonstrate what works with this population and where effective alternatives to the status quo existed to support better system and individual child well-being outcomes.

In particular, the document led with the following statement and laid out ten key findings tied to fiscal implications to provide the rationale for policy reforms: "Taxpayers currently bear the burden of a series of practices and policies that could benefit from strategic, substantive reforms with both immediate and long-term cost-benefits. Consider the following costs . . ." The facts were then used as building blocks in the Rightsizing JJ reform agenda focused on several content areas. The juvenile justice social problem in Ohio, not unlike many social problems that capture political attention, was essentially framed as an economic one comparing the high social and fiscal costs of Ohio's ineffective juvenile justice system to the better return on investing in effective programs. Further, developmental psychologist Aletha Huston (2005) notes that it is essential to ensure that policy research is tied as directly as possible to actions that policymakers can take. The Rightsizing JJ publication accomplished all of these points, making it particularly useful for its intended purpose: to inform policymakers of what the research tells us about effective juvenile justice policy and practice.

All of this led the core team to create research policy principles, which guided all recommendations for legislative change:

1. **Realign** public dollars from costly, ineffective ODYS institutions to cost-effective, community-based alternatives.
2. **Reinvest** in proven-effective, research-supported and evidence-based interventions.
3. **Revise** certain key sentencing schemes to restore some of the fundamental qualities of the juvenile justice system based on principles of adolescent development and the discretionary role of juvenile court judges and to deter deeper system involvement.

Specific policy solutions included the adoption of fiscal realignment language in the state budget to apply savings from juvenile corrections (either through the further elimination of correctional facilities or through other cost savings realized through downsizing of population and personnel) to be reinvested in EBPs, specifically naming at least two efforts currently supported by ODYS. The policy agenda also sought to ensure that all community-level interventions funded through the ODYS RECLAIM state–local cost-sharing formula be "research-supported, outcome-based" programs by adding specific language to the state code. This comprehensive policy agenda for juvenile justice reform was grounded in research to ensure its likelihood of success and credibility, and ultimately better outcomes for the young people involved. Presenting the policy solution as a trifold set of strategies—realignment, reinvestment and revision of law to reflect core values of the juvenile justice system and principles of adolescent development—provided a useful organizing framework for the reform agenda that also helped to advance its political viability.

The success of HB 86 involved leveraging the ongoing activities of many individuals working for juvenile justice improvements in different capacities ("policy entrepreneurs" described by Kingdon) into strategic partnerships. Figure 2.1 illustrates these areas of ongoing juvenile justice reform efforts as "key influencer activities." Typically, the entities engaged in these influencer activities were dedicated to systems change that was supported in part by private funders that helped provide resources to harness collective efforts for effective reform.

Although these activities overlapped at times through existing partnerships, the policy change in HB 86 occurred as a result of a deliberate, coordinated alignment of these strategic activities with the guidance of a core campaign team. The core team was composed of professional "campaign" staff, including communication consultants and lobbyists, and key practitioners, advocates and other policy subject matter experts (several of whom were among

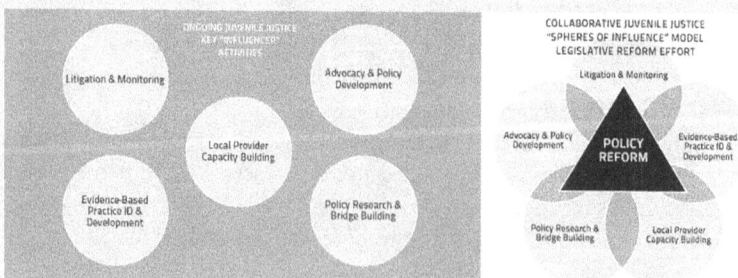

Figure 2.1 Key Influencer Activities

these "influencer" entities). The select nature of the team facilitated the trust and nimbleness needed to respond to the pace of the legislative process in order to move a clear, concise juvenile justice reform agenda forward in the immediate budget cycle.

Leveraging the critical, existing "influencer activities" in order to advance shared priorities for juvenile justice reform required an understanding of what that work entailed and its potential role in a collective reform effort. "Litigation & Monitoring" included several class-action lawsuits concerning unconstitutional conditions and treatment of youth in ODYS juvenile facilities and related matters, which resulted in a settlement agreement with the state. This settlement agreement provided the groundwork for a developmentally informed approach to treatment and rehabilitation of youth and helped to identify and shape specific policy reforms sought in HB 86. For instance, several statutory provisions within the juvenile code were inconsistent with the guiding principles adopted in the settlement agreement, such as how youth were considered eligible for release from correctional facilities, requiring a legislative remedy. The settlement agreement also advanced the movement of youth back into programs in local communities under a continuum of care based on risk and need levels, seeking input from a number of stakeholders to help change the reliance on confinement.

The "Evidence-Based Practice Identification & Development" activity involved university partners such as those from the Center for Innovative Practice with the Begun Center at Case Western Reserve ("CIP"), helping to disseminate a variety of resources and best practice treatment models to support successful interventions with particular populations, behavioral health and juvenile justice interventions, as part of their technical assistance role to public and private agencies. Importantly, CIP brought attention to some of the evidence and rationale for investing in effective community-based alternatives for youth with serious behavior issues, including work from the Blueprints for Violence Prevention at the University of Colorado and analysis completed by the Washington State Institute for Public Policy, which examines costs and benefits related to evidence-based practices. Coupled with ongoing, high-level policy discussions regarding children's behavioral health in Ohio, this expertise helped inform the development of appropriate policy language to encourage cost-effective programming for youth in the juvenile justice system.

"Provider Capacity Building" was another critically important area of activity needed in order to effectively downsize the incarcerated juvenile population, which was occurring as a result of several variables, including provisions in the settlement agreement, the continuing decrease in the juvenile crime rate and the impact of RECLAIM and other diversionary efforts to disincentivize use of state correctional facilities. Because many of the community-based programs to date were not using EBPs, capacity needed to be built around helping these programs be more effective and having the ability to measure child well-being outcomes. University support (CWRU and University of Cincinnati) was vital to providing the technical assistance needed to implement and evaluate effective programs. Policy efforts concerning local program capacity building involve several elements: creating and operating cost-effective community programs, integrating outcome-based and EBPs within community programs to ensure quality outcomes, using research and evaluation to measure the "success" of these programs and identifying potential, sustainable funding streams to develop the local capacity to serve children and young people. At its core, however, forging relationships among critical partners—juvenile court judges, probation and court administrators, evaluators and technical assistance providers and ODYS management—is vital to building an effective state–local system of care. Strong partnerships are built over time, through a series of dialogues, information sharing, training and other collaborative activities. Policy reforms focused on expanding these efforts.

"Advocacy & Policy Development" occurred through the engagement of several organizations, public and private, in order to build broad alliances. These relationships, many of which were developed over years of professional and grassroots engagement, were integral to the success of this legislation. Activities were undertaken to gather feedback from the public (a large survey was distributed to stakeholders and community members), conduct media outreach and public education and involve other key stakeholders in the juvenile justice system. Critically, the core campaign team also had professional lobbyists with credibility and access to the current political leadership to successfully move the policy agenda through HB 86.

"Policy Research & Bridge Building" is the last sphere of activity noted in this strategic model and represents multifaceted work. In this context, it required a comprehensive grasp of the social science literature and specific data related to the juvenile justice system; access to subject matter experts and working relationships with key stakeholders in the field; analysis, translation and applied policy capabilities; an understanding of political feasibility; and a capacity to articulate a collective vision for change into an actionable proposal. The Shubert Center at CWRU served this function as the coordinating entity of select "influencer" partners in order to develop a juvenile justice reform policy agenda with an eye toward influencing the state budget and supported with relevant secondary research and data analysis to make the case for reform. This work was guided by the following values:

1. Policymaking should be **research-informed**.
2. Child-related policies should be aligned with **principles of child and adolescent development**.
3. **Collaborative, bidirectional processes** lead to more effective policy development.
4. Policy proposals must be actionable and **relevant to the current political climate**.

The policy research and bridging function facilitated real-world policy change through reliable access to expert policy analysis. In doing so, it connected the professional "campaign" team and long-term Ohio-based advocates and practitioners to broker an ambitious yet pragmatic agenda that could be turned into concrete legislative proposals and embraced by a broad range of stakeholders. The day-to-day challenges of managing various elements of the campaign, engaging critical influencers and political leaders, being responsive to new developments and negotiations and communicating to different partners and stakeholders while methodically moving a policy reform agenda can be all-consuming. The ability to utilize the core campaign team and its advisors for guidance and strategic intervention as the legislative process unfolded was essential to the success of the policy reform effort.

Finally, local and national funders were vital to the success of this policy effort. Without funding, as well as content expertise, important components of managing strategies would have been out of reach. The National Campaign for State Juvenile Justice Reform, led by the MacArthur Foundation with support from other national funders and the Cleveland-based Gund Foundation, provided resources otherwise unavailable for strategic management, professional government relations services and communications support needed to craft and propel the intensive, sophisticated and time-limited state legislative campaign resulting in the passage of HB 86.

Similar to the other two cases in this chapter, the Ohio juvenile justice reform partnership case captures a host of partnership principles related to motivation, as well as to the notion of key conditions needed for partnership success. A feature of this case is the clear importance of principles and values that are jointly determined and documented by the core members of the partnership team. In the context of achieving policy reform—the primary motivation for this partnership—it makes sense that being strategic was of particular importance and perhaps of greater importance than in other partnerships for which there is less of a tangible goal with known urgency in terms of available windows for action and results, as was the case in Ohio.

Key Takeaways

The three cases shared here reflect a diversity of motivations for researcher–policymaker partnerships. Importantly, none of them stem from requirements imposed by their own or other institutions. Rather, each of these partnerships grew out of desires for developments that would have impact beyond the activities of the partnerships themselves. They were motivated by a need for knowledge to inform policymaking, improving a context for useable research and affecting legislative change. Collectively, they reveal the following five questions that partnership-seeking individuals and entities would do well to consider as they embark on collaboration:

- Will the motivation inspire true partnership or forced collaboration?
- What is the nature of preexisting relationships between key individuals connected to each of the primary partner institutions?
- Can the value for each partner entity be ensured?
- Can agreements be established early on?
- Is there a willingness by both/all parties to adapt throughout the partnership?

It is worth considering that each of the three cases featured in this chapter—and many throughout the book—came about as the result of individuals and institutions seeking to solve problems or challenges that neither sector—research or policy—could solve alone but that both would benefit from in terms of the jointly pursued solution. Massachusetts had a research challenge. DPS and Duke had a systems challenge. Ohio had a policy challenge. In each case research and policy informed each other. In each, the contexts and drivers were slightly different, but each partnership had initially to determine a willingness to work together on a shared policy area or problem.

We conclude this chapter by sharing two examples of the helpful guides, tools and checklists that exist to support entities that are motivated to partner and need to explore the feasibility of doing so. Among other values, these tools often prompt potential members of a partnership to reflect on their willingness to work outside of their typical realm with individuals and entities that may be very different from them. We share two of many examples here. First, the Substance Abuse and Mental Health

Services Administration's (SAMHSA) Center for the Application of Prevention Technologies offers an online worksheet to help assess readiness for collaboration and partnering. This resource is one in a series of collaboration tools offered by SAMHSA and is available at https://captcollaboration.edc.org/sites/captcollaboration.edc.org/files/attachments/Are%20You%20Ready_0.pdf. We share it as an example of a resource provided by the public sector as well as an example of a brief checklist, which in barely more than a page, raises questions about readiness that all potential partners would do well to consider. The second resource was developed by the White House Council for Community Solutions and The Bridgespan Group. The *Toolbox Overview for Building Needle-Moving Community Collaborations* presents a detailed listing of resources related to community collaboratives. Although our focus is not on community-based efforts, the resources pertain to cross-sector partnerships and fit well with several of the researcher–policymaker partnership themes that we highlight, including motivation and implementation. The *Toolbox Overview* is available at http://www.serve.gov/new-images/council/pdf/Community-CollaborativeToolkit_all%20_materials.pdf. Particularly useful in terms of motivation for researcher–policymaker partnerships, it includes organization self-assessments to determine contextual factors and organizational and individual readiness to partner.

References

Abdulkadiroglu, A., Angrist, J.D., Dynarski, S., Kane, T.J., & Pathak, P.A. (2011). Accountability and flexibility in public schools: Evidence from Boston's charters and pilots. *Quarterly Journal of Economics, 126*(2), 699–748.

Abdulkadiroglu, A., Angrist, J.D., Hull, P.D., & Pathak, P.A. (2014). Charters without lotteries: Testing takeovers in New Orleans and Boston. *Edlines.* Retrieved from: http://www.doe.mass.edu/research/reports/2014/12EdLines-TestingTakeovers.pdf.

Abdulkadiroglu, A., Angrist, J.D., Hull, P.D., & Pathak, P.A. (2015). *Charters without lotteries: Testing takeovers in New Orleans and Boston* (Working Paper No. 20792). Retrieved from National Bureau of Economics website: http://www.nber.org/papers/w20792.

Abdulkadiroglu, A., Angrist, J.D., Narita, Y., & Pathak, P.A. (2015). *Market design meets research design* (Working Paper No. 21705). Retrieved from National Bureau of Economics website: http://www.nber.org/papers/w21705.pdf.

Angrist, J.D., Cohodes, S.R., Dynarski, D.M., Pathak, P.A., & Walters, C.R. (2016). Stand and deliver: Effects of Boston's charter high schools on college preparation, entry, and choice. *Journal of Labor Economics, 34*(2), 275–318.

Angrist, J.D., Pathak, P.A., & Walters, C.R. (2013). Explaining charter school effectiveness. *American Economic Journal: Applied Economics, 5*(4),1–27.

Brownson, R.C., Royer, C., Ewing, R., & McBride, T.D. (2006). Researchers and policymakers: Travelers in parallel universes. *American Journal of Preventative Medicine, 30*(2), 164–172.

Choi, B., Pang, T., Lin, V., Puska, P., Sherman, G., Goddard, M., Ackland, M.J., Sainsbury, P., Stachenko, S., Morrison, H., & Clottey, C. (2005). Can scientists and policy makers work together? *Journal of Epidemiology and Community Health, 59*(8), 632–637. http://doi.org/10.1136/jech.2004.031765.

Conaway, C.L. (2013). The problem with briefs, in brief. *Education Finance and Policy, 8,* 287–299.

Cousins, J., & Simon, M. (1996). The nature and impact of policy-induced partnerships between research and practice communities. *Educational Evaluation and Policy Analysis, 18*(3), 199–218.

Gatta, M., & McCabe, K.P. (2008). The "new" policy partnership: Academic researchers and government officials partnering toward social equity. *Equal Opportunities International, 27*(2), 129–131.

Gerardi, D., & Wolff, N. (2008). Working together: A corrections-academic partnership that works. *Equal Opportunities International, 27*(2), 148–160.

Golden-Biddle, K., Reay, T., Petz, S., Witt, C., Casebear, A., Pablo, A., & Hinings, C.R. (2003). Toward a communicative perspective of collaboration in research: The case of the researcher-decisionmaker partnership. *Journal of Health Services Research and Policy, 8*(2), 20–25.

Gooden, S.T., Graham, F.S., & Martin, K. (2014). Research partnerships at the state level: Bridging the academic-practitioner divide. *State and Local Government Review, 46*(3), 184–196.

Huston, A. (2005). Connecting the science of child development to public policy. *Social Policy Report, 19*(4), 3–18.

Kingdon, J. W. (2011). *Agendas, alternatives, and public policies* (updated 2 ed.). Boston, MA: Longman.

Lindblom, C.E., & Cohen, D.K. (1979). *Useable knowledge: Social science and social problem solving.* New Haven, CT: Yale University Press.

Setren, E. (2015). *Special education and English language learner students in Boston charter schools: Impact and classification* (Working Paper No. 2015.03). Retrieved from MIT Economic website: http://economics.mit.edu/files/11208.

Substance Abuse and Mental Health Services Administration Center for the Application of Prevention Technologies. *Prevention collaboration in action. Identifying needs and opportunities for collaboration.* Retrieved from the SAMHSA website: https://captcollaboration.edc.org/sites/captcollaboration.edc.org/files/attachments/Are%20You%20Ready_0.pdf.

Walters, C.R. (2014). *The demand for effective charter schools* (Working Paper No. 20640). Retrieved from the National Bureau of Economic Research website: http://www.nber.org/papers/w20640.pdf.

White House Council for Community Solutions and The Bridgespan Group. (2012). *The toolbox overview for building needle-moving community collaborations.* White House Council for Community Solutions, Washington, DC. Retrieved from the Corporation for National and Community Service website: http://www.serve.gov/new-images/council/pdf/CommunityCollaborative Toolkit_all%20_materials.pdf.

3 Implementing Effective Partnerships

Making Partnerships Happen

In the previous chapter, we learned about motivations for researcher–policymaker partnerships. As the three cases in that chapter illustrate, certain motivations may increase the likelihood of stronger and longer-lasting partnerships. But even when the partners' motivations are aligned and the policy and research climates are optimal, the business of implementing a partnership across sectors and institutions can be daunting and complex. There are a host of good reasons for this. Among them is the fact that the partners' organizational policies and practices may differ significantly with regard to required protocols, even law. In addition, reporting, accountability and financial record-keeping mechanisms of the partnering institutions may not naturally complement each other. This can add challenges to the collaboration that may not reflect the partners' willingness and desire to be productive and successful together.

This chapter features two partnership cases that provide windows into the intricacies of implementing a partnership. They expose the elements that were required, including who is involved, their roles and how they went about forming the partnership. Although not written as how-to guides, the cases here, combined with the others throughout the book, collectively offer a road map for "making" a researcher–policymaker partnership. Many of the principles and components of partnership implementation that have contributed to the success of these two partnerships undoubtedly would apply to different types of partnerships as well. They also reflect what the literature says about partnerships more broadly.

What the Research Says

Although there is an extensive literature on the challenges of and strategies for designing and implementing research-practice partnerships (Palinkas, Short, & Wong, 2015), there is considerably less regarding researcher–policymaker partnerships (Stone, Maxwell, & Keating,

2001). For purposes of this book, however, thinking of policymakers as a type of practitioner is useful. Likewise, considering many public-sector practitioners as policymakers makes sense. The Washoe-CASEL case, for example, is described as a researcher-practitioner partnership. In that partnership, we meet school district representatives working in the public sector in a realm where policy and practice are intertwined. In sum, many differences between research and *practice* that have implications for partnership implementation apply to research and *policy* as well.

A frequent finding concerns the importance of creating formal organizational components of the partnership, as opposed to assuming that the partnership's leaders will naturally default to a reliable structure and methods for interaction. In this context, being organized means building the practical structures that are necessary for a successful project plan: scope management, stakeholder identification and management, creating a communications plan, establishing roles and responsibilities and creating a plan for dealing with issues and risks (Bowen, 2002). Research also shows clear benefits from establishing processes and systems in advance of the partnership launch and then modifying those systems collaboratively as needed throughout the partnership. Gatta and McCabe (2008) point to the importance of a clear feedback loop between the researcher and policymaker partners to ensure regular and consistent communication about progress and any needed course corrections.

Perhaps not surprisingly, there is literature in the field of community-based participatory research on the challenges of partnerships between academics and community partners that reflects precisely the same types of challenges often experienced in researcher–policymaker partnerships. A common challenge is that information about implementing the partnership may reach each of the partners through separate methods and sources of communication (Andrews et al., 2013). In this situation, those representing the policymaker partner may hear almost solely from the individuals leading their "side" of the partnerships, whereas the researchers hear almost exclusively from the leaders of their "side." Furthermore, one partner might communicate primarily in writing and the other primarily verbally, thus perpetuating both the use of sector-specific jargon that only one partner understands well and a lack of consistency in terms of the content of the communication. This can reinforce differences between the partners, making it harder for them to integrate their efforts and leverage each other's strengths. We do not propose that partners abandon their language or preferred means of communication. Adopting joint communication processes as part of the partnership's implementation plan, however, can be critical to the partnership's eventual success.

Much of the partnership implementation literature focuses on implementation of programs by practitioners who provide direct services such as health care (Harrison & Graham, 2012). Although perhaps seemingly less relevant to researcher–policymaker partnerships, implementation science research has much to offer to collaboration in this realm. In particular, the National Implementation Research Network's "Implementation Drivers" tool could largely be applied to researcher–policymaker partnerships (NIRN, 2013). As part of the tool, "organization drivers" are described as "mechanisms to create and sustain hospitable organizational and system environments for effective services." The notion of hospitable organizational and system environments for services is equally persuasive when considering the elements for successful partnerships in a policy context.

We would argue that although context may not make or break every partnership, it is an important component of every partnership. For both of the cases featured in this chapter, the context is one of researchers partnering with school district policymakers, though the research partners in the two cases represent different types of organizations. In one, the research partner is a university. In the other, it is a nonprofit organization that includes researchers, policy analysts and practitioners. These two examples illuminate the diversity of partners that exist within the research realm, a reminder that multiple types of organizations in each sector can be party to researcher–policymaker partnerships.

Partnership Implementation Cases

The following partnerships both received financial support from the Institute of Education Sciences (IES). This was not intentional in terms of our selection of cases for the book. Yet we do intentionally focus on partnerships in the social and education policy spheres, and the IES has devoted substantial human and financial resources to studying and catalyzing partnerships between research and policy. It is not surprising, therefore, that the IES features in both of the following cases about implementing partnerships, as well as in the case by Heinrich and Good about the University of Wisconsin–school districts partnership in Chapter 4 on sustaining.

The first case in this chapter is that of the Collaborative for Academic, Social, and Emotional Learning (CASEL) and Washoe County School District (WCSD). In this case, we learn about the high degree of intentionality employed by members of the partnership to establish processes, both leading up to the partnership and once it was underway. The research partner devoted extensive time to developing a relationship with the school district partner and laying a foundation of strong buy-in before the intensive research began. This project planning was clearly a critical component of the partnership and contributed to its success and long-term sustainability.

Creating a Monitoring System for School Districts to Promote Academic, Social and Emotional Learning: A Researcher-Practitioner Partnership

Robert Schamberg, Celene E. Domitrovich, Laura Davidson, Ben Hayes, Trish Shaffer, Rachel A. Gordon, Marisa Crowder, Randal Brown, Ann McKay Bryson and Roger P. Weissberg

The Collaborative for Academic, Social and Emotional Learning[1]
Georgetown University
Washoe County School District
University of Illinois at Chicago

Imagine a partnership between two organizations that will affect education reform across the nation. By developing an assessment of student social and emotional competence, this group of ten people has advanced the field of social and emotional learning, enabling school districts and states throughout the country to measure the personal and social characteristics of students that are increasingly recognized as key to success in school and life (Pellegrino & Hilton, 2012).

Utilizing student self-report ratings gathered with this new tool and an extensive district data set, the partnership analyzed the associations between social and emotional skills and student behavior, academic success and graduation rates. The results are significant. Students with higher social emotional competence (SEC) have significantly lower suspension rates, have significantly higher mathematics and language arts achievement and graduate from high school at a much higher rate than those with lower SEC.

This is the story of that partnership.

Social and emotional learning (SEL) is the process through which children and adults learn and practice the skills to manage themselves, their relationships and their work effectively and ethically. These skills include recognizing and managing emotions, developing care and concern for others, establishing positive relationships, making responsible decisions and handling challenging situations constructively (Weissberg, Durlak, Domitrovich, & Guolotta, 2015).

The primary goals of the partnership between WCSD and CASEL were to conduct research on social and emotional factors that promote student learning and achievement and to use the findings to create a robust graduation monitoring system that includes indicators reflecting students' strengths as well as risks.

Prior research demonstrates that students who are socially and emotionally competent perform better in school, are more likely to stay in school and graduate and function better in adulthood (Farrington et al., 2012; Jones, Greenberg, & Crowley, 2015; Valiente, Swanson, & Eisenberg, 2011). Students who enter school with a lack of social emotional competence or high levels of behavior problems often fall behind their peers over the early elementary years and are at risk for a range of poor outcomes in adolescence, including social adjustment problems, academic failure and dropping out (Arsenio, Adams, & Gold, 2009; Barry & Reschley, 2012).

CASEL (based in Chicago, Illinois) is an organization of practitioners, researchers and policy analysts, with the mission to advance the science and practice of SEL and to make it an essential part of pre-K–12 education in the United States. In 2013–2014, WCSD was ranked the fifty-ninth largest school district in the United States, serving 65,550 students in sixty-two elementary schools, fourteen middle schools, twelve high schools, one magnet school, five alternative schools and eight district-sponsored charter schools in and around the city of Reno, Nevada.

The Partnership Context

The Collaborating Districts Initiative

The WCSD–CASEL research–practice partnership evolved out of an existing relationship between the organizations. In September 2012, when the two organizations jointly applied for funding from the Institute for Education Sciences to fund their research agenda, CASEL and WCSD had already been working together to implement SEL in WCSD in the context of a large-scale initiative designed to advance knowledge of how school districts can make SEL an integral part of every student's education. In 2011, CASEL and the NoVo Foundation launched the Collaborating Districts Initiative (CDI) to build capacity in eight large urban school districts to systematically provide support for SEL in all schools and classrooms, enhancing the social and emotional competence of all pre-K–12 students and the adults who serve them. The goals of the CDI are to demonstrate that a district can implement SEL with fidelity at scale across a system; to collaboratively develop and refine practical tools that promote the effective implementation and assessment of SEL; to promote students' social, emotional, and academic competence; and to strengthen the research base related to this work.

Each of the school districts developed a three-year SEL implementation plan, utilizing a six-month planning grant. Subsequently, the NoVo Foundation provided each collaborating district with an annual grant of $250,000 and the ongoing support of two CASEL consultants, one with specific expertise in systems and policy and the other with SEL professional development expertise. Each district was initially funded for three years. In 2014, grants were extended for an additional three-year period, including continued funding for CASEL consultants.

As part of the CDI, the two CASEL consultants assigned to WCSD spent time in the district supporting the SEL department and district professional developers in engaging key stakeholders, including the superintendent and the superintendent's cabinet, principals, district educators and staff, families and community members by helping to grow their knowledge about SEL, the factors that support its development, and its relevance for academic learning. Building an enthusiastic constituency for SEL was integral to these engagements.

WCSD adopted a model of SEL implementation that includes three primary approaches that build on their districts' strengths and philosophy (Figure 3.1). The first element focused on teaching SEL skills as part of core academic curricula, such as mathematics and language arts. The second element involves direct instruction on social and emotional skills through use of evidence-based programs in grades K–12. The third emphasizes promoting a physically, socially and emotionally safe climate and culture conducive to learning in all classrooms and schools.

As the CDI progressed, CASEL become aware of WCSD's unique strengths in the areas of research, assessment and accountability. The focus on instructional methodology and accountability, along

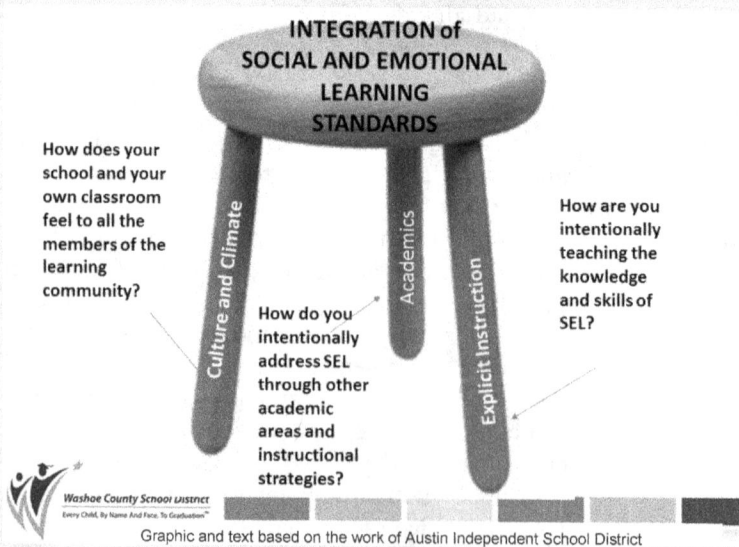

Graphic and text based on the work of Austin Independent School District

Figure 3.1 WCSD SEL Primary Approaches

with their commitment to data-driven decision-making, has been a strength of the WCSD SEL implementation.

WCSD Preexisting Strengths around Data Collection and Use

Over the course of several years prior to the beginning of the CDI and the partnership, WCSD devoted time and resources to building an extensive electronic data warehouse, containing all longitudinal student achievement data, student behavior data, demographic information and student school climate survey results. The accountability department uses this integrated database to provide data to school personnel in a variety of formats aggregated at the individual, classroom, school and district levels. For example, the online student profile provides a one-page snapshot of data and performance levels of each student for use in parent–teacher conferences (see Figure 3.2), and the school dashboard provides a summary of

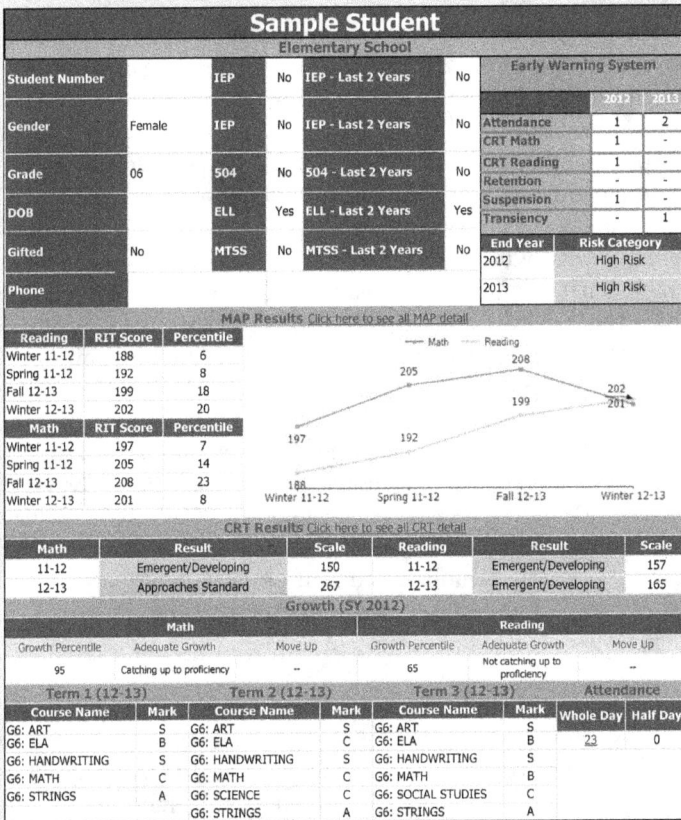

Figure 3.2 WCSD Online Student Profile

an entire school's performance that can be searched and viewed at different levels (i.e., classroom, school).

In addition to the online data warehouse the district generates printed annual school profile books, school climate reports and trend data on key indicators such as graduation rates, math and reading proficiency, credit attainment and student behavior. Schools use this information to develop their annual school improvement plan, with data literacy support provided by the accountability department.

Since 2009, WCSD has held annual data summits to comprehensively review student and system outcomes, evaluate district progress and determine how to use the information for district and school improvement. During the annual summits, the board of trustees; district leadership; and community, parent, student, principal and teacher representatives come together for a full day of facilitated conversation around district performance data and initiatives.

When CASEL and WCSD began this partnership WCSD was already in the third year of administering its annual Student Climate Survey to all students in grades 5–9 and 11. When they joined the SEL Collaborating Districts Initiative, WCSD integrated a student self-report rating of social and emotional competence into its existing Climate Survey. The SEL student self-report items were drawn from existing measures by CASEL and the American Institutes of Research (AIR), who were the evaluators of the Collaborating Districts Initiative (Kendziora & Osher, 2016).

Over the past decade, school districts across the nation have increasingly turned to the use of graduation monitoring systems to ensure that students who may be at risk for dropping out are identified early and receive interventions to keep them on track and successful. One of the most empirically supported models of a monitoring system was developed by Robert Balfanz (Balfanz & Byrnes, 2012; Balfanz, Herzog, & Mac Iver, 2007). Balfanz identified four academic indicators that were most highly associated with academic risk and demonstrated that student outcomes were significantly improved when these factors were used to identify which students were at risk and in need of services (Balfanz et al., 2007).

In 2009, WCSD developed its own Early Warning Risk Index (EWRI) based, in part, on the Balfanz model and validated the system by demonstrating that the indicators were effective in predicting academic outcomes, including next-year GPA, on-track status for graduation, disciplinary outcomes and, most importantly, graduation outcomes. The decision to develop the risk index was driven by several years of stagnant cohort "on time" graduation rates that hovered around 56 percent each year. The district was also concerned about pronounced achievement gaps in the graduation rate between various student populations, including different racial/ethnic groups. Several of the reasons many students failed to graduate (e.g., short by only one or two credits or exams) seemed amenable to intervention if identified earlier.

In 2014, WCSD was able for the first time to conduct a longitudinal analysis of its EWRI among ninth graders to determine how effectively the formula predicted four-year graduation outcomes. The index did a remarkable job predicting academic outcomes, finding that "high-risk" students identified in ninth grade were thirteen times as likely to drop out compared to students identified as "no risk" in the ninth grade. That said, only one-third of all "high-risk" ninth-grade students beat the odds and graduated four years later. These findings suggested that although the risk index had predictive utility, it failed to identify all the factors that helped some at-risk students demonstrate resilience and overcome obstacles to graduation.

The Partnership Grows

The Institute for Education Sciences (IES) Research Practitioner Partnership Grant

The CASEL research team became aware of the request for proposals for the IES Research Practitioner Partnership Grant and wanted to find a partner to help further their goals to improve SEL assessment. CASEL surveyed all eight CDI districts as to their interests and qualifications to partner on a project.

WCSD was fine-tuning its risk index as it began its partnership with CASEL and became more aware of the relevance of SEL for developing the social skills, attitudes and behaviors that facilitate positive educational outcomes. The members of the accountability department were hopeful that the risk index could be improved by recognizing and accounting for protective factors in order to explain some of the as-yet-unexplained variance in student outcomes. Although research and intervention studies suggest that social and emotional skills promote positive outcomes, there is little research on how to effectively measure these competencies in the context of district assessment systems or how to combine academic and nonacademic indicators to create monitoring tools for decision-making. Answers to these important problems of practice were important to both WCSD and CASEL, so these served as the basis of their research partnership. A combined team of WCSD

WCSD-CASEL Research Aims

WCSD and CASEL are interested in developing reliable measures of the social and emotional skills, dispositions and behaviors in students that promote academic learning, incorporating them as an SEL indicator into their student monitoring system, and ultimately using such research-based evidence to guide interventions and decision-making at the individual, classroom and building level.

- **Aim 1.** To develop reliable and valid teacher and youth self-report measures of social and emotional skills, dispositions and behaviors that are appropriate for use in educational decision-making.
  - o   **Subaim 1a:** Do the SEL items measure five separate conceptual competencies or one single competency?
  - o   **Subaim 1b:** Do the SEL items capture different levels of SEL competencies, following conceptual expectations?
- **Aim 2.** To examine how different dimensions of social and emotional skills, dispositions and behaviors are associated with academic outcomes (GPA and standardized achievement test scores).
  - o   **Hypothesis:** SEL is expected to operate as a promotive factor against poor academic outcomes such that students with higher levels of SEL will demonstrate better grades and higher scores on standardized achievement tests than students with lower SEL (i.e., positive main effect).
- **Aim 3.** To examine whether social and emotional skills, dispositions and behaviors serve as protective (i.e., interactive) factors moderating the relationship between student individual risk and academic outcomes.
  - o   **Hypothesis:** We expect that students with high Balfanz risk scores and/or high demographic risks (English language learner; free and reduced lunch receipt) in one academic year are expected to perform worse academically in the next academic year than those with low Balfanz or demographic risk, but that this association between high risk and lower achievement will be smaller (buffered by) higher SEL competencies.
  - o   **Research question:** Does the way in which SEL moderates the relationship between risk and outcome vary by grade?

Source: C. Domitrovich, et. al. February 2014.

---

leaders, CASEL researchers, CASEL consultants and university research partners developed a proposal. Paul LaMarca of WCSD and Roger Weissberg of CASEL were designated as the primary investigators of the grant application, which was funded in July 2013.

The Partnership Team Is Established

Soon after receiving the funding letter the work began in earnest, and the core team, who are the authors of this case study, was established. The team remained remarkably stable during the partnership. Several others provided expertise and leadership to the committee, most notably, University of Illinois, Chicago professor,

Dr. Everett Smith, who shared his expertise with WCSD researchers in applying Rasch measurement and related psychometric measurement techniques.

Partnership Activities

Because team members lived in four different states, partnership meetings took place every two weeks via conference calls or by webinar. The team came together in person twice a year, often in conjunction with a CASEL CDI meeting or a national research conference of interest to the group. At the first partnership meeting held at the school district, the research aims and a set of partnership guidelines created to support the functioning of the team were presented to the WCSD SEL Advisory Council. The council, composed of a diverse group of stakeholders from the district and community, was established by WCSD and provided consultation regarding SEL implementation.

Initial tasks of the team centered on development of reliable and valid measures of the five SEL competencies developed by CASEL.

The work began with the researchers from the University of Illinois teaming with the WCSD researchers to apply advanced statistical strategies (such as Item Response Theory, Latent Class Analysis and Rasch Analysis) to the WCSD social and emotional competence (SEC) student self-report data that had been collected over the two previous years through the Student Climate Survey. These analyses indicated that several of the items were redundant, enabling the partnership to develop survey items that explore additional aspects of SEC. Also, it was demonstrated that over 80 percent of students rated themselves high in these competencies, suggesting that some questions were "too easy." With these data in hand, the team developed a bank of items that were intended to more accurately measure each competency and would provide more discrete separation between students with lower, moderate and higher levels of SEC.

These items were iteratively refined over a span of two years. New and revised items were sampled in successive administrations of the survey. Detailed statistical analysis was then used to analyze the results, indicating which items from the bank had the greatest evidence of local reliability and validity. During this process, the team also considered the reading level of each item because items would be used in grades 5–11 and by students for whom English is not their first language. The revision process also led to disaggregating results into eight constructs (see Figure 3.3) to assess independent skills embedded in each of CASEL's five competencies, yielding a core set of seventeen anchor items and 150 trial items. This enabled further sampling

Emotion Knowledge:
   "I can predict how I will feel in most situations."
Self-Concept:
   "I am satisfied with who I am as a person."

Schoolwork:
   "I come to class prepared."
Emotion Regulation:
   "I can calm myself down when I get upset."
Goal Management:
   "I try hard to do well in school."

"I learn from people whose views are different from my own."

"When I make a decision, I think about what might happen afterwards."

Answer Choices
1 = Never True for Me
2 = Rarely True for Me
3 = Somewhat True for Me
4 = Usually True for Me
5 = Always True for Me

"There are very few people I don't get along with at school."

Figure 3.3 WCSD Five SEL Competencies

in the next administration of the survey of four to five trial items for each construct in addition to anchor items that were administered to all students. The seventeen anchor items were selected judiciously from the larger bank of 150 items. Rasch item-difficulty ratings were used to help the team select one challenging item and one easier item in each of the eight constructs. Items were chosen because they best represented the competency and because they were psychometrically sound (no concerns with reading level, high reliability, no differential item functioning across student subpopulations). The seventeen items created a scale that could be used as a short-form assessment of overall SEC that tested a range of ability.

The research and accountability members of the partnership performed technical analysis and shared results with practitioner members, who then contributed to developing, editing and fine-tuning the items. The analytic members of the team also examined the response options and survey mode used by students through quantitative means and through focus groups with students. Ten student focus groups with 100+ students in grades 5–12 provided important feedback on items, survey modes, response options and the climate survey-taking environment at schools.

The findings from these quantitative and qualitative analyses led to several changes. For example, student response options were modified from students choosing one of five ratings (1 = "Never true for me" to 5 = "Always true for me") to choosing one of four ratings (1 = "Very difficult for me" to 4 = "Very easy for me"), as it was determined students did not reliably distinguish between "Never true for me" and "Rarely true for me." Focus group feedback also led to a change in the survey mode. The team tested various survey modes designed to promote more engagement in the assessment task in order to combat disengagement and missing data, discovering that more engaging formats (e.g., using a slider format to provide responses) reduced attrition when compared with more traditional, multiple choice survey modes.

The group spent four months analyzing spring 2015 results and refining the instrument further. Three rounds of individual prioritization of items and follow-up discussions yielded an intermediate-sized bank of 150+ items to measure competence within the eight categories. Field testing of a short-form, 40-item assessment with 12,000 WCSD students was conducted in April 2016.

The partnership has presented its work several times within WCSD at conferences and at national meetings. This included conducting an invited panel at the Society for Educational Effectiveness (SREE) in September 2014 and serving in December 2014 as one of several model programs for a consortium of Illinois organizations, including the Illinois Governor's Office of Early Learning, who were considering developing a *Partnership for Children and Families: Connecting Research, Practice and Policy*.

In February 2016, a keynote presentation about the work of the partnership was shared in Reno at the CASEL Collaborating Districts Annual Meeting. Along with a recap of the development of the instrument, the partnership team presented initial research findings that related academic and behavioral outcomes with students' social and emotional competencies as measured by the survey. Superintendents from ten leading districts participated in the two-day event, along with curriculum and instructional leaders, board members, policy makers and SEL leaders. A second, more technical breakout session was provided for accountability, research and evaluation leaders from each district, as well as other interested attendees. The IES partnership offered access to the banks of items and student focus group protocols to the other CDI districts, as well as technical assistance in analysis and use of student SEC data to drive district- and school-level planning and programming.

Partnership Accomplishments

Benefits to CASEL

Several tangible products represent the accomplishments of the WCSD–CASEL partnership. The first is an improved version of the student self-report rating of social and emotional competence that is being used to evaluate the CDI (AIR, 2014). The second is the technical report that describes the new WCSD-CASEL SEC assessment tool, documents the analyses that were conducted by the researchers on the team, and provides practitioner-oriented guidelines for conducting climate surveys, including formative use of the results (WCSD-CASEL Partnership, 2016).

The Nevada State Department of Education and the Association of Alaska School Boards became aware of the SEL work being implemented in the CDI districts in their states and of the SEC assessment tool specifically and inquired with CASEL about whether they could implement these measures. The agencies were given free access to the SEC assessment tool created by the WCSD–CASEL partnership, and in the spring of 2016, both states administered it on a state-wide basis. The state-level inclusion of SEC in their assessment program aligns with and furthers CASEL's mission to provide social and emotional learning in all schools and classrooms across the country. In July 2016, CASEL announced that eight states, including Nevada, would take part in the CASEL Collaborating States Initiative (CSI). Through this partnership and in collaboration with national experts, CASEL will develop comprehensive standards for SEL, model SEL policies, practice guidelines and other implementation tools.

As an organization, CASEL benefitted greatly from the partnership with WCSD in several ways. First, the experiences helped to inform CASEL regarding the importance of including accountability/assessment leaders in systemic SEL implementation efforts. Second, the methodologies employed by the partnership in analyzing and altering the student competence measure have now been applied to CASEL's staff survey of school-level implementation, which is used to gauge staff perceptions regarding SEL enactment at a school site. Third, the experience CASEL had working with WCSD has led the organization to pursue similar research–practice partnerships with several other CDI districts.

Benefits to Washoe County School District

Through the Collaborating Districts Initiative, WCSD began measuring social and emotional competence by including SEC items on their climate assessment. At the February 2016 State Education Address, the Washoe County School District Superintendent highlighted the district goal of graduating 90 percent of students annually by 2020 (Davis, 2016). The district now has actionable

SEC data to support that goal. The district is using these data to make policy decisions and to support instructional improvement at the school and classroom levels. The results of implementing an improved measure of SEC will enable them to measure the social and emotional growth of students and help evaluate the effectiveness of SEL programs and practices.

WCSD has strategically utilized this partnership to engage stakeholders and build the constituency to support SEL. They hosted two SEL advisory committee meetings with over forty leaders, community members and district employees engaged in learning dialogues about SEL and the assessment of student social and emotional competence in order to improve conditions for learning and instructional practice. Over a hundred WCSD students participated in focus groups providing guidance and input on the SEC assessment (Blad, 2016). Approximately 100 teachers and principals participated in an SEL assessment workshop presented at the January 2016 SEL quarterly mini-conference, learning about the new assessment and exploring the resulting data. At each of these events, there was evidence of increased stakeholder support toward making SEL a part of the education of all students.

In an innovative use of partnership grant funds, the WCSD Accountability Department hired two part-time social science PhD students who attended the University of Nevada, Reno. These two graduate researchers, along with other members of the WCSD accountability department, received world-class training and support in advanced statistical methods. By the second and third year, the graduate students were the district leaders in implementing these analytical methods.

Benefits to the Field

The development of a no-cost SEC assessment tool with local evidence of validity and reliability is a key development for K–12 education. CASEL is constantly asked about cost-effective assessment tools that are easy to administer, provide actionable data for policy and program development and provide useful data for teachers and principals. We expect that over the next two years, many states and school districts will begin utilizing this tool to measure student competence and will use these data to guide their SEL implementation and to inform instruction. One upcoming step for the partnership is to develop a toolkit to support districts in implementing the assessment and using the data to inform policy, instruction and programming.

The field of education requires scientifically sound data to make the case for infusion of SEL into pre-K–12 instruction. WCSD obtained approval through their internal review process and their legal department to allow for the collection of student identifiers on student SEC responses so that the relationship between SEC and student achievement, demographic and behavioral data could be studied. A passive parental permission process was utilized. Analyses indicated that SEC has a significant association with student school success in Washoe County School District:

- Students who rate themselves as lower in SEC are more than twice as likely to be at risk for dropping out than students with high SEC scores.[2]
- Seventy-three percent of 2013–2014 WCSD eleventh-grade students with low SEC scores graduated from high school in June 2015, whereas 89 percent of the 2013–2014 eleventh graders with high SEC scores graduated in June 2015.
- In 2014–2015, students with low SEC scores had an in-school suspension rate of 4.6 percent, whereas students with high SEC scores had a 2.7 percent in-school suspension rate. SEC accounted for almost two-thirds of suspensions from school, even while controlling for previous patterns of suspensions and demographics (gender, poverty, participation in special education services and English language learner services).
- On the 2014–2015 Smarter Balanced Assessment Coalition (SBAC) assessment of the Common Core State Standards administered in WCSD, 45 percent of students with high SEC scores earned a 3 or 4 in mathematics, whereas just 23 percent of students with low SEC scores earned a 3 or 4. In English language arts, 61 percent of students with high SEC scores earned a 3 or 4 in mathematics, whereas 40 percent of students with low SEC scores earned a 3 or 4.

Factors that Contributed to Partnership Success

Existing Relationship of Partner Organizations

The partnership grew out of the CASEL Collaborating Districts Initiative. With the exception of two colleagues from the University of Illinois at Chicago, all relationships were already rooted through the work of systematically making SEL a part of the education of all K–12 students in Washoe County. Through this work, team members already had gotten to know and trust one another. Group norms emphasized valuing all group members, as well as psychological safety to express views and take risks. This new partnership enabled deeper work and provided the time and context for relationships to grow and flourish.

Research–Practice Integration

The partnership was a unique combination of a school district; the staff of a nonprofit that is devoted to advancing research, practice and policy; and action researchers. A strength was that each primary organization has members with both research and practice experience, who identify as belonging to both worlds and were capable of communicating with multiple stakeholders. As a result, the partnership was not a one-way street of research to practice, but a two-way street between research and practice with constant interchange among researchers and practitioners, both within and across the organizations. This was a critical factor that facilitated the improvements that were made to the student report of SEL competence.

Often an organization's priority and the perspective of its members are not aligned. The WCSD team members worked hand in hand with CASEL researchers, clinicians and practitioners. WCSD's research and practice staff were already integrated before this partnership was formed. WCSD's Office of Accountability and the Social and Emotional Learning (SEL)/Multi-Tiered Systems of Support Department (MTSS) regularly partnered to foster and evaluate initiatives, to seek grant funding and to co-implement strategies to benefit students and staff. This lack of silos within these two school district departments is highly unusual; their alignment of purpose, goals and teamwork were essential elements of the successful partnership.

The CASEL consultants brought their skills and experience of leading and guiding SEL evidence-based practices, their backgrounds in assessment and as educational practitioners and their existing relationships with all stakeholders.

The lead academic member of the partnership, Dr. Rachel A. Gordon, was very experienced with bridging research, practice and policy. She is not only an expert in measurement and the analytic methods that were critical for developing our assessment of student social competence, but is also very experienced at working with practitioners and policymakers to utilize research findings to make data-driven decisions.

Existing Data Warehouse and Access to Data

The partnership was able to make use of a much larger data set. The design of the data warehouse provided a rich tool enabling multivariate analysis of SEL competence data matched to behavioral, academic, demographic, climate, transiency and graduation data. The designers of district-wide assessments and the data warehouse were core members in the partnership and well versed in appropriate use of data in research. Issues that could take weeks to resolve in other circumstances were often resolved immediately. WCSD was also able to rapidly implement revisions to items and quickly organize focus groups to gain direct input from students. Often researchers working on measure development would take months or years to complete these processes.

Analytical/Research Orientation

WCSD's Accountability Department houses a team with strong analytical, statistical and research expertise. CASEL's research team is nationally respected for the many studies they have authored and for the development of the CASEL Guides to Social and Emotional Learning Evidence-Based Programs (CASEL, 2013, 2015). Rachel A. Gordon and Everett Smith are both nationally recognized social science and measurement experts. In addition, the practitioners on the team with classroom teaching and school administration experience have all been involved in multiple research studies involving SEL and other academic and nonacademic issues. This partnership had great depth and breadth when it came to research expertise, both within and across organizations.

A Shared Focus on SEL

A cornerstone of the partnership's success was its focus on social and emotional learning. SEL creates a climate for and approach to collaboration that addresses many of the hurdles other partnerships might face. The CASEL consultants and WCSD leaders who are also experts in SEL are "bridging" individuals who are extremely aware of their own and others' processes. Throughout each day, members of the partnership attended to group dynamics while always keeping the focus of the work on implications for practice.

Meetings of the partnership included opening activities that focused on self-awareness, social awareness and setting personal and group intentions for the day. Often, in daylong meetings, a "brain break" activity would be introduced by one of the practitioner members of the partnership. These short activities, which ranged from meditations, to physical movement, to team-building activities, have been demonstrated to relieve stress, bring joy into learning and working together and help learners and collaborators continue to focus (Willis, 2007). Reflections at the closing of each day built optimism and group commitment to the work. Some participants indicated that this group facilitation style was new for them, made them feel good and they enjoyed these meetings as a result.

The "integrated practice" model that characterizes "the Washoe Way" of approaching SEL was very conducive to research–practice integration. Because social and emotional learning provides both content to learn and strategies to model and practice, it is essential to have effective formative as well as summative measures. Classroom teachers and leaders at every level work diligently to continually align academic outcomes, assessment measures and effective teaching and communication about student growth and challenges. The expectation of having practical, accessible and effective outcomes was a driving force in crafting an assessment that would be useful to students, families and educators.

Several members of the partnership have integrated SEL into their leadership toolkit. An in-depth example illustrates how the skills of listening, empathy and compassion affected the work of the partnership. The WCSD Accountability Department conducted focus groups with students about their reaction to previously having taken the social and emotional competence survey, which was embedded in the Student Climate Survey. Focus groups revealed that some students reported that they were told by their teachers that the survey was not important and were not told that their survey responses would be kept confidential. Students also felt frustrated that they had never seen the results of their Climate Survey responses.

Within weeks of the focus groups, the Office of Accountability developed a training in collaboration with the SEL Department to disseminate these important findings to educators and leaders, incorporating it into a larger SEL training on assessment. The training occurred just prior to the following administration of the district's Climate Survey. The training focused both on the importance of a well-controlled survey environment for students and on encouraging educators to generate ideas about potential uses for Climate Survey results.

Additionally, shortly after the focus group findings, WCSD's Office of Accountability decided to host its first Annual Data Symposium for students so that students would have an opportunity to reflect on Climate Survey results and offer input and recommendations based on the data. Inspired by the incredibly valuable information, or "data" gleaned from students in this and other student voice projects, the WCSD Office of Accountability worked to establish the district's first student voice coordinator position to be housed within their office. In addition, student voice has become a mainstay component of SEL professional development in the district. These examples convey the WCSD Accountability Department's strong philosophy that data should shed light on areas in need of improvement and that educators should be empowered with data to drive effective change.

Federal Funding for the Partnership

The WCSD–CASEL partnership was funded with an external federal grant from the Institute of Education Sciences (IES), the statistics, research and evaluation arm of the U.S. Department of Education. The funding was essential to the success of this partnership. One of the most important aspects of the grant was funding the partnership members to travel to one another's locations for deep, interactive collaborative work and to attend national conferences that expanded the team's thinking around substantive issues.

IES funding also provided the resources needed to expand the capacity of the WCSD Office of Research, Accountability and Evaluation research department to conduct new measurement, field testing and analyses. The district achieved this by using the funds to hire the two graduate students, building their capacity and benefiting from their growing expertise. The researchers from the University of Illinois at Chicago mentored the graduate students so that they were knowledgeable and able to work independently over time. Finally, the WCSD members of the team felt that the flexibility of the IES funding was very helpful and different from previous federal grants under which there had been very little room to deviate from the original plan as the actual work unfolded.

Even though CASEL received the federal award, both CASEL and WCSD were designated specific funds from IES so the district was assured its portion and had control over how it was spent, avoiding a possible imbalance in the partnering relationship.

According to the partnership members from WCSD, this federally funded work with CASEL brought additional legitimacy to the district and its SEL implementation that helped them develop buy-in with schools, district leadership and at the state level.

Key Questions for Partnerships to Consider

Perhaps all successful partnerships feel unique. But it is our contention that, just like social emotional skills, vibrant effective partnerships can be intentionally built and effectively nurtured. Based upon our experience, we encourage other partnerships to consider these questions, which certainly applied to our partnership:

- Are there mutually interesting, important, and beneficial outcomes to the proposed partnership?

- Is there clarity regarding why the organization or individuals are partnering? (Is it more than a means for acquiring funding?)
- What are the existing relationships between the partners? Does your structure enable a free flow of ideas, including strategies for respectful disagreement, and does it foster innovative thinking?
- What is the partnership doing to build relationships within it and with other entities? Are you facilitating activities to promote self-awareness, goal setting, empathy and reflection?
- As a researcher, are you open to adjusting the questions that you examine if the focus of your partner changes?
- From the practitioner side, beyond building the national research base, how will this project directly benefit organizations, schools or stakeholders, whether through trainings, products or actionable information? Do the benefits outweigh the effort expended by and the demands to the schools or organizations?
- Is there long-term commitment to the partnership? Will your partnership continue when the initial funding is over? Can your partnership's purpose change over time?

The excitement, commitment and pride about this work among all WCSD and CASEL collaborators are palpable and contribute to the project's success and the continued level of engagement. The complex CDI work over years and the strong and continuing relationships across organizations—embedded in important and effective work—have made this a powerful and productive partnership.

Summary and Future Directions

The broader context of the CDI was an important factor that enabled the partnership to be successful. The CDI itself has continued beyond its original three-year funding. Although there is an ending date for the current funding cycle (June 2018), it appears that CASEL and the CDI districts have found a mutual benefit (nationally and in their communities) in continuing their prominent roles of building the SEL movement, even if there is not yet specific funding to continue the CDI.

The CDI provided the opportunity to establish a foundation for this in-depth partnership that enabled us to get ahead of the game once we actually received the resources needed to start our research. That foundation included familiarity, trust, common priorities and a shared language for engaging with one another.

Another reason for the success of the partnership was its shared purpose. We focused our partnership research on measurement of SEC and the application of these data to local and national educational policy and strategy. Both WCSD and CASEL have a keen interest in the development of SEL assessment tools and developing scalable strategies for using data to inform policy and instruction.

The WCSD–CASEL partnership continues to be very strong, and its work is expanding. One WCSD member of the IES team is serving on CASEL's national assessment work group. The *Work Group to Establish Practical Social-Emotional Competence Assessments* seeks to provide immediate support and guidance to educators on selecting and using currently available SEC assessments, while also sharing a clear vision for the future of SEL assessment. The results of this initiative will ensure that current and future SEL policy and practice are scientifically sound and actionable. This individual will be able to share information between the partnership and the work-group, advancing the work of both.

WCSD hosted CASEL's 2016 CDI annual cross-district meeting (Social Emotional Learning from Implementation to Scale: Spotlight on Equity & Assessment), with the work of the partnership prominently featured. Each year, superintendents and other district leaders from each of the eight CDI districts engage in this two-day meeting, sharing emerging best practices and hearing updates from CASEL on the state of SEL in the nation. As a measure of the value of the work of this partnership, one of CASEL's funders provided the financial support for each CDI district to bring an additional participant to the meeting representing each district's accountability, research, assessment or evaluation department. A special job-alike session was held for these attendees that drilled into the technical aspects of the partnership's work. The meeting served as an important launching point to disseminate the new self-report measure and to gather feedback from practitioners about its implementation and use.

One key take-away from this partnership is the importance of focusing on building capacity and sustainability from the beginning. For example, WCSD strategically used their funds to train and support the two graduate students to work in the Research and Evaluation Department. During the second and third years, the students were leading the data analysis for the group. Their work will also benefit other districts in the CDI that might choose to adopt the student rating.

The partnership is applying for funding from new sources to further work that they have been doing together. CASEL and WCSD believe that developing a practical and collaborative system for classroom-based formative assessment for student social and emotional competencies will champion a new process of ongoing learning and instruction in the SEL field By designing such a system and demonstrating its value for both student and teacher learning and making it practical and authentically applicable for teachers and students, we will highlight how the results of classroom-based formative assessments can inform instruction and teacher practices to improve social and emotional learning. Our project will result in valuable lessons learned and tangible strategies and tools for use in classrooms across the country.

The CASEL/Washoe case features multiple partnership implementation strengths in addition to the importance of "pre-work" noted earlier. The strengths include a recognized, shared purpose and focus, which appear pertinent to implementation of the partnership and to having certain capacities in place. Without team members possessing specific needed expertise, the work of the partnership would not be possible at a high quality, if at all. Although many elements for successful partnership implementation are intangible, tangible components exist as well. In the CASEL/Washoe case, they included material capacity in the form of the large data set, without which implementation may have been impossible. Other tangible components were the development of the "research aims" and "partnership guidelines," both foundational components of partnership planning. Most prominent among the characteristics of this partnership that highlight its commitment to thoughtful implementation are the numerous communications components, including regular partnership team meetings by conference call and in person, team members with knowledge of how to communicate in both the research and practice "worlds" and "constant interchange" between the partners.

The second case in this chapter features SanDERA, the San Diego Education Research Alliance. The SanDERA partnership has developed and evolved consistently since its first iteration emerged nearly two decades ago primarily as a research-only endeavor. It is now a deep collaboration that not only fulfills critical needs of both the policymaker and the researcher partners, but also shares its findings and accomplishments in ways that increase the potential for policy impact beyond the San Diego schools. It is no accident that in addition to "partnership," terms that appear throughout the case include "jointly," "communication," "relationship" and "together." Each of these represents important attributes of SanDERA, and all are products of concerted effort and thoughtful deliberation. The partners are careful to convey, however, that it should be feasible for other entities preparing to implement a strong researcher–policy partnership to do so in part by emulating many of SanDERA's characteristics and components.

The San Diego Education Research Alliance[3]

By Karen Volz Bachofer, Peter Bell, Julian R. Betts,
Dina Policar, Ronald G. Rode and Andrew C. Zau

The San Diego Education Research Alliance at the University of California, San Diego (SanDERA at UCSD) is a researcher–policymaker partnership that has grown over the last sixteen years. It is a collaboration between the Department of Economics at UCSD and the San Diego Unified School District (SDUSD), the second largest district in California. This case describes the evolution of the partnership from a traditional university research activity to a true and deep collaboration, and distills lessons we have learned about creating and sustaining partnerships. Some of the factors that led to the growth of SanDERA were happy accidents, such as the good chemistry between team members, all of whom genuinely want to know what works in public education and how to improve student outcomes. But many of the other factors contributing to the success of SanDERA resulted from deliberate decisions we made at various points in our trajectory. It is these decisions about how we choose research questions, how we communicate during a project and how we share the results at the end of a project that we think are most worth sharing.

The Evolution from Research to Deeper Collaboration

SanDERA is the product of two waves of research that have led to the present configuration.

Wave 1 (1999–2008)

Julian Betts, an economist at UCSD, who at the time was also a Senior Fellow at the Public Policy Institute of California (PPIC), wanted to develop a research relationship with a school district in order to study education policy in a richer and more timely way than is possible using only existing longitudinal data sets. David Lyon, then president of the PPIC, approached then SDUSD Superintendent Alan Bersin with a proposal to study the district's *Blueprint for Student Success*, a reform initiative launched by Bersin and Chancellor of Instruction Anthony Alvarado in 1998. Participants in the initial meeting included Bersin, Lyon, Betts, Karen Bachofer (SDUSD Executive Director of Research and Evaluation) and, by phone, Lauren Resnick (University of Pittsburgh Institute for Learning), a consultant to Bersin/Alvarado. Following that initial conversation, Betts and Bachofer began meeting to discuss a range of possible research topics/projects, including evaluation of the *Blueprint*. By early 2000 Betts, Lyon and the district, with key input from Bachofer, had developed an initial memorandum of understanding (MOU). It outlined specific research questions, but did not create a broader partnership of the sort that would emerge over the ensuing years.

Betts was very experienced in conducting education research and was keen to work with a large district to assist it in making decisions related to policy and practice. Moreover, Betts realized that access to individual student, teacher and program data was essential to understanding the impact of policy and practice on student outcomes. The size of SDUSD's student population (approximately 135,000 students) made this possible. (Use of state- and national-level data sets, though useful, did not provide student-, teacher- or program-level data necessary for deep understanding of outcomes of programs, policies and practices.)

Bersin wanted an external review of the *Blueprint*; Betts wanted to conduct research that would lead to improved district policy, practice and outcomes. In the early years, the researcher–district relationship was fairly typical. Betts submitted research requests to the district's Research Proposal Review Panel (RPRP), the specified data were provided by the SDUSD, the research proceeded and results were published, in this case usually by PPIC.

Given the unprecedented access that Betts and his colleague Andrew Zau obtained, it is natural to ask "What was in it for the district?" Superintendent Bersin clearly wanted an arm's-length independent evaluation of his reform. In addition, many district staff members were imbued in the research ethos and wanted to see the work succeed. The research and evaluation staff in the district were and are extremely skilled and more than capable of conducting highly sophisticated research on their own, but funding cuts, mandated reporting responsibilities and shifting district priorities have meant that sustained focus on long-term research projects has become less possible over time.

Given that the *Blueprint* was just getting underway and there would not have been enough data in 2000 to evaluate the reform convincingly, Betts focused the first report on a regression analysis of factors related to gains in individual students' test scores (Betts, Zau, & Rice, 2003). This was of some use to the district but was at the same time an academic study. Even at this early stage, though, both sides invested in the relationship. The district investment came in the form of training on the data it collected. The UCSD research team responded to Superintendent Bersin's desire to see how much difference there was across student demographic groups in the qualifications of students' teachers. It was not easy for district staff to answer this question because information on teacher qualifications resided in the Human Resources Department, which was not linked to student data. Although taking on this project slowed the publication of the first report somewhat, the UCSD research team felt that this work represented a show of good faith—an investment in what it hoped would be a long-standing relationship.

From the start, good communication facilitated a productive and healthy working relationship. Bachofer and Betts met monthly to discuss research projects and findings. Primary benefits included 1) Bachofer providing clarification of district policies and practices to assist Betts in research; 2) Betts sharing initial findings and early drafts with Bachofer to ensure "no surprises" for the district and to identify potential misunderstandings of data, programs and practices; and 3) an emerging relationship of trust and mutual goals.

One early decision regarding personnel has, in retrospect, turned out to be pivotally important. Betts originally proposed hiring graduate students to acquire and clean data. David Lyon of PPIC, as the funder of the initial work, worried that administrative data from a large public entity such as SDUSD would be complex and instead suggested hiring a full-time person to work with the district. Andrew Zau, a statistician who is today the senior statistician for SanDERA, was hired in summer 2000. Over the course of writing a first book with Betts on school resources and student outcomes, Zau received extensive training from district staff on data sources and data issues. Instead of training a succession of graduate students, district personnel could focus on making sure that Zau understood data sources, how policy changes affected data, variable definitions and any limitations of the data. (In later years Zau and Betts took the responsibility for training other university staff, mostly graduate students, who became involved in the research.) In the long run, this approach has reduced burden on district staff as Zau and Betts developed a long-term memory of data availability. And on several occasions, Zau has spotted issues with data that district colleagues were able to correct early on before beginning to use each new year's worth of data they acquired.

With each passing year, new research ideas came up, sometimes originating with Betts and his UCSD colleagues, but equally often generated jointly with district staff, especially Karen Bachofer, who had become the main district liaison to the research team. Among other items, the UCSD team published two studies of the *Blueprint for Student Success* and a lottery-based study of the impact of major school choice programs in SDUSD.[4]

Over time, several studies examined state or national education policies using SDUSD as the context for data gathering. One study examined early implementation of the accountability provisions in the federal No Child Left Behind law in San Diego (Betts & Danenberg, 2004). Later, two studies of the impact of the California High School Exit Examination focused on SDUSD (Betts, Zau, Zieleniak, & Bachofer, 2012; Zau & Betts, 2008).

Several Betts/SanDERA projects have evolved into longer-term studies and relationships. First, in 2007, Betts and his team were contracted by the U.S. Department of Education to conduct a two-part, multiyear study on career and technical education (CTE) in San Diego, as part of a national evaluation required by the Perkins Act (Betts, Zau, McAdams, & Dotter, 2014). In 2009, given the promise of the initial research, the U.S. Department of Education asked Betts to undertake a descriptive case study examining CTE outcomes in San Diego (Bachofer, Betts, & Zau, 2014). Second, a California Academic Partnership–funded study of the impact of diagnostic mathematics testing led to two related studies on the impact of using Mathematics Diagnostic Testing Project assessments in SDUSD (Bachofer, Zau, & Betts, 2012a, b; Betts, Hahn, & Zau, 2011).[5]

Another factor that has enriched the collaboration over the years is the growing number of UCSD doctoral candidates who have contributed to SanDERA work. In many cases, one or more thesis chapters have been based on work with SanDERA. A particularly exciting development is that several graduate students over the years have had ideas and approached Betts, who has facilitated those studies with the district. The results have been original and included thorough evaluations of district programs such as its Breakfast in the Classroom program or the impact of the California High School Exit Examination on student outcomes. Others have included more basic research, for instance, on which types of students gain more from smaller class size in elementary school, and some technical problems in using student test scores to evaluate teacher effectiveness, a policy that has not been used in SDUSD (Babcock & Betts, 2009; Koedel & Betts, 2010, 2011).[6]

SanDERA researchers publish widely and often present results at regional and national research conferences, enhancing the value of the work outside San Diego. The publications have been peer reviewed, and many are published by the PPIC. Results have been presented at meetings of the Association for Public Policy Analysis and Management (APPAM), the Allied Social Science Association meetings (ASSA), the California Educational Research Association (CERA) and the American Educational Research Association

(AERA), among others. All PPIC publications have led to public release events in Sacramento, the state capital. Funding sources also broadened, with the PPIC providing funding for all of the initial work and a growing list of foundations and institutes, including the PPIC, funding much of the later work.

The partnership between Betts and the district continued to strengthen due to 1) the utility to the district of the research products, which it judged to be of high quality; 2) the personal and professional connections that developed between Betts, Zau and district staff; and 3) the ongoing demonstration of confidentiality, transparency and respect for district staff and students.

Wave 2 (2009–2016)

Between 2000 and 2009, the district experienced several changes in leadership. Betts and Bachofer wanted to ensure the stability and longevity of the partnership and understood the need to formalize the relationship so that it would survive future changes in leadership.

In 2008, representatives from the university and district were invited to attend a conference hosted by the Chicago Consortium on School Research focused on developing district–university research partnerships. A team attended and began planning to establish a formal UCSD–SDUSD research alliance. The team realized that over eight years it had essentially developed a thriving researcher–practitioner partnership in all but name. In December 2009, Bachofer left SDUSD to begin working with Betts and his research team at UCSD.

In May 2010, SanDERA was created via a five-year MOU between SDUSD and UCSD. Whereas the strong preexisting working relationships between district staff and UCSD researchers formed the blood and muscle that enable the research, the formal MOU provided the backbone that gives the collaboration its form, structure and strength.

Although the team did achieve its initial goal to evaluate the *Blueprint*, over time the relationship that developed between Betts and district staff became far broader, resulting in a true partnership that has launched dozens of mutually beneficial research projects over the years. As such, SanDERA is distinctly different from other researchers who apply to conduct studies in the district—mostly to conduct "one-off" projects that are not necessarily aligned with the district's research needs. SanDERA aims to "conduct rigorous and relevant research that contributes to the development of education policy and informs, supports, and sustains high-quality educational opportunities for all students in San Diego and beyond" (SanDERA Mission Statement). The relationship has therefore been mutually beneficial.

How Creation of an Organizational Structure Has Positively Influenced SanDERA

Much of the SanDERA structure developed from the articulation of a mission statement and the SanDERA operating guidelines, the latter of which is included as an appendix to this chapter. (More information on SanDERA is available at http://sandera.ucsd.edu.)

A first key component of the operating guidelines is the executive committee. Over the years, six key people, three at SDUSD and three at UCSD, have convened regularly to discuss research and district policy issues. These six people, listed next along with their current titles, formed the SanDERA executive committee, which initially met once a month, and with the expansion of research activities, now meets twice monthly:

- Julian Betts: UCSD Researcher and Team Leader; Executive Director of SanDERA
- Andrew Zau: PPIC and subsequently UCSD Statistician; current SanDERA Senior Statistician
- Karen Bachofer: Former SDUSD Executive Director of Research and Evaluation and current Director of SanDERA
- Ronald G. Rode: Current SDUSD Director of Research and Development
- Peter Bell: Current Director of Data Analysis and Reporting
- Dina Policar: Current Director of Instructional Data Support

Amazingly, these six individuals have worked together consistently over the more than fifteen-year history of the UCSD–SDUSD relationship, though roles have shifted since 2000. The executive committee discusses proposed research and the progress of ongoing projects, writes grant proposals, plans SanDERA board of advisors meetings, discusses issues with data and data systems, manages grant-related reporting requirements, prepares presentations and generates ideas for future projects. Each of the three district representatives plays a key role. Rode is the liaison with the superintendent, networks with staff throughout the district to ensure that SanDERA research meets district needs and is well informed and shares his knowledge of state policy mandates. Bell's intimate knowledge of the student data systems and state testing programs and quantitative research background allow him to help steer the researchers in the right direction. Policar keeps the executive committee up to date on evaluations she is conducting of district programs, and she also oversees various testing and surveys related to a current SanDERA project we mention later. As for the UCSD members of the committee, all three are involved in conducting research, but with slightly different emphases. Betts plays a key role in design and conduct of research and grant writing. Bachofer regularly interacts with district staff, stays abreast of district and state policy, administers grants and plays the lead role in a number of administrative functions, such as compliance with human subjects requirements. Zau has the key role of working with a variety of district staff, acquiring, cleaning and managing data and performing statistical analysis. All three play key roles in integrating graduate students and other affiliated researchers into SanDERA work. Many thesis chapters that have been written over the years would quite simply have been impossible without the direct involvement of Bachofer and Zau.

The formalization of the executive committee has clearly increased the quality and frequency of exchanges among these six stakeholders.

In addition to the creation of an executive committee, SanDERA created a board of advisors that meets twice per year. The board draws upon expertise from both the district and the community. From the district, the board includes district teacher and administrator representatives and the superintendent. From the community, the board includes representatives from the Parent Teacher Association, Latino and African American advisory groups, postsecondary institutions and the business community. At each meeting, SanDERA members present results from ongoing research and discuss potential new work.

A particularly effective exercise at an early board meeting challenged members to prioritize among potential research topics that board members and/or the SanDERA executive committee had previously mentioned. In order to avoid having each respondent identify every single topic as important, Bachofer used a "spend-a-dot" approach in which she gave each board member a limited number of red adhesive dots, which they could affix in any way they wanted to the list of proposed research topics. In other words, respondents had a budget constraint. This led to a number of clear focal points, such as English learners, which SanDERA has subsequently studied. Appendix C shows the list of topics that board members had suggested at previous meetings, along with the final votes. Since 2011 when this initial "spend-a-dot" activity was conducted, we have not had the resources to study each of these topics, but it is accurate to say that many of our activities have responded directly to the top two items as voted upon by the board of advisors. This exercise has also entered the vernacular of board conversations, with one member at a recent meeting telling us that he would spend his "red dots" on one aspect of our English learner agenda before the other.

Meanwhile, the creation of regular meetings of the executive committee—something the partners agreed to on paper—started to have tangible effects on the research. Although arm's-length studies of district or state reforms have continued, the executive committee meetings have germinated true collaborative research by the six district and university members. The next section highlights two key projects that have resulted.

Evolution toward More Deeply Collaborative Research

Modeling Academic Trajectories

In 2012, the team developed a proposal to study the academic trajectories of SDUSD students, with the goal of alerting teachers and administrators at district schools about which students are off track to meet major academic milestones. The proposal won funding from the Institute for Education Sciences at the U.S. Department of Education in 2013 under its Researcher-Practitioner Partnerships in Education Research competition. This project moved SanDERA into new territory, as the three district members of the San-DERA executive committee, Bell, Policar and Rode, now became co-principal investigators with Betts.

This project used historical data to model whether students achieved various milestones including, among many others, reaching proficiency in California math and English Language Arts (ELA) standards by a certain grade, completing the expected number of courses as freshmen in high school (which we refer to as "being on track in grade 9") and graduating on time. The results were then used to predict the likelihood that each student currently in the district will achieve these milestones.

Each element of this project was designed jointly by the six executive committee members, and ideas on how to perform the analysis evolved over time, in particular due to comments from the SDUSD members of the team. Further, the project convened numerous focus groups at which teachers were asked to comment on the outcomes the team had selected to model and the graphical depictions of data. At one meeting, teachers expressed the concern that because students arrive at each school with different levels of academic readiness, looking only at the percentage of students on track to meet a given goal could give a misleading picture of how well a school was performing. The team realized that the teachers in effect were requesting the team to use "value-added" models that

Trends in the % of Students Predicted to Meet the Goal:
Being on Track at the End of Grade 9
By Grade for Various (Expected) Graduating Classes as of Spring 2014
All Students at School ZZZ

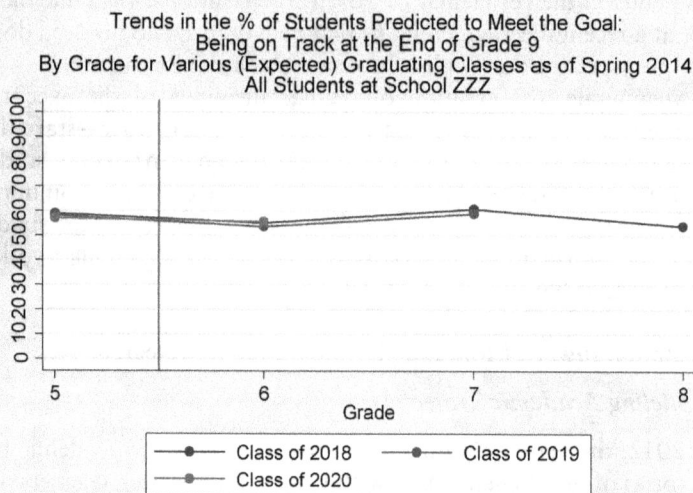

Note: Grade 5 data show performance the year before students entered the school in grade 6

Figure 3.4 Example of a Middle School Data Display Showing Grade-by-
Grade Mean Likelihood that Students Will Succeed in Grade 9

in some form took into account students' academic performance before they arrived at the given school.

Figure 3.4 shows the graph created in response to this teacher concern. It shows for an actual district middle school the percentage of students on track to complete expected coursework when they become freshmen in high school. The key innovation is that for grade 6 students, their predicted likelihood of being on track in grade 9 is shown not only in grade 6, their first year at the middle school, but also in grade 5, the year before they arrived at the school. Grade 5 likelihoods, appearing to the left of the vertical line in Figure 3.4, indicate that many students enter the middle school with low predicted likelihood of being on track at the end of grade 9. The graph shows that students, once they arrive in grade 6 at this school, experience a very modest decrease compared to grade 5 in the predicted likelihood that they will be on track after their freshman year in high school.

Another example of the value of the teacher focus groups is that when teachers saw some of the variations in likelihoods of being on track among various groups of students, they asked us: "What accounts for these differences?" The research team already had a plan for showing what factors mattered in the underlying logit model for predicted outcomes, and this comment motivated the team to produce school-level, student-level and district-level

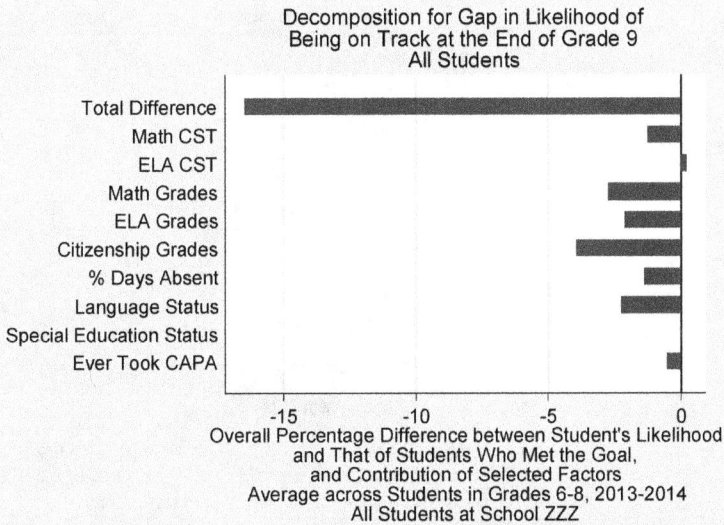

Decomposition for Gap in Likelihood of
Being on Track at the End of Grade 9
All Students

Overall Percentage Difference between Student's Likelihood
and That of Students Who Met the Goal,
and Contribution of Selected Factors
Average across Students in Grades 6-8, 2013-2014
All Students at School ZZZ

Figure 3.5 Decomposition of the Gap between Predicted Likelihood of Student Success in Grade 9 at a Given Middle School and the Predicted Likelihood of Older Students Who Did Succeed in Grade 9

decomposition graphs. Figure 3.5 illustrates the factor decomposition for the same middle school shown in Figure 3.4. The top bar in this graph shows the gap in predicted likelihood between students at the middle school and "successful" students, by which we mean all students in the district who had already reached grade 9 and had completed enough courses, with good enough grades, to be on track. At the given school, the average student's likelihood was about 17 percentage points below that of older successful students (on track in grade 9) when they were in middle school. The remaining bars further quantify this gap into explanatory factors we used in the underlying model, including test scores (the "CST" refers to the California Standards Test), grades, citizenship grades, attendance, English Learner and special education status and an indicator for whether the student had even taken the "CAPA" test for students in special education who needed special accommodations. For this school, the biggest factors contributing to the predicted 17-percentage-point deficit were citizenship grades (a measure of classroom behavior), English Learner status and ELA grades.

The Academic Trajectories project also produced graphs and tables depicting results for the district as a whole and for individual students. Figure 3.6 shows trends in the percentage of students off track and on track for another of our outcomes—graduating from

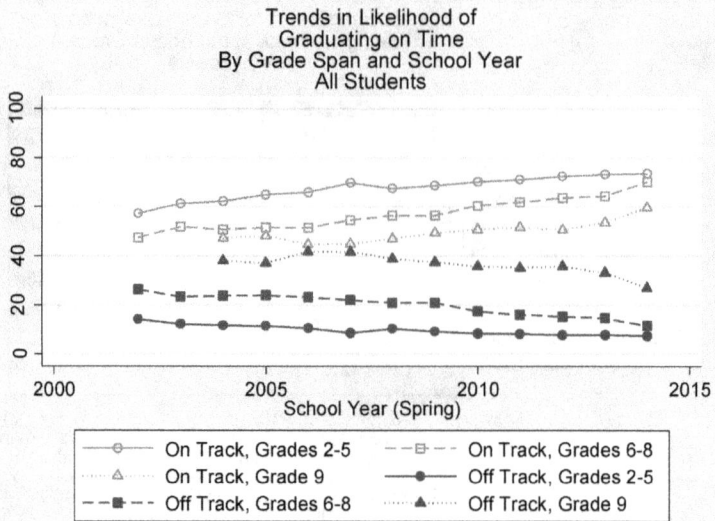

Figure 3.6 Trends in the Percentages of Students On Track and Off Track to Graduate on Time

Note: A student is deemed "on track" if the predicted likelihood of success is 75 percent or higher, and "off track" if it is less than 50 percent.

high school on time—for three separate grade spans. The figure shows that for elementary and middle grades, as well as grade 9, the percentage of students on track to graduate on time has risen quite steadily.

Our ultimate goal is to give teachers and administrators tools for early identification of students who may require additional supports to meet a given goal. Key questions for the district include: "If I give additional support to students whose predicted likelihood is below, say, 50 percent, how many students would that be? How many of those students are likely not to meet the goal without help? How many students who don't really need help would I be providing supports to?" One tool we have generated is a graph and accompanying table that answers these questions using historical data.

Figure 3.7 shows the predicted likelihood for students of being on track in grade 9, using information from when they were in grades 3–5. We separately show these predicted likelihoods for students who did not and who did meet this goal once they reached grade 9, shown in the top and bottom panels, respectively. Formally, this graph demonstrates whether our model has "discriminant validity": Is it the case that most of those who in fact succeeded had high predicted

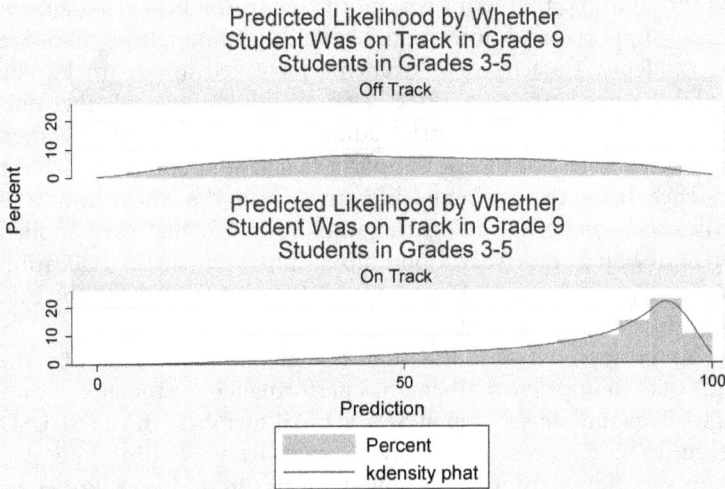

Figure 3.7 Histograms of the Predicted Likelihoods of Being On Track in Grade 9 for Grade 3 to 5 Students Who in Fact Were Not on Track and Were on Track When They Reached the End of Grade 9

likelihoods and that most of those who did not succeed had low predicted likelihoods? The figure shows that this is indeed the case.

Suppose that district administrators want to provide academic supports to students below a certain predicted likelihood of meeting a given goal. Using a table based on data from previous cohorts of students, administrators will be able to estimate answers to the earlier questions for various potential cut points. For instance, for the goal of being on track in grade 9 shown in Figure 3.7. If administrators picked a cutoff of 60 percent likelihood of being on track in grade 9, historically, here is what would have happened: They would have selected 37 percent of grade 3 to 5 students for additional supports. They would have provided supports to 65 percent of those who would not meet the goal in grade 9 without help. And they would have provided supports to 19 percent of those who would have succeeded in grade 9 even without help. Overall, of the students they selected for supports, 62% would not have been on track in grade 9 without additional help.[7]

Changing the Odds

In our *Academic Trajectories* work, we never assumed that predicted likelihoods that a student would succeed were deterministic.

On the contrary, that work was motivated by the belief that appropriate supports and interventions could meaningfully improve the academic trajectories of students identified as off track. The SanDERA executive committee began to think about whether university researchers and district administrators, working together, might create new academic supports that would combine the best evidence from the academic literature with the know-how and professional expertise of district staff. In 2015, the team applied for and won a four-year Continuous Improvement in Education Research grant from the Institute for Education Sciences of the U.S. Department of Education.

This project, which is less than a year old at the time of writing, seeks to improve mathematics performance of students in four high-needs middle schools in SDUSD. All members of the SDUSD executive committee are involved, with Rode, Policar and Bell again serving as co-principal investigators. In addition, Professor Amanda Datnow of the Department of Education Studies at UCSD, an expert on data-driven decision-making and professional learning communities (PLCs), joined the team to observe PLCs and to interview math teachers at the four participating schools. Bruce Arnold and his successor, Kim Samaniego, as state director and UCSD representative of the Mathematics Diagnostic Testing Project (MDTP), provided twice-yearly diagnostic readiness tests and worked with teachers in the four schools to diagnose individual student areas of strength and weakness. The project also included funds for the district to hire a math resource teacher, Kira Rua, who has worked closely with mathematics teachers at the four middle schools to help them diagnose math weaknesses and design lesson plans and, in some cases, differentiated instruction to address those weaknesses. Policar plays a key role in surveying the math teachers at the four schools regularly to learn about progress of the reforms, while at the same time her office provides training to teachers in various aspects of online data use.

This project brings the university researchers and the district staff even closer together. In the words of Bell, who coined the title of the project, the earlier *Trajectories* project "calculated the odds" that students will succeed; the new project aims instead to "change the odds" that students will succeed.

One indication of how the interactions between the university and the district are strengthening even further is the level of participation at the monthly Changing the Odds Steering Committee Meetings. In addition to SanDERA executive committee members listed earlier, area superintendents, Wendy Ranck-Buhr (SDUSD Director of Teaching and Learning Support) and resource teachers from SDUSD regularly attend the meetings along with, from UCSD, Datnow and Samaniego.

What Makes SanDERA Research Different from Other Second-Party Research?

SanDERA represents just one of many research groups and individuals conducting research that use SDUSD data. What is the distinction between the SanDERA approach and the more typical research project in which a researcher requests district data?

Bachofer is well situated to address this key question. For more than ten years, she served as executive director of SDUSD's Research and Evaluation Division where, among other duties, she oversaw the district's Research Proposal Review Panel (RPRP), the group responsible for reviewing all applications to conduct research in the district and monitoring the progress/products of that research. In 2009, Bachofer left SDUSD and joined Betts and his team at UCSD; she is now director of SanDERA.

The typical scenario at the district proceeds in this fashion:

a. An external researcher (e.g., graduate student, research group or professor) requests permission to conduct research in the district from the RPRP. Quite often, the research project is not aligned with district priorities or programs and the researcher has no context/understanding of the district or the environment in which the research is conducted.
b. The RPRP requires that the researcher find a district sponsor to ensure that the research is appropriate and will yield some useful information (to balance the time of "subjects" involved in the research). Often, the RPRP chair must assist the researcher in identifying a possible sponsor.
c. If approved (some proposals are of poor quality and/or not deemed suitable and are not approved), district staff must work with researchers/sponsors to ensure that the project moves forward. In some cases, this means making introductions to appropriate district staff, providing data, helping researchers understand district programs/practices and even troubleshooting for the researcher.
d. The RPRP chair follows up with each researcher to track progress and obtain a copy of any publications/presentations that result from the research.

These types of projects usually require significant investments of district time and talent, often with little useful return to the district.

By contrast, SanDERA projects, which must also receive RPRP approval, feature the following distinct characteristics:

a.   Researchers who have come to know district personnel, practices, policies and programs well and have little need for "hand-holding."

b.   A SanDERA statistician who knows district data structures and characteristics and plays a key role in initiating new projects once approved. District staff seldom extract new data (unless the project involves program data not previously acquired by SanDERA).

c.   Trust built up over nearly sixteen years, leading to frank and respectful give-and-take on issues related to data, programs, policies, personnel and research plans. There is the assurance of complete confidentiality of data and conversations.

d.   District assurance of high-quality, rigorous research that is useful to the district and, where possible, linked to the district's strategic plan.

e.   "No surprises" access to drafts of research products, with expected feedback on procedures, data and conclusions, helps ensure accuracy.

f.   A board of advisors made up of district leadership, teachers'/administrators' association reps, members of the business, philanthropic and parent communities and a range of advocacy groups (e.g., Latino Advisory Committee), ensuring relevancy.

g.   Mechanisms for publishing and sharing research findings (e.g., through PPIC and journal articles) to inform the work in San Diego and beyond.

h.   A mutually beneficial partnership focused on improving student achievement and professional practice.

Remaining Challenges

The Importance of Individuals

A natural question to ask is whether the formal agreements and organizational structures forming the backbone of SanDERA are enough to keep the alliance functioning, regardless of staffing, or whether there is something unique about the individuals who manage SanDERA that make them essential to its survival. The executive committee members discussed this question at length. We concluded that we could survive one member retiring or leaving at a time, but that it would take planning and effort to replace that member with a person who possesses a comparable combination of skills, knowledge and openness to policy research. Not all school districts are as open as SDUSD has been to being studied over many years with finely detailed data. The main difference is that both university and district participants respect rigorous research and want to improve the quality of education.

Funding

Funding has been an enduring challenge. SanDERA (and the work of Betts, Zau and colleagues prior to the establishment of SanDERA in 2010) has never sought nor received funding from SDUSD. Rather, each research project has had its own independent source of funding. Over the years, Betts/SanDERA has been supported by entities like the U.S. Department of Education, the PPIC, the William and Flora Hewlett Foundation, the Bill & Melinda Gates Foundation, the Atlantic Philanthropies, the San Diego Foundation, the California Academic Partnership Program, the Yankelovich Center for Social Science Research and the Smith Richardson Foundation to conduct research related to school choice, career and technical education, English learners, the state's high school exit examination, charter schools, diagnostic testing in mathematics and continuous improvement. SanDERA's current two grants from the U.S. Department of Education's Institute of Education Sciences are a researcher–practitioner grant and a four-year partnership grant focused on continuous improvement. Before that the U.S. Department of Education funded both a quantitative and qualitative study of CTE in the district.

There are pros and cons associated with this funding model. First, the pros. 1) SanDERA was established as an external research entity and, as such, concerns related to conflict of interest or impartiality have never arisen. If the district had funded SanDERA, this might not have been the case. 2) SanDERA's board of advisors (a twelve-member board with university, district, parent, community, philanthropic and teacher/administrator association representation) has established (and continues to update) a research agenda broadly aligned with district goals, interests and needs, but not limited or constrained by the district. 3) Research findings and products are not influenced by the district, and findings are always distributed freely by SanDERA, not the district. Of course, SanDERA abides by a "no surprises" policy, whereby district leadership is briefed on research findings prior to publication or presentation to the public. SanDERA has never felt pressure to modify research findings, even if its reports might cause discomfort for the district.

Now the cons. 1) Even though we have established a research agenda, we must secure funding prior to beginning work on any topic. For example, the board of advisors' highest-priority research topic is English learners. However, although we have published one solid report on English learners, and English learners receive attention as a subgroup in all of our studies, until sufficient funding can be found to support additional research, further work specifically on this topic must be placed on hold (Hill, Betts, Chavez, Zau, & Bachofer, 2014). 2) SanDERA spends substantial amounts of time writing research proposals which, when successful, fund only activities directly related to a specific research topic. Short-term, quick-turnaround projects that would help the district aren't usually possible, the infrastructure for our research group (e.g., website, networking, conferences) has considerable room to grow and sharing research findings with parents and community is limited. Obtaining sustaining funding is an ongoing priority for us.

Positive Impacts on the Host District

With a decade of an informal collaborative relationship followed by six years as a formal, researcher–practitioner collaboration, has SanDERA made a difference in terms of the school district itself? The district has viewed some publications as more academic than policy oriented and some as quite policy relevant. Of the latter, some studies have been helpful in confirming that the district was on the right course. Occasionally, reports have suggested that improvements could be made, and the district has on several occasions responded by making policy adjustments.

A prime example is the first publication on the *Blueprint for Student Success—the* reforms, mostly in reading, implemented by former Superintendent Alan Bersin. At the time, there was a tremendous amount of backlash from the teachers' and administrators' associations due to the "top-down" nature of the implementation, the increased accountability for student outcomes, vastly different professional development requirements in frequency, expected change in instructional practice and content and the introduction of peer coaches and classroom observation. New student course placement guidelines, new after-school and summer programs for at-risk and severely at-risk students and benchmarks linked to retention and promotion were also instituted. Bersin and Alvarado needed to know whether the *Blueprint* was having an impact on student achievement—were students' needs being met, even if teachers and principals were unhappy and, if so, how and where?

Betts and his colleagues modeled student test scores over time, explaining test scores as a function of student and teacher characteristics and interventions available to each student at any given time. The findings suggested that additional resources devoted to low-performing elementary schools, the Extended Day Reading Program and double-length English classes in middle school had all contributed to faster gains in academic achievement. However, at the high school level, students exposed to triple-length English classes actually performed worse relative to their past achievement and relative to high school students in earlier cohorts who had not been exposed to the reforms. In short, overall the program was a success at the elementary and middle school levels, but some elements were a failure at the high school level. In part based on a briefing the district received before this publication, the district dropped the triple-length English classes in high school (Betts, 2009; Betts et al., 2005; Betts, Zau, & Koedel, 2010).[8]

Another example of SanDERA research influencing district policy was a series of reports on the role of career and technical education (CTE, formerly vocational education) in the district (Bachofer et al., 2014; Betts et al., 2014). The reports, funded by the U.S. Department of Education, showed that much of the stigma that sometimes accompanies CTE was flat out wrong. It was not true, as sometimes assumed, that only students with the lowest academic grades took CTE courses. Most district students took at least one CTE course while in high school, and students in the middle of the academic grade distribution took the most CTE courses, not students at the very bottom or top. Second, taking CTE coursework was not related to academic success or failure. The reports followed students after high school graduation and measured their enrollment in postsecondary institutions around the country. Students who took CTE coursework were as likely to enroll in postsecondary institutions, and if anything, more likely. In 2009, Bachofer joined UCSD to spearhead a qualitative companion study of CTE in the district. This work not only brought a new case study approach to our work, but also brought us memorable vignettes from student focus groups about the role that CTE plays in keeping many students engaged in high school.

These findings proved useful to the Office of College, Career, and Technical Education at a time when the district was in the throes of financial crisis brought on by the economic downturn of 2008 and 2009. The rich set of CTE course offerings at SDUSD were at some risk due to cutbacks in the district, but survived until funding recovered.

A third and more recent example deals with reclassification criteria for English learners (Hill et al., 2014). When the California Standards Test (CST) was phased out in California, there was no "basic skills" assessment given statewide (in spring 2014). At the same time, the California English Language Development Test (CELDT), a statewide measure of English fluency, continued but was due to be phased out several years later in preparation for the launch of a new test to measure fluency that would be aligned with the Common Core State Standards for English learners. State guidelines require that a measure of basic skills be used as one of the criteria for reclassification, but no test existed in 2014 to fill this need. At the same time, district leadership was worried about relying on the CELDT without any basic skills test in English to make reclassification decisions, because the CELDT was not aligned with the Common Core. SanDERA research on the relationship between CELDT scores, reclassification decisions and future student outcomes reassured the district that it could use CELDT scores with local assessments—but without CST scores—to reclassify students.

A fourth example of positive policy impact relates to new graduation standards. The school board of SDUSD passed a new higher "college preparatory" high school graduation requirement in spring 2011, to go into effect with the class of 2016. SanDERA members have published three reports on this new college prep requirement. The reports have noted that this promising policy, which could help more San Diego students become eligible to attend the California State University and University of California systems, at the same time poses a risk that less academically inclined students may not graduate on time. The first report looked back at the class of 2011 and found that only 61 percent of students would have graduated had they been subject to the new requirements (Betts, Zau, & Bachofer, 2013). This, of course, created a lower bound for the class of 2016 because students in the earlier class were not required to take the so-called "a–g" college preparatory courses, and the class of 2016 was. A second report, issued in early 2015, examined the class of 2016 through the end of grade 9 and showed that although students in the class of 2016 had started to complete more of the required courses, they would need to accelerate their coursework markedly in the later grades (Betts, Young, Zau, & Bachofer, 2015). A third report in early 2016 followed the class of 2016 through August 2015 and found that just before starting their senior year about one in four students were at risk of not graduating on time. The report showed that certain student subgroups, especially English learners and those receiving special education services, were at the greatest risk of not graduating on time (Betts, Young, Zau, & Bachofer, 2016).

The district reacted to these analyses, as well as internal data analysis conducted by district staff, by implementing a series of reforms. It allowed rigorous written and oral language exams to serve as a replacement for the World Language course requirement, typically for those students with a non-English home language. Then in 2015–2016 the district assigned additional counselors to high schools with the most students at risk of not completing the "a–g" requirements. They were to monitor students' progress toward meeting graduation requirements and ensure that they took the courses needed to accomplish that. Equally important, the district signed a contract with an online provider of credit recovery courses that had been approved by the University of California as meeting the "a–g" course requirements.

SDUSD Superintendent Cindy Marten has acknowledged that the series of reports helped the district mobilize this extraordinary series of interventions. An online report indicated that

> (The SanDERA) researchers were the ones who combed district records and concluded in the PPIC report many students were three semesters behind as of August 2015 on completing the required seven courses. Marten said early reporting from the researchers informed district efforts to add online courses and expand summer school for students needing to make up courses. (Burks, 2016)

Lessons Learned: Factors that Have Been Essential to SanDERA's Success and Longevity

Two key agreements fostered the growth of mutual trust between the researchers and practitioners. An arm's-length policy, which guaranteed the researchers the right to publish, was built into the initial agreement with PPIC, as well as into subsequent individual project agreements between Betts and SDUSD. Second, Betts made a "no surprise" commitment to the district, meaning that he and other researchers would always show the district staff member acting as official "sponsor" for a given research project the results and draft papers before presenting them at conferences or submitting for publication. These two policies—a "no surprises" policy combined with the right to publish—represent the two pillars upon which SanDERA was later built and have provided the foundation of mutual trust that has supported the work over almost two decades.

The policies did more than build mutual trust: The no-surprise policy has on numerous occasions benefited the researchers or the district. For example, an early draft of a report on how students were faring with the California High School Exit Examination showed a fairly large number of students who had not graduated in grade 12, due to not completing the exam, re-enrolling the following year (Betts et al., 2012). (The state had mandated that schools should accept these nongraduates, but the researchers were surprised that many re-enrolled.) One of the district colleagues advised the research team to separate non–diploma-bound students—students who due to a major disability were not expected to receive a regular diploma—from other students. Sure enough, the former students, whom the state funds for several years after grade 12 to master life skills, constituted a meaningful fraction of the students the team had been counting as reacting to the state mandate for those who had not passed the exit exam to re-enroll.

Conversely, the district benefited from the no-surprise policy when in the study of the *Blueprint for Student Success*, early evidence the team compiled about the negative effect on high school students of triple-length, pull-out classes in English contributed to the district's policy change. The policy change came a year before the appearance of the official refereed publication.

In seeking to find the key components of the collaboration, the executive team compiled the following list:

- **Building trust.** Researchers have built trust by 1) developing a deep understanding of district policies, practices, procedures, data systems, district leadership, program managers and schools (knowing the district); 2) keeping district leadership informed about the status/findings of research projects (no surprises policy); 3) being good stewards of all information/data collected while conducting research (confidentiality); and 4) working with district leadership to address issues of concern (research agenda aligned with district priorities). The district has built trust by 1) taking time to ensure that researchers have access to, and understand, district policies, practices, procedures, data systems, district leadership, program managers and schools; 2) facilitating access to data and individuals necessary to conduct high-quality research; 3) serving on advisory/steering committees and creating opportunities for sharing findings with district and community; and 4) allowing researchers to share research findings without being censored (right to publish).
- **Developing data expertise.** SanDERA could not function without access to a range of student-, teacher- and program-level data. District staff coached Andrew Zau for nearly five years as he mastered the complexity of both the data structures and the data themselves. During this time, Zau was introduced to key district personnel who taught him what information was available and how to use it.
- **Valuing true collaboration.** The SanDERA executive committee— composed of three district and three university members—feels like its own entity. Although members bring the background knowledge and expertise of their home organizations to the table,

the team itself seems to be an independently functioning group. Some members of the team have been working together for more than twenty-five years, and the newest member of the group has a history of over ten years. Each member of the team is an equal partner, and each feels free to challenge and question data, findings, processes or plans, resulting in much stronger outcomes.

- **Shared belief in the value of policy-oriented research.** The expertise and openness of district staff have contributed significantly to the success of the partnership. District partners are curious, focused and knowledgeable perfectionists—just what is required to produce meaningful, quality products.

We suspect that many readers will be contemplating a partnership about issues other than public education. Regardless of the focus of the researchers and the government partners thinking about collaborating, the following checklist of questions could prove helpful in deciding whether to commit jointly to building a researcher–practitioner partnership. If potential partners can honestly answer each of these questions in the affirmative, they are already well on their way to a lasting collaboration.

1. Are you ready to check your ego at the door?
2. Are you ready to commit to this for multiple years? Are you willing to commit to regular partnership meetings and impromptu meetings as data or policy issues arise?
3. Have you identified a funding source to start up the collaboration and then to sustain it?
4. Do you agree on a research agenda? Are there one or two burning questions both sides want to answer?
5. Do you have a plan to disseminate results?
6. Do you have the patience and persistence to see projects through to the end, when the academic audiences that the researchers typically communicate with and the government decision-makers whom the practitioners typically communicate with may need the same information written in different styles and on different timelines?
7. Do the researchers realize that in administrative data generated by government entities, standards, procedures and data collection efforts constantly change? Are they willing to invest the time to find solutions when the way data are stored or coded changes, or when the data gathered change in more dramatic ways over time?
8. Can both sets of parties foresee "gains from trade" at the outset, in which each partner enriches the understanding and capabilities of the other partner?

There are no doubt a thousand ways to build a thriving researcher–government practitioner partnership. That said, this case study recounts one approach. It has proven remarkably robust for us, and we hope that others will find in this account elements that prove useful in building their own unique partnerships.

Reflecting on the implementation history and now ongoing policy impact of SanDERA, the terms noted earlier—jointly, communication, relationship and together—continue to stand out. Another set of terms features prominently as well. These include trust, mutual benefit, longer-term and policy impact. The case expresses that the success and impact of SanDERA's research endeavors have not come at the expense of its policy partner. As pointed out early on, this is unlike a "fairly typical" researcher–policymaker relationship that revolves around the researcher requesting approval for a study, receiving that approval and completing the research with little, if any, during-study or follow-up interaction with the policymaker. By establishing agreements about publication and review prior to publication (the "no surprises" rule), SanDERA partners created ground rules for managing and using information in a mutually respectful and beneficial way. SanDERA had other forms of project governance in place, with the establishment of advisory boards and less formal, but equally critical, accountability through teacher focus groups. Incorporating practitioner (teacher) input ensured that research results were relevant and more likely to be used. What comes through clearly in this case from an implementation standpoint is that a carefully crafted infrastructure and cultivated relationships have combined to solidify both the substance of SanDERA's work and the structure that allows it to function.

Key Takeaways

The SanDERA partnership illuminates many of the themes also present in the CASEL/Washoe partnership. Among them, successful implementation of a partnership means that both partners benefit. Both cases in this chapter document a combination of perceived and real benefits. The CASEL case acknowledges benefits to CASEL, to Washoe and to the field. In addition, researcher candor about when some research may not always be of as much use as others to the policymaker illustrates awareness of partner needs and a reflective approach to the work that is essential to building relationships and trust. Moreover, the case notes that the success of the partnership has led to CASEL's pursuit of similar partnerships with other districts. SanDERA notes that there are consistently benefits to the researchers and to the district.

Both cases also emphasize the importance of being deliberate about partnership processes. They formalized their partnerships through documentation, thus explicitly stating expectations and responsibilities and reducing the likelihood of confusion and misunderstanding that can easily stem from the different cultures, languages, practices and policies that often define researchers and policymakers. Both cases established regular communications and meeting schedules as well as formal processes for initiating work (e.g., time for writing grants, identifying research topics) and moving work forward (e.g., creating clear role delineation, embedding permanent staff within partner systems). The planning and formalizing aspects of the implementation is a feature of both partnerships.

An attribute of both cases that we are optimistic will play an increasingly prominent role in future researcher–policymaker partnerships is equity. In their tool, *Building Equity in Research Practice Partnerships,* Ryoo et al's description of equity in partnerships could well be describing SanDERA (Ryoo, Choi, & McLeod, 2015). Among other characteristics, they emphasize that equity exists when partners "[c]ollaboratively define research questions, purpose, goals, and definitions of success" and when they "[a]ttend to the changing needs of the collaboration as research questions and educational strategies shift over time." SanDERA features both of these among the reasons for its success and sustainability. Likewise the CASEL/Washoe partnership discusses its cross-district meeting entitled *Social Emotional Learning from Implementation to Scale: Spotlight on Equity & Assessment,* a testament to the attention paid to equity as a focus area of the partnership.

Finally, both the CASEL/Washoe and SanDERA partnerships have gifted readers of this book with questions to consider upon entering into a researcher–policymaker partnership. It is telling that, unsolicited, they produced these guiding considerations. Together, they offer fifteen questions that researchers, policymakers and—as SanDERA points out—entities of any multisector partnership—might do well to consider as they propose, design and then implement a partnership. That SanDERA's executive team of researchers and policymakers developed the guidance speaks to the collaborative approach that both cases bring to their implementation and to the overall work of their partnerships.

Given the importance of regular communication and short- and long-term planning, partnerships may benefit from participating in basic project management training or using project management tools. Free software is available at a variety of sites, and some common office products are available as add-ons to current packages. These tools can be technology based (i.e., software) or paper based and will involve calendaring of regular activities, including communicating and work-team check-ins as well as deliberate scheduling of tasks that need to be completed to reach key milestones. More complex packages may also include analyses of project risk and mitigation strategies and resource allocation tracking.

As is true for every case in this book, the cases in this chapter could also be featured in other chapters. The CASEL case, for example, provides extensive insight relevant to research utilization, whereas the SanDERA case has much to say about sustaining researcher–policymaker partnerships. We encourage readers of these and all of the cases to pay attention to and learn about the partnerships, not only with respect to the theme of the chapter where they are situated, but also for the other ways in which they educate and provide guidance about planning, establishing, carrying out and benefitting from researcher–policymaker partnerships.

Notes

1 This research was supported with a grant from the Institute of Education Sciences (R305HI30012).
2 Students with low SEC scores are those who score more than one standard deviation less than average, while those with high SEC scores are those who score more than one standard deviation greater than average.
3 Links to many of the studies listed here can be found at http://sandera.ucsd.edu/research-and-publications/index.html.
4 The *Blueprint* studies include Betts (2009), Betts, Zau, and King (2005) and Betts, Zau, and Koedel (2010). For the main school choice study see Betts, Rice, Zau, Tang, and Koedel (2006). For a history of how school choice operates in San Diego, see Zau and Betts (2005). Koedel, Betts, Rice, and Zau (2009) study how school choice programs affect socioeconomic and racial integration in SDUSD. As another example of school choice research, Betts, Tang, and Zau (2010) use charter school data from SDUSD to show how superficial comparisons that do not take into account students' initial achievement are likely to lead to biased estimates of the impact of charter schools on achievement.
5 Betts, Hahn, and Zau (2011) provide the quantitative study. Bachofer, Zau, and Betts (2012a, b) present results of a survey and a set of interviews of secondary school math teachers.
6 See Babcock and Betts (2009) for the class-size study. Koedel and Betts (2010, 2011) address some technical issues with using student test scores to evaluate teachers. It is notable that SDUSD was a district that did not follow this controversial path to evaluating teachers, and yet district staff were open to us conducting academic studies of the issue.
7 Unsurprisingly, the predictions are even more accurate for middle school students than for elementary school students because when observed the former are closer to reaching grade 9. If a middle school provided supports to students who are below 60 percent likelihood of being on track in grade 9, historically it would have supported 39 percent of middle school students, including 71 percent of those who would not be on track in grade 9 without additional help and only 15 percent of those who would be on track without help.
8 See Betts, Zau, and King (2005) for the first study of which a draft version influenced district policy, and a follow-up in Betts, Zau, and Koedel (2010). For a retrospective summary on the impact of the reform, see also Betts (2009).

References

American Institutes for Research (AIR). (2014). *CASEL/NoVo collaborating districts initiative: 2014 cross-district implementation summary.* Washington, DC: AIR.
Andrews, J.O., Cox, M.J., Newman, S.D., Gillenwater, G., Warner, G., Winkler, J.A., White, B., Wolf, S., Leite, R., Ford, M.E., & Slaughter, S. (2013). Training partnership dyads for community-based participatory research: Strategies and lessons learned from the Community Engaged Scholars Program. *Health Promotion Practice, 14*(4), 524–533.

Arsenio, W.F., Adams, E., & Gold, J. (2009). Social information processing, moral reasoning, and emotion attributions: Relations with adolescents' reactive and proactive aggression. *Child Development, 80,* 1739–1755. doi:10.1111/j.1467-8624.2009.01365.x.

Babcock, P., & Betts, J.R. (2009). Reduced-class distinctions: Effort, ability, and the education production function. *Journal of Urban Economics, 65*(3), 314–322.

Bachofer, K.V., Betts, J.R., & Zau, A.C. (2014). *An evaluation of the outcomes of career and technical education in San Diego Unified School District: A descriptive case study.* San Diego, CA: San Diego Education Research Alliance at UCSD.

Bachofer, K.V., Zau, A.C., & Betts, J.R. (2012a). *The impact of the use of the Mathematics Diagnostic Testing Project in San Diego Unified School District: Teacher survey component.* Long Beach, CA: California Academic Partnership Program.

Bachofer, K.V., Zau, A.C., & Betts, J.R. (2012b). *The impact of the use of the Mathematics Diagnostic Testing Project in San Diego Unified School District: Teacher interview component.* Long Beach, CA: California Academic Partnership Program.

Balfanz, R., & Byrnes, V. (2012). *Chronic absenteeism: Summarizing what we know from nationally available data.* Baltimore: Johns Hopkins University Center for Social Organization of Schools.

Balfanz, R., Herzog, L., & Mac Iver, D.J. (2007). Prevention student disengagement and keeping students on the graduation path in middle-grades schools: Early identification and effective interventions. *Educational Psychologist, 42,* 223–235.

Barry, M., & Reschley, A.L. (2012). Longitudinal predictors of high school completion. *School Psychology Quarterly, 27,* 74–84.

Betts, J.R. (2009). The San Diego blueprint for student success: A retrospective overview and commentary. *Journal of Education for Students Placed at Risk, 14*(1), 120–129.

Betts, J.R., & Danenberg, A. (2004). San Diego: Do too many cooks spoil the broth? In F.M. Hess & C. Finn (Eds.), *Leaving no child behind? Options for kids in failing schools* (pp. 213–238). New York: Palgrave MacMillan.

Betts, J.R., Hahn, Y., & Zau, A.C. (2011). *Does diagnostic math testing improve student learning?* San Francisco, CA: Public Policy Institute of California.

Betts, J.R., Rice, L., Zau, A.C., Tang, Y.E., & Koedel, C.R. (2006). *Does school choice work? Effects on student integration and achievement.* San Francisco, CA: Public Policy Institute of California.

Betts, J.R., Tang, Y.E., & Zau, A.C. (2010). Madness in the method? A critical analysis of popular methods of estimating the effect of charter schools on student achievement. In J.R. Betts & P.T. Hill (Eds.), *Taking measure of charter schools: Better assessments, better policymaking, better schools* (pp. 15–32). Lanham, MD: Rowman and Littlefield Publishers, Inc.

Betts, J.R., Young, S.M., Zau, A.C., & Bachofer, K.V. (2015). *The "College Prep for All" mandate in San Diego: An examination of new graduation requirements in the context of San Diego: Part I.* San Diego, CA: UC San Diego.

Betts, J.R., Young, S.M., Zau, A.C., & Bachofer, K.V. (2016). *College prep for all: Will San Diego students meet challenging new graduation requirements?* San Francisco, CA: Public Policy Institute of California.

Betts, J.R., Zau, A.C., & Bachofer, K.V. (2013). *College readiness as a graduation requirement: An assessment of San Diego's challenges.* San Francisco, CA: Public Policy Institute of California.

Betts, J.R., Zau, A.C., & King, K. (2005). *From blueprint to reality: San Diego's education reforms.* San Francisco, CA: Public Policy Institute of California.

Betts, J.R., Zau, A.C., & Koedel, C.R. (2010). *Lessons in reading reform: Finding what works.* San Francisco, CA: Public Policy Institute of California.

Betts, J.R., Zau, A.C., McAdams, J., & Dotter, D. (2014). *Career and technical education in San Diego: A statistical analysis of course availability, students' course-taking patterns, and relationships with high school and postsecondary outcomes.* San Diego, CA: The San Diego Education Research Alliance at UCSD.

Betts, J.R., Zau, A.C., & Rice, L. (2003). *Determinants of student achievement: New evidence from San Diego.* San Francisco: Public Policy Institute of California.

Betts, J.R., Zau, A.C., Zieleniak, Y., & Bachofer, K.V. (2012). *Passing the California high school exit exam: Have recent policies improved student performance?* San Francisco, CA: Public Policy Institute of California.

Blad, E. (2016). Students help design measures of social-emotional skills. *Education Week.* Retrieved from: http://www.edweek.org/ew/articles/2016/04/13/students-help-design-measures-of-social-emotional-skills.html.

Bowen, H. Kent. *Project management manual.* Harvard Business School Background Note 697–034, September 1996. (Revised March 2002).

Burks, M. (Producer). (2016, May). *San Diego unified high school graduation rates higher than expected.* Online article. Retrieved from: http://www.kpbs.org/news/2016/may/11/san-diego-unified-high-school-graduation-rates/.

Collaborative for Academic, Social, and Emotional Learning (CASEL). (2013). *CASEL guide: Effective social and emotional learning programs: Preschool and elementary school edition.* Chicago, IL: CASEL.

Collaborative for Academic, Social, and Emotional Learning (CASEL). (2015). *CASEL guide: Effective social and emotional learning programs: Secondary school edition.* Chicago, IL: CASEL.

Davis, T. (2016). *WCSD state of education address.* Retrieved from: http://www.washoeschools.net/Page/3618.

Farrington, C.A., Roderick, M., Allensworth, E., Nagoaka, J., Keyes, T.S., Johnson, D.W., & Beechum, N.O. (2012). Teaching adolescents to become learners: The role of non-cognitive factors in shaping school performance: A critical literature review. *University of Chicago Consortium on Chicago School Research.* Retrieved from: http://ccsr.uchicago.edu/publications/teaching-adolescents-become-learners-role-noncognitive-factors-shaping-school.

Gatta, M., & McCabe, K.P. (2008). The "new" policy partnership: Academic researchers and government officials partnering towards social equity. *Equal Opportunities International, 27*(2), 129–131.

Harrison, M.B., & Graham, I.D. (2012). Roadmap for a participatory research-practice partnership to implement evidence. *Worldviews on Evidence-Based Nursing, 9*(4), 210–220.

Hill, L.E., Betts, J.R., Chavez, B., Zau, A.C., & Bachofer, K.V. (2014). *Pathways to fluency: Examining the link between language reclassification policies and student success.* San Francisco, CA: Public Policy Institute of California.

Jones, D.E., Greenberg, M., & Crowley, M. (2015). Early social-emotional functioning and public health: The relationship between kindergarten social competence and future wellness. *American Journal of Public Health, 105,* 2283–2290. doi.org/10.2105/AJPH.2015.302630.

Kendziora, K., & Osher, D. (2016). Promoting children's and adolescents' social and emotional development: District adaptations of a theory of action. *Journal of Clinical Child and Adolescent Psychology. Special Issue: Good enough? Interventions for child mental health: From adoption to adaptation—from programs to systems, 45*, 797–811. doi: 10.1080/15374416.2016.1197834.

Koedel, C.R., & Betts, J.R. (2010). Value-added to what? How a ceiling in the testing instrument influences value-added estimation. *Education Finance and Policy, 5*(1), 54–81.

Koedel, C.R., & Betts, J.R. (2011). Does student sorting invalidate value-added models of teacher effectiveness? An extended analysis of the Rothstein critique. *Education Finance and Policy, 6*(1), 18–42.

Koedel, C.R., Betts, J.R., Rice, L.A., & Zau, A.C. (2009). The integrating and segregating effects of school choice. *Peabody Journal of Education, 84*(2), 110–129.

National Implementation Research Network (NIRN). (2013). *Implementation drivers: Assessing best practices.* Retrieved from: http://implementation.fpg.unc.edu/sites/implementation.fpg.unc.edu/files/NIRN-ImplementationDrivers AssessingBestPractices.pdf.

Palinkas, L.A., Short, C., & Wong, M. (2015). *Policy partnerships for implementation of evidence-based practiced in child welfare and child mental health.* Retrieved from: http://wtgrantfoundation.org/library/uploads/2015/10/Research-Practice-Policy_Partnerships.pdf.

Pellegrino, J.W., & Hilton, M.L. (2012). *Education for life and work: Developing transferable knowledge and skills in the 21st century.* Washington, DC: The National Academies Press.

Ryoo, Jean J., Choi, M., & McLeod, E. (2015). *Building equity in research-practice partnerships.* Research and Practice Collaboratory. Retrieved from: http://research andpractice.org/wp-content/uploads/2015/10/BuildingEquity_Oct2015.pdf.

Stone, D., Maxwell, S., & Keating, M. (2001). *Bridging research and policy.* An international workshop funded by the UK Department for International Development Radcliffe House, Warwick University. Retrieved from: http://www2.warwick.ac.uk/fac/soc/pais/research/researchcentres/csgr/research/keytopic/other/bridging.pdf.Valiente, C., Swanson, J., & Eisenberg, N. (2011). Linking students' emotion and academic achievement: When and why emotions matter. *Child Development Perspectives, 6*(2), 129–135.

WCSD-CASEL Partnership. (2016). *Guidance for using the student self-report social and emotional competency assessment tool.* Unpublished Technical Report.

Weissberg, R.P., Durlak, J.A., Domitrovich, C.E., & Gullotta, T.P. (2015). Social and emotional learning: Past, present, and future. In J.A. Durlak, C.E. Domitrovich, R.P. Weissberg, & T.P. Gullotta (Eds.), *Handbook of social and emotional learning: Research and practice* (pp. 3–19). New York, NY: Guilford.

Willis, J. (2007). The neuroscience of joyful education. *Educational Leadership, 64.* Retrieved from: http://www.ascd.org/publications/educational-leadership/summer07/vol64/num09/The-Neuroscience-of-Joyful-Education.aspx.

Zau, A.C., & Betts, J.R. (2005). The evolution of school choice. In F.M. Hess (Ed.), *Urban school reform: Lessons from San Diego* (pp. 223–241). Cambridge, MA: Harvard Education Press.

Zau, A.C., & Betts, J.R. (2008). *Predicting success, preventing failure: An investigation of the California high school exit exam.* San Francisco, CA: Public Policy Institute of California.

4 Sustaining Successful Partnerships

In this chapter we discuss partnerships that last. We are particularly interested in understanding how individuals and teams who are situated in different sectors such as academia and policymaking manage to build relationships and work together over long periods. What are the common ways in which these very different professionals work together? How do they succeed in working with one another on multiple types of projects? In the two case studies shared in this chapter, we observe a set of attributes shared by partnerships that continue over time.

Short-Term Partnerships

Before we examine these long-term working relationships, we first contrast them with shorter-term arrangements. Short-term partnerships are usually built upon a single work product or consultation, are time limited and are often, but not always, between specific individuals.

These types of arrangements often have defined start and end dates and can frequently involve a formal contract. They may or may not be funded. Some examples might include the following:

- An evaluation for a child welfare intervention that is part of an evaluation studies graduate class at a local university. The evaluation work lasts the length of the semester, and the students and perhaps the instructor have contact with the child welfare agency only for the length of the study. When the final report is completed, so is the partnership.
- A county court needs a literature review on a set of policy options to help the court explore new sentencing alternatives based on the most effective treatments for juvenile offenders. A local university faculty member offers to complete the review and presents the results before the county bench.
- A state agency needs a descriptive report of state- and county-level child data, such as low birth weight rates, child protection investigations and kindergarten entry assessment results. Because the state

agency is short-staffed and cannot complete the report, it issues a request for proposal (RFP) for completion of this one-time document, and a local university receives the grant. The university in turn assigns the work to undergraduate sociology students to complete in time for the legislative session.

In each of these brief examples there is a succinct start and end date and the need for a clear and accessible product that can usually be provided within a short timeframe. In addition, these types of products are sometimes learning experiences for students who are under the guidance of faculty or graduate students. They typically do not last beyond the length of the course or a contract end date.

Although some of these partnerships may provide the foundation for additional projects in the future and some actually become part of a larger collaborative arrangement, as we will see in the case study on the Hennepin-University Partnership, by and large they do not sustain beyond the completion of immediate work. Individuals are less likely to maintain their connections, and these relationships are only about the short-term work required.

Long-Term Partnerships

When we consider what types of partnerships are "short term" and which are "long term," we struggle a bit with a clear definition in terms of timeframes or types of work. It is almost better to define long-term partnerships around the changes in individuals' behaviors related to information seeking and problem-solving. When faced with a policy problem, public agencies that are part of long-term partnerships consider the research partner as among the pool of information sources to tap, in addition to internal experts, high-level government leadership or leaders of direct service agencies. Likewise, when researchers with established policy partnerships seek a research opportunity to test a theory or replicate other research, they consider among their potential partners a specific agency or set of agencies with whom they have worked before. The "other side" then becomes part of the landscape of thought partners who can help achieve the goals of problem-solving or exploration.

In addition to collaborative partnering becoming normative and almost a habit for problem-solving, the other attribute we anticipated for sustaining partnerships over time was that the relationships move beyond individuals and become institutionalized. If the individuals who have started up the partnership or who have been highly engaged leave the organization, other staff and leaders are aware of, support and already participate in the partnership, which allows it to continue. In this way, the partnership becomes part of the fabric of collective problem-solving and exploration around a shared area of interest.

The following case highlighting the long-running Family Impact Seminars at the University of Wisconsin-Madison shows the vitality of a researcher–policymaker partnership that has lasted over two decades and has become a national model. Using a specific seminar to illustrate the partnership, Karen Bogenschneider and her colleagues describe its origins and share the attributes of this partnership that has sustained its place in Wisconsin's policymaking landscape.

Connecting Research and Policy: The Story of a Wisconsin Family Impact Seminar on Jobs

Karen Bogenschneider, Hilary Shager, Olivia Little and Stephanie Eddy

Calls for stronger connections between research and policy often are no more than lofty words and pious platitudes. In Wisconsin, though, these words take on a special significance as part of a long and strong tradition that the mission of a public university is to serve the public good. This century-long tradition is proudly known to citizens of the state as the *Wisconsin Idea—making* the boundaries of the university the boundaries of the state. As early as 1904, University of Wisconsin-Madison President Charles Van Hise boldly proclaimed that he "would never be satisfied until the beneficent influence of the university reaches every family in the state." In 1910, the Wisconsin Republican platform characterized the university as the "people's servant," commending the research that it conducted and that it carried to people around the state (Stark, 1995, p. 11). This legacy continues in Wisconsin today, where the need to connect research and policy is not only something you say, but something you see. State Street is the iconic seven-block pedestrian mall that connects the university campus and the state legislature. The university and the legislature are only blocks apart in geographic distance, yet they seem worlds apart in the amount of communication that occurs between the two. In Wisconsin, the aim of the Family Impact Seminars is to connect the two ends of State Street.

Officially, the story of the Wisconsin Family Impact Seminars began in 1992. In reality, however, it is an outgrowth of the Wisconsin Idea, which has deep roots in the state and has come to be respected by faculty and expected by policymakers. In fact, the seminars grew out of a discussion in which legislators questioned whether the Wisconsin Idea was still alive and well. We turned to these very legislators in our exploratory interviews to assess whether the seminars would meet a need in the state. The enthusiastic response from every state legislator and agency official we interviewed spoke volumes. The Family Impact Seminars would serve an important purpose similar to other offshoots of the Wisconsin Idea. However, the seminars would differ in taking direct aim at connecting the research produced at a state university to decisions being made at the state capitol.

Even without the fertile soil of the Wisconsin Idea, the Family Impact Seminars have spread across the country to a couple dozen states. The seminar model first took root in Congress under the leadership of Theodora Ooms and was expanded to state legislatures under the leadership of Karen Bogenschneider. Currently, leadership for the national headquarters, The Family Impact Institute, is being provided by Shelley MacDermid Wadsworth of Purdue University.

In most states, the Family Impact Seminars operate as a partnership that serves as a knowledge broker between researchers and policymakers. The seminars are a series of presentations, discussion sessions and briefing reports that communicate high-quality, nonpartisan research to policymakers on topics they identify. The goals of the seminars are to build greater respect for and use of research in policy decisions; to encourage policymakers to examine policies and programs through the lens of family impacts; and to provide neutral, nonpartisan opportunities for legislators to engage in open dialogue for fostering relationships and finding common ground. In this case study, we illustrate the success of the Family Impact Seminars in achieving these goals with the story of one seminar in Wisconsin.

Previous writing on the Family Impact Seminars has focused on their theoretical underpinnings (i.e., community dissonance theory, Kingdon's (2003) theory of open policy windows, structural family systems theory), the core components that undergird their effectiveness and the track record of the seminar model across almost two dozen states (Bogenschneider, 2014; Bogenschneider & Corbett, 2010a). In this case study, we drill down on how the Wisconsin Family Impact Seminars, situated at the University of Wisconsin-Madison, partners with state legislators, executive agency officials and policy analysts at the legislature's nonpartisan service agencies. We argue that this partnership model is fundamental to the success of the seminars in an era of increasing specialization where it appears that society has problems, legislatures have committees and universities have disciplines (Kellogg Commission, 1999). Legislative policy expertise varies according to legislators' interests and is further subdivided by the narrow jurisdictions of the legislature's committee structure. Similarly, researchers, executive agency officials and legislative analysts develop expertise in distinct areas and operate in their own cultures (Simmons, 1996). Yet most social problems are not so easily divided and compartmentalized. By partnering across institutions, the seminars offer a uniquely broad interdisciplinary perspective that is needed in policy discourse to break through what has been aptly coined the "iron curtain of specialization" (Bellah, Madsen, Sullivan, Swidler, & Tipton, 1996, p. 301).

In the pages that follow, we tell the story of Wisconsin's thirtieth Family Impact Seminar, *Positioning Wisconsin for the Jobs of the Future*, held in October 2011. The leadership for this seminar, similar to most other states, consisted of a bare-bones staff including about 25 percent of a faculty director's time along with a coordinator, graduate student and consultant, each of whom devoted part-time effort over a couple of months. In this case study, we begin at the end with selected impacts detailing, in the policymakers' own words, how research from this seminar influenced policy decisions and the policymaking process. Then we circle back to describe the partnership model and its pragmatic processes and procedures that are at the core of executing a successful seminar. We conclude by specifying how the partnership model is central to the success of the seminars in building better public policy for families.

How Was the Wisconsin Family Impact Seminar on Jobs Designed and What Were Its Impacts?

This seminar featured three experts: Jonas Prising, Executive Vice President and President of the Americas for Manpower Group headquartered in Milwaukee, Wisconsin; William Symonds, Director of the Pathways to Prosperity Project at the Harvard Graduate School of Education in Cambridge, Massachusetts; and Ron Haskins, Senior Fellow of Economic Studies and Co-Director of the Center on Children and Families at the Brookings Institution in Washington, DC. The presentations were followed by a reactor panel that included Wisconsin's chief economist and three state employers. This seminar highlighted strategies for building a foundation for Wisconsin's economic success—what jobs are hardest to fill, which industry sectors are projected to face the highest skills gaps in the state, how well the current workforce training system is working and what evidence-based programs help businesses improve productivity and equip workers with the education and skills they need (e.g., Career Academies, Manufacturing Extension Program, preschool education and sector strategies). About one-quarter of seminar time was devoted to Q&A. The seminar was followed by two "invitation only" discussion sessions—one targeted to state legislators and another to high-ranking agency officials.

One sign of the success of the Family Impact Seminars is the engagement of dozens of policymakers. For example, the jobs seminars attracted eighty-six participants, including twenty-six legislators, sixteen legislative aides, twenty-three agency officials, ten university and extension faculty and four nonpartisan service agency analysts. In keeping with the nonpartisan nature of the seminars, lobbyists and the press were not invited. Twelve legislators participated in a 75-minute discussion session with the speakers and nine high-ranking agency officials participated in a separate 90-minute discussion. Overall, 36 of 132 legislative offices participated in some aspect of the day's activities.

The seminar received high marks on an end-of-session evaluation (N = 64, 74 percent response rate). On a scale of 1 (poor) to 5 (excellent), participants assigned a rating of 4.5 to the quality of the research, 4.4 to its relevance, 4.4 to objectivity and 4.3 to usefulness. Policymakers praised the uniqueness of the seminar and the quality of the speakers in a follow-up phone evaluation (N = 32 legislators, aides and executive agency officials, 77 percent response rate; unless otherwise noted, comments in this paper are from the follow-up evaluation, which were written down during phone interviews and are as close to the respondent's own words as possible):

> I thought it was excellent. I was amazed at the kind of experts you got to speak—well balanced, and some of the top people in the field. It was an experience like none other I've experienced. (legislative aide)
>
> I was very impressed by the people (the speakers)—their background and how well informed they were. They were very good, knew what they were talking about, and had very good data to support what they were saying. (legislator)

Impacts on Policy Decisions

Granted, the research presented at this seminar was highly rated, but do legislators *really* use information from a seminar in their jobs? It would be naïve to suggest that research from a seminar would directly cause a complex, multiply determined process like a policy decision. However, it would be equally naïve to ignore when research from the seminars *may* have influenced policy decisions. Following this seminar, the legislature passed two bills that policymakers attributed, in part, to research provided by the

seminar—a law that provided grants to technical schools for training in advanced manufacturing skills and an alternative diploma
law whereby disengaged students participate in work-based learning in technical trades while earning high school diplomas. In the
words of two legislative aides:

> The really useful discussion at this last seminar was the mis-
> match between the skills that are available in the workforce and
> the skills that are needed in advanced manufacturing and other
> technical areas, and how to address that. That has turned out to
> be one of the major economic development themes of this year.
> We used the information from this seminar to support a bill that
> we introduced on advanced manufacturing.
>
> We used the information when working on devising a com-
> promise bill for alternative diplomas. This was influenced by
> the Pathways to Prosperity [Symonds] talk and the ideas from
> the seminar as a whole.

Beyond being used to draft legislation, the seminar influenced legislators' views of the ideas behind the legislation:

> It helped me to stop and think about what we're doing at the
> educational level and even at the K–12 level. For instance, the
> idea of alternative high school diplomas. Now the state is head-
> ing down that road, which I think is good.

Impacts on the Policymaking Process

The seminar also influenced the way policy issues are debated and
discussed. This seminar occurred at a contentious time about one
year after an election in which the assembly, Senate, and governor's
office all switched from Democratic to Republican control. A few
months after the election, a controversial budget repair bill that
included cuts to collective bargaining caused mass protests, intense
political divisions in the state and heightened partisanship and
polarization within the legislature. One legislator said, "We need to
start bringing people together, so it's really positive that you guys
are so bipartisan." Another legislator explained how the seminars
have risen above partisanship:

> We tried to get input on what things were going to be important
> and, in this atmosphere, not "game" the ending, and I think
> it [the seminar] accomplished that. These Seminars (focusing
> on evidence, research, with respected experts, etc.) are really

good for focusing us on issues in times of political turmoil and contentiousness.

Both a legislator and an aide credited information from this seminar with the creation of a legislative study committee on *Improving Opportunities in High School*, which is an important outcome because it leverages a legislative infrastructure for carrying forward the ideas presented at the seminar. Legislators explained that the seminar "gave us a shared framework to talk about the issue," which is "helpful for talking to colleagues on the other side of the aisle":

> There are few opportunities that we have to do this besides the Seminars and legislative study committees. Other settings are more confrontational and more partisan.

Legislators' claims that this seminar helped them reach across the aisle reflect the meticulous attention the Family Impact Seminars pay to providing high-quality, nonpartisan research and opportunities for discussion in a neutral, off-the-record setting, without the potentially polarizing presence of lobbyists or the press.

The seminar also played a role in changing how W-2, the state's welfare program, was implemented. An agency official explained the ways that ideas from the seminar influenced administration of the program:

> It's more the big concepts, and that is impacting the way I administer the W-2 program—we're focusing more on training and other activities that create a fit between participants and employers . . . The material presented is consistent with the data we're seeing for our program, but this gave me better labels and better ways of explaining it to other people.

How Did Seminar Information Influence Policymakers' Decisions?

From seminar testimonials like this, we were aware of the research input early in the lawmaking process and the policy output later in the process. Yet what remained unclear were the pathways through which this research was incorporated into policy deliberations and decision-making. Obviously, it was not a linear process whereby legislators heard research on the input end and a policy change emerged on the output end. What was the black box between research input and policy output?

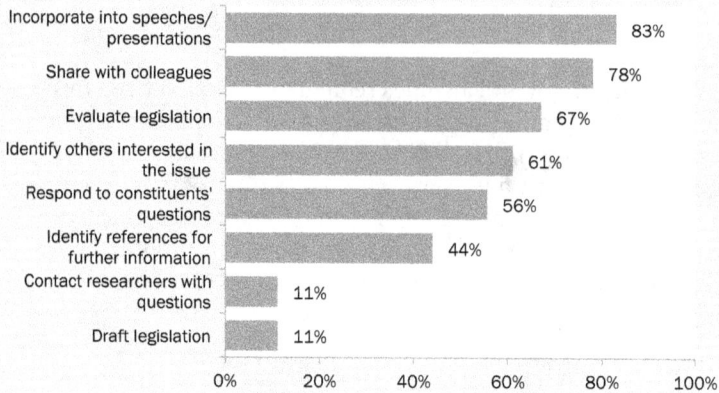

Figure 4.1 Ways Legislators Used Information from a Family Impact Seminar on Jobs

Note: N = 18 legislators, 69 percent response rate.

To sort out how seminar information is used in the policy process, seminar staff conducted follow-up phone evaluations five to seven months after the seminar with all legislators, aides and state agency officials who attended the seminar (N = 32, response rate = 77 percent). Figure 4.1 displays the responses of only the legislators in the sample regarding how they used information from the seminar. These data provide some insights about several ways that research winds its way through the policy process. We use the legislators' own words to describe three main uses of research from the seminar: incorporating it into speeches and presentations, sharing it with colleagues and evaluating pending legislation. We also detail what policymakers say about how the use of seminar research in their decisions results from the multiple delivery methods of the Family Impact Seminars.

Incorporating Research into Speeches and Presentations

The vast majority of legislators (83 percent) incorporated seminar information into their speeches and presentations. One idea from the seminar that influenced legislators' thinking was the data on dropouts. In the words of a legislator: "The key thing that jumped out at me was the high school dropout rates. I had no idea—it was shocking (how high they were)." When a Republican legislator explained why the seminar information was valuable to him, he clearly revealed how the *speaker's* words became *his* words:

I have used it in a number of speeches and ideas. Particularly the idea of concentrating on high school dropouts, making sure that everyone graduates. It is important for two reasons—one, we need their input into employment for the economy, and two, if they don't graduate they become a drain on the economy. I've used this a lot in my talks and my thinking.

Another legislator observed that concerns about dropouts came up "in several ways and in several conversations" during the session. Notably, this was the first time that legislators expressed interest in dropouts in over two decades of conducting Wisconsin Family Impact Seminars.

Sharing Research with Colleagues

What is obvious from the evaluation is that the use of research in the policy culture is not a straightforward process, whereby research is incorporated into a policy decision by a single policy-maker (Tseng, 2012). Policymaking is a team sport. Thus, inspiring legislative action is often predicated by sharing research with others. In the follow-up evaluation, almost all agency officials (94 percent) and four-fifths of legislators (78 percent) reported sharing information with colleagues. One legislator described a specific example:

I did mention the seminar on the floor of the Assembly, when something was proposed that went against what the seminar information told us would work. I knew that others who were present had also attended the seminar, so I used it to call them out.

Over two-thirds of legislators (67 percent) reported using seminar information to evaluate legislative proposals. One legislator used seminar research to decide how to vote on a pending bill, and another used it as a "measuring stick" to assess legislation for its consistency with the speaker's "evidence, data and expertise." Legislators mentioned three different instances where they used seminar information to refute proposed budget cuts. As one example, a legislator explained learning about the importance of "a nimble education system that is able to respond quickly to the needs of employers. When cuts were being made, I was informed about the issue and how this was going to affect my community."

Beyond using seminar information to weigh the merits of a bill, legislators also reported using seminar information to build up a general knowledge base. Two aides mentioned that seminar information is particularly useful when their boss either chairs or serves on committees that deal with the seminar content because it helps them understand what the problems are, which solutions are available and what bills to introduce.

Finally, the influence of research on policymakers' decisions results not only from the content of the seminars, but also from the seminar processes and products. Respondents often commend the multiple delivery methods the seminars use. For the jobs seminar, one aide was impressed with how the seminar "seemed to flow really well from speaker to speaker" and how their presentations complemented each other. Respondents praised the "good give-and-take" at the seminar, noting how well the panel of employers worked to get the conversation flowing. A legislative aide requested the CD of the seminar and shared it with another office. Agency officials mentioned how useful the seminar briefing report was for writing a cross-institution grant because it informed people about the work others were doing so they could support each other instead of "staying siloed."

What Pragmatic Processes and Procedures Does the Partnership Take to Achieve Seminar Success?

The Family Impact Seminars are more than an event. The seminars are a process that is built around a partnership among the organizers, university researchers and a number of state policy actors, including legislators, agency officials and nonpartisan service agency analysts. We review here the five main components of the partnership model.

First, one essential element of the partnership model is that a bipartisan panel of state policymakers (consisting *only* of legislators and one governor's representative) identifies the topic of the seminar. This eleven-member advisory panel, many who serve for several years, includes one representative of the governor's office and an equal number of Democratic and Republican legislators. Each advisor is individually interviewed to identify a topic that is rising on the legislative agenda and would benefit from research-based information. The topic that received the most bipartisan votes in spring of 2011 was jobs.

Second, after selecting the topic, seminar staff pull together a one-time, seminar-specific, expert planning committee of executive agency officials, nonpartisan legislative analysts and university/ extension faculty. At this stage in the planning process, no legislators are included to avoid a focus on a single favorite issue or a particular partisan agenda. The expert planning committee for the jobs seminar included the secretary and the chief economist of the Wisconsin Department of Revenue, the president of the Wisconsin Technical College System, the chief economist and the executive assistant of the Wisconsin Department of Workforce Development, a division administrator of Family Economic Security in the Wisconsin Department of Children and Families, the president of the Wisconsin Technology Council, the director of the Wisconsin Legislative Fiscal Bureau, a senior staff attorney of the Wisconsin Legislative Council and several heads of relevant university and extension institutes. The agenda included exploring a number of directions the seminar could take and seeking input on which directions would best map onto the policy infrastructure and political climate in the state.

Building on input from the seminar's legislative advisors, the expert planning committee reached consensus on having seminar speakers address (1) what jobs Wisconsin should position itself for in the next five years and beyond and (2) evidence-based jobs programs and policies. Two issues arose at the meeting that required another contact with the legislative/gubernatorial advisors. First, the expert planning committee was uncertain which direction for the third speaker would be most politically and economically viable. Second, the experts suggested that we include (for the first time) an employer reactor panel, but were uncertain whether legislators would find it useful. This expert "meeting of the minds" also serves other valuable purposes, such as providing ready access to suggestions for speakers for the seminar and employers for the reactor panel. Each agency or organization also provides names of high-ranking officials to invite to the seminar and discussion session.

Following the expert planning meeting, we recontacted our legislative advisors via email for their advice on the employer panel and on whether the third speaker should focus on (1) how the needs of employers match up with available workforce training or (2) how Wisconsin should position itself for innovation and entrepreneurship. Based on their feedback, we focused the third speaker on the match between employer needs and workforce training. In addition, we proceeded with organizing a first-time ever employer reactor panel, which was introduced with data on employment and wages in Wisconsin presented by the state's chief economist.

Fourth, based on advice from the expert planning committee and our network of contacts, we identified the speakers and employer panel with an eye toward providing a comprehensive, nonpartisan view of what policymakers can do to position Wisconsin for the jobs of the future. We made several contacts with the speakers and panelists to write their briefing report chapters and to brief them on relevant Wisconsin data and the current policy context in the state. We coached them via phone and written materials on what makes an effective seminar presentation, such as including stories and personal experiences and laying out several policy options rather than making a specific recommendation. We organized a dinner so speakers could overview their presentations, making it easier for them to build on each other's ideas during the seminar.

The final step is shifting our finely tuned marketing machine into full gear. To recruit legislators and their staff, we make about five contacts with each office, including a save-the-date flyer, an invitation from legislative advisors, personal reminder calls a couple days before the seminar and so forth. High-ranking agency officials received special invitations to the seminar and discussion session. As we detail next, the partnerships formed at each step of the planning process are integral to identifying seminar participants and encouraging their attendance at the seminar and discussion session.

How Does a Partnership Model Contribute to the Success of the Family Impact Seminars?

In the give-and-take that is the hallmark of any good partnership, university organizers of the seminars benefit from the contributions of their partners and, at the same time, provide valuable contributions to the partnership. We know from the evaluation that the jobs seminar was useful to policymakers for four main reasons: (1) the ability to bring relevant policy actors to the table, (2) timely topic and content, (3) big ideas broken down into manageable pieces and (4) practical research that establishes facts and destroys myth. We review here how the partnership contributed to each of these aspects of the seminar's success.

Ability to Bring the Relevant Policy Actors to the Table

One value added of the seminars is the capacity to convene high-ranking policy actors on issues of common interest. For the jobs seminar, a legislator explained that the seminars are "good for legislators" because they get them "talking to people outside of the legislative process." Similarly, an agency official reported how reaffirming it is to learn that business and industry leaders are committed to the same goals that they are, which reinforces the knowledge "that we need one another to make this really work." The only way that the seminars can engage participants inside and outside the legislature is by using a model that deliberately partners with state policy actors, including legislators, executive agency officials and nonpartisan legislative service agency analysts. The university has the power to convene these stakeholders, who have surprisingly few opportunities to interact with each other, even though they are addressing the same policy issues, albeit from distinct institutional vantage points. Members of the planning committee have agreed to brief speakers on the Wisconsin context on the seminar topic and also have written briefing report chapters summarizing Wisconsin law or the cost of and participation in relevant state policies or programs. In essence, the seminar model is an iterative process that shuttles back and forth to seek advice and contributions from each partner and, in so doing, to secure their buy-in to the success of the seminar along with their commitment to participate and promote participation among their colleagues.

Seminar staff also are intentional in taking steps to connect the speakers by providing written and face-to-face opportunities for familiarizing them with each other's work and the contributions each of their perspectives makes to the seminar topic. Speakers consistently provide positive feedback about the format of the seminar that allows them to present their ideas to policymakers and engage in audience give-and-take following their presenta-tions. Also, speakers appreciate the opportunity for in-depth exploration of their ideas in targeted discussion sessions that hone in on the specific information needs of both legislators and agency officials.

Timely Topic and Content

Timeliness is a key component of the success of the seminars. For the jobs seminar, a legislative aide verified the importance of tim-ing: "Obviously, this is the #1 topic for everyone in government and policy right now, so it was well attended." A legislator concurred: "It's so relevant to what we're trying to do right now. Those sta-tistics (about employment in the state) are something all legislators should know about." In addition to the timeliness of the seminar topic, a legislator commended the timeliness of the seminar content in this comment on the end-of-session evaluation: "Very informa-tive, speakers really boiled down to the basic issues our state needs to focus on."

The only way that a university-based effort, like the seminars, can deliver research on topics that are percolating up on the policy agenda is by partnering with elected and appointed policymakers in the state. Without this partnership, it would not be possible to identify real problems nor to zero in on evidence-based responses that are most economically and politically feasible.

Big Ideas Broken Down into Manageable Pieces

In studies, the utilization of research in policymaking depends on bringing big ideas to policymakers' attention. In a cluster analysis that compared four different types of research users, the state legislators most likely to value, seek and use research placed a significantly higher priority on research that challenges the status quo and provides unexpected, new ways of thinking about an issue (Bogenschneider, Little, & Johnson, 2013). The seminars are known for introducing big ideas that challenge policymakers' thinking. Legislators likened the research presented at the jobs seminar to a "mindset change" and to a "leap forward." A legislator characterized the seminar as "energizing" claiming "[i]t kick starts your thinking." An agency official concurred that seminar research "challenges the norm in policy thinking," such as its short-term focus:

> There's something that stuck with me from Manpower, around the notion that we need to think probably much more broadly about workforce solutions and most policymakers tend to be more short-term focused. And while there certainly is a need to do short-term solutions, it's really looking at long-term systematic change that's important. If we don't solve it at that level, we'll keep coming back.

Policymakers also were challenged to consider the complexity of the issue due to the way speakers situated it within state, national and global contexts. One state legislator reported being "impressed and scared" that we are not keeping up with the world:

> That really bothered me. We're looking for people to be educated and to do the jobs, and we're in a worldwide situation now, not just the state of Wisconsin. People are moving all over the world to do the work, and it doesn't seem like we're keeping up with our end of the deal—with what we need to do . . . things are changing so fast in regards to technology, computer skills, what is needed to compete globally.

Respondents reported hearing ideas that they do not come across in their "regular media consumption." One legislator reflected that we may have "heard some of the things piecemeal," but the speakers provided information on "really all the important pieces of the puzzle" and brought it together in a "holistic" way.

Policymakers are always looking for a silver bullet solution, but the speakers bring up the macro issues and trade-offs and the limitations of state policy in the global economy. It shows us that the world is more complicated than we would like to think. Seminar organizers were able to walk a fine line in presenting the complexity of issues without portraying them as so complex that policymakers lose hope that anything can be done. In the follow-up evaluation, many policymakers reported that because of the Family Impact Seminars, they were "quite a bit" more likely to "see how complex problems can be broken down into manageable pieces" (the response of 57 percent of legislators and 47 percent of agency officials).

One way that the seminars demystify complex problems is by identifying malleable factors and specific considerations that can serve to overcome the sense of hopelessness that can pervade problems and choke off any meaningful response. For example, one important factor that a legislator mentioned in the end-of-session evaluation was that "families are at the core of a healthy society." A routine consideration of the seminars is whether the issue has disparate effects on diverse populations depending on different circumstances. In this seminar, respondents appreciated the emphasis on how education is "losing the boys" and on "youth who maybe don't cope as well to the regular school format." The only way the seminars can carry off a model that presents big ideas broken down into workable responses is by collaborating with partners who are in close contact with policymakers and know which policy directions are politically possible.

Partnering with policymakers and policy analysts also provides access to a spectrum of speakers with expertise ranging from economics to education, from workforce to welfare, employment to entrepreneurship, families to finances. These cross-disciplinary partnerships allow the seminars to connect the dots across disciplinary silos in order to present big picture ideas, as well as to identify speakers who are at the forefront of visionary thinking on the issue. For example, two speakers for this seminar were suggested by members of the expert planning committee. In addition, the chief economist who introduced the employer panel with Wisconsin data was a member of the planning committee, which gave him access to inside information on legislators' interests, experts' insights on the topic and the specific goals of this seminar.

Practical Research that Establishes Fact and Destroys Myth

Paradoxically, the seminars are seen as providing big picture ideas, yet are simultaneously perceived as being practical. In the follow-up evaluation, almost six in ten (56 percent) legislators reported that because of the seminars, they are "quite a bit" more likely to see the practical value of research. What made the research presented at the job seminars practical was that it provided baseline facts and down-to-earth program models. For example, one legislator reported how important it was to learn that the jobs of the future would require both technical and socioemotional skills:

> All employees are going to need more computer skills, more basic skills . . . Kids need training not necessarily just in a school setting . . . They need the skills to present themselves in an interview, to show up for work on time, be punctual, respectful to their employers, etc.

As another example, an aide mentioned how the evidence-based programs featured at the seminar can help policymakers make data-driven decisions for establishing "good economic development programs." One agency official was "intrigued" by the outcomes of the evidence-based programs, and another said the Department of Workforce Development was considering implementing some of the programs in the state.

In addition to establishing factual information, the seminars destroy myths that a Nobel Laureate has noted "thrive in environments without data" (Heckman, 1990, p. 301). The seminars' myth-busting capacity is exemplified in this comment from an agency official:

> You're familiar with the fields your expertise is in, where you spend your time, but to have other peoples' comments, questions, reactions—it sometimes reaffirms what you're thinking and sometimes creates some questions or some different ways of looking at things. I always like that, and that has happened each time.

Legislators explained that the seminars destroy myth through the messengers—the "honesty and candor" of the speakers—as well as the message—research-based information. An aide reported relying on the seminars to "fact check" the accuracy of information their office receives. Specifically, participants reported that the jobs seminars changed misperceptions of manufacturing, outdated understandings of what educational directions could have the biggest impact on the state economy and misinterpretations of Wisconsin's unemployment numbers. As explained by an agency official:

> Because there is such a large pool of unemployed people, I have assumed any job opening has many, many potential

candidates, given the economy, and instead I've learned that's not the case.

This capacity to establish fact and destroy myth is a contribution that universities can make to the seminar partnership in a couple of ways. First, universities are society's main research engine (Kellogg Commission, 1999) and one of few institutions that can play a role as an "honest knowledge broker" to help overcome partisan paralysis. Legislators attest to the capacity of universities to serve in this nonpartisan role: "I tend to trust the information from the Family Impact Seminars" and "My impression of the Family Impact Seminar is that it is not biased."

Second, university staff can coach the speakers on the latest evidence on communicating research to policymakers, such as including stories and personal experiences in their presentations. The value of this coaching was observed by a state legislator:

> I found it compelling when the employers and presenters talked about their children's experiences and what they had chosen to do educationally—the idea that a "default to college" mentality might not be the best for all people, but how entrenched that is in parental thinking. I had heard before the statistic that only a third of jobs in the future will require a B.A., but hearing it at the seminar and hearing it through the stories of how people's children had grappled with that really drove it home.

Summary

The Wisconsin Family Impact Seminars are one "new" outgrowth of the century-long tradition of the Wisconsin Idea. The idea that universities should serve the public good runs deep in the state. In 1912 when Theodore Roosevelt accepted the presidential nomination, he proclaimed that "the University of Wisconsin has been more influential than any other agency in making Wisconsin what it has become, a laboratory for wise social and industrial experiments in the betterment of conditions" (Roosevelt, 1912, para. 41). Today's state legislators and citizen activists situate the Wisconsin Family Impact Seminars in the long-standing legacy of the Wisconsin Idea. In fact, one legislator made that exact point:

> The researchers at UW [the University of Wisconsin] . . . have always been approachable to me. But I think the seminar does open the eyes for other legislators. When I talk to legislators from other states, they find this idea intriguing, and don't feel it is a part of their legislative experience. I think that is both

because of the proximity between the university and the state capitol in Wisconsin, and the history of Wisconsin (e.g., in valuing research . . .). I feel that the Family Impact Seminars keep that tradition alive.

Similarly, an unsolicited blog from Bill Kraus (2013), the leader of a nonpartisan, grassroots group that focuses on good government, characterized the seminars as a "latter day re-creation" of the Wisconsin Idea:

> What the experts bring to the discussion are facts. What the legislators and staffers do is turn the facts and research into legislative policy. The magic is that people who disagree philosophically and politically see that collaboration is not only possible but desirable when the focus is on the facts . . . The goal becomes finding solutions rather than seeking political advantage . . . Because the Seminars are only about solutions, they somehow engender civility and mutual respect as well.

The beauty of the Family Impact Seminar model is that it works, even in states without a strong "Wisconsin Idea" tradition—in red and blue states, in northern and southern states, in poor and prosperous states. The transcontextual success of the Family Impact Seminars is attributed, in large part, to the partnership model on which it is built. Foundational to the success of convening seminars designed to cross disciplinary and cultural boundaries is seeking advice from experts in diverse fields such as economics, education, family studies, health, human development, law, political science, psychology, social work and sociology. Drawing on the experience and expertise of elected and appointed officials along with nonpartisan legislative analysts is also foundational to identifying what issues are rising on the political agenda and which research-based solutions are politically and economically feasible. Because universities have a reputation for producing nonpartisan research, they are positioned as a trusted repository of new knowledge that has the potential to transform even the most entrenched societal problems of our times (Kellogg Commission, 1999).

The Family Impact Seminars are similar to other university–policy partnerships in that they benefit the university by demonstrating to policymakers in a concrete way the value of the university and how useful research can be in providing big picture ideas that are down to earth and practical. Yet the seminars' partnership with policymakers may differ in one respect that deserves mention here. The seminars were formed with the primary intention of using research to inform the policy enterprise. Perhaps the biggest surprise of working on the seminars is how the effort has also unexpectedly ended up informing the research enterprise. In our ongoing work at close quarters with policymakers, we have developed trusting relationships with them, which have resulted in response rates in our research studies of 65 percent or higher in a field where 20 percent is typical and 30 percent is considered good (Browne, 1999). What we have learned about communicating research to policymakers has resulted in several journal articles and books on evidence-based policymaking, family policy, the family impact lens, what research evidence policymakers need, how to make a global case for family policy and so forth (Bogenschneider, 2014, 2015; Bogenschneider & Corbett, 2010a, 2010b; Bogenschneider et al., 2012; Bogenschneider et al., 2013; Friese & Bogenschneider, 2009; Hines & Bogenschneider, 2013). What's more, the lessons learned have been featured at policy trainings for national professional societies, including the National Science Foundation, the American Psychological Association, the Society for Research on Child Development and the National Council on Family Relations.

One unique challenge for universities when they partner with policymakers is funding. With many partnerships, it is common, and often expected, that partners would secure or provide financial support. However, when the primary partners are policy actors (e.g., legislators, agency officials), funding conceivably could come with political strings. This funding stream would be inappropriate for a model like the seminars where success depends on a strong, nonpartisan reputation. In Wisconsin, the initial funding to launch the seminars was from the university, which made it possible to attract foundation funding. Most recently, the funding has come from the university and a private philanthropist.

The capacity of the university to convene partnerships of state policy actors on an ongoing basis is due, in part, to the concerted attention the seminars pay to evaluation. Recruiting policy actors to participate in evaluations is a daunting task. Yet data on the impact of the seminars are critical to convincing partners that the time and effort they invest will be well spent. The evaluation data from the jobs seminar inspire confidence, given its impressive 77 percent response rate and given the countless concrete examples of how the research was used that respondents were able to recollect five to seven months later. Participants indicated many ways the seminar was effective, such as contributing to two new laws, the implementation of current laws and discussion of future laws through a formalized Legislative Study Committee process. Participants also indicated ways the seminar could have been more effective, such as focusing less on skills and more on solutions, particularly for rural parts of the state.

The results of this evaluation of a Family Impact Seminar on jobs is consistent with evaluations of several seminars in Wisconsin and other states that transcend a range of topics, speakers and participants. From the perspective of policymakers themselves, research from the jobs seminar was used to share with colleagues, incorporate into speeches and presentations and evaluate and draft legislation that ended up having several impacts on policy decisions and the policymaking process. Another indicator of the value of the seminars to policymakers is that 69 percent of the respondents in the follow-up evaluation had attended a previous seminar. This "repeat business" signals the success of the seminars in achieving its goal of improving policymakers' respect for research evidence and indicates the value policymakers find in participating in neutral, nonpartisan discussions for fostering relationships and finding common ground.

The exact ways in which research winds its way through the policy process is unclear, but one thing is clear: It is possible to use research to build better public policy for families on the important issues of the day. What it takes to be successful is a commitment to communicating high-quality and nonpartisan research through strong partnership-based models like the Family Impact Seminars.

Strategies for Sustaining FIS

We focus on two broad areas with respect to the ingredients needed to make the impressive success of Wisconsin's long-running Family Impact Seminars last.

Cultivating a Fertile Context

Wisconsin's commitment to applying research to policy has deep roots. To extend Bogenschneider, Shager, Little and Eddy's metaphor, Wisconsin's soil was fertile for this work thanks to the rich history of engaged scholarship set forth early by the University of Wisconsin's President Van Hise in 1904. National activity around this type of partnership taking place over the late 1980s and 1990s further supported the framework of the Wisconsin Idea that helped create favorable conditions for the Family Impact Seminars when they came to be during the same period.

The authors describe how conditions outside and within the state of Wisconsin helped set the stage for this work. This broader ongoing commitment to research-informed policymaking, which was cultural to Wisconsin, helped ensure the ongoing expectations of researchers and policymakers that this type of partnership would continue. Most encouraging, we learn that this type of partnership is also possible in states without Wisconsin's tradition of working across these two sectors for the benefit of family and social policy, as many other states have adopted and now operate Family Impact Seminars.

Usefulness and Legitimacy

Bogenschneider and her colleagues' description of the intensive planning of the Family Impact Seminars using their seminar on jobs as an example illustrates the critical importance of making research useful to policymakers. To provide a seminar experience that ensures "legislators understand the needs of a changing workforce," they engage in key steps every year—many of which occur months before the seminar itself takes place: identifying speakers who can address the topics that are of interest to legislators; working to acculturate researcher speakers to the world of the policymaker (helping them understand how to "think like a policymaker") and remove their own biases and recommendations; and producing digestible, written summaries of relevant research.

The perception of the legitimacy of research is also essential. Legislators are willing to listen and participate in meaningful discussions around potentially contentious policy issues in part because the university is a trusted source of unbiased research.

Through their evaluations, Wisconsin Family Impact Seminar sponsors continuously affirm the usefulness of their events to inspire action through information use in legislation, speeches and the customization of topics that have relevance and meaning to elected officials. Bogenschneider and her team receive consistently positive feedback from policymakers and faculty as to the usefulness of the seminars. They note that some of the unanticipated benefits include building relationships across researchers and policymakers and facilitating relationships within the policymaking sector, all of which help to bridge the persistent cultural divide between these two groups in the interest of making better policy. Importantly, the Family Impact Seminars may be helping to mitigate some of the negative communication effects attributable to political polarization. (This theme is also present in the case study on Minnesota's Early Childhood Caucus in Utilizing Research in Chapter 5.)

Making the Family Impact Seminar experience worthwhile to policymakers ensures its ongoing support. In fact, we learn that a number of Wisconsin elected officials regularly work closely with the seminar planners to build the best possible seminar each year and invite colleagues who are concerned about family policy issues.

We next turn to a case study that describes a formalized structure between the researcher and policymaker communities that spans multiple disciplines, including education and social policy. Minnesota's Hennepin-University Partnership (HUP) was established to streamline the processes needed to help make these types of partnerships happen. This particular arrangement was developed to streamline collaborative initiatives that were frequently occurring between one local government and its university and, like Wisconsin's Family Impact Seminars, took advantage of fortuitous conditions in the local landscape that supported such efforts. Before sharing Minnesota's Hennepin-University Partnership case, we note a few of the common barriers to establishing researcher–policymaker partnerships that stem from the literature and our experiences and which HUP addresses.

Barriers to Researcher–Policymaker Partnerships

A number of scholars, including Bogenschneider and colleagues from the previous case study, have noted the cultural and physical separations between researchers and policymakers when it comes to using research in public policy and practice (Drabble, Lemon, D'Andrade, Donoviel, & Le, 2013; Jaynes, 2014; Jones & Sherr, 2014). In the case study that follows, we use a comparatively broad definition of the term "policymaker" to include not only elected officials, but also government agencies that do public work. In the Hennepin-University Partnership, or HUP, the "policymaker" entity involved is a large Midwestern metropolitan county and its elected officials, which in this case are county board members.

We have both worked in academia and in policymaking and in so doing have been involved in partnerships with "the other side." We know first-hand the challenges that can arise when seeking out, creating and sustaining these partnerships. Broadly, we pursued this book project because of a desire to share insights about how to address those challenges. However, some of the specific and often mundane concerns that arise when working through these types of partnerships are critically important and can make or break a collaborative opportunity if they are not successfully navigated.

Finding an Expert

A policymaker who needs help exploring or understanding an issue of importance to constituents might consider reaching out to a university researcher for assistance. A local public university is a reasonable place to start—they are, after all, public. The policymaker might begin by asking colleagues if they know of any local university researchers who specialize in that issue. Alternatively, the policymaker may go online and attempt to learn who among local university faculty may be researching this topic. However, universities are large, multilayered, multidepartmental organizations; even a small private college or university can be difficult to navigate. Research centers are numerous, and their areas of focus may not be obvious by name alone. Finding a university expert can be a challenge.

A researcher dedicated to researching education or social policy needs to be able to test theories or replicate the work of others in the field. A researcher also knows the importance of evidence-based policy approaches that research elsewhere in the country is showing to be particularly effective and may also know that the local social services agency does not use these practices. The researcher might also intend to apply for a federal grant to study effective implementation and evaluation of this practice. To the researcher, government agencies are bafflingly complex with impossible hierarchies. What is the best way to connect with the right person in direct practice to do this? If a researcher does not already have connections and relationships with people in the other sector, figuring out where to begin can be overwhelming.

Dealing with Funding and Resources

Regardless of the sector, exploration, research and evaluation require resources. Researchers can conduct limited research pro bono, but full-scale studies are expensive and time consuming. Further, if that research involves an evidence-based practice, it is difficult for public agencies at both the policy and direct service levels to operationalize new tasks associated with an evidence-based approach without additional funding. A host of other resource and funding questions can emerge depending upon perspective. Figure 4.2 details a few common questions that reveal the different perspectives of policymakers and researchers.

Researcher	Policymaker
Why do policymakers have such a hard time understanding that I can't say for sure what the research shows?	*The researchers say they won't know for sure what we can learn from the study until they finish it in three years. But I'm working on the issue now. Can't they tell us what they think at this point, even if it's not completely proven?*
Why can't we hire temporary staff for the pilot without going through a complex contract hiring process?	*What are "indirects" and why are they 52%?*
We'd like to pay staff a stipend to do the pilot work. Can we?	*If almost all of the funding is going to the researchers, what are we going to get out of this?*
I don't know if I'll be able to get a peer-reviewed publication out of what the policymakers want to study. Should I still help them?	*Will a researcher want to help us with something that may not include experimenting with people or testing out a new theory? We just want to know how we can improve our work.*

Figure 4.2 Common Partnership Questions

Like the questions themselves, the likely answers reflect differences between research and policy institutions that can present barriers to partnership. If these and other resource and funding issues are not addressed up front, they can be early barriers to working together. Yet there are researchers and policymakers who have successfully overcome these barriers. The following case study of the Hennepin-University Partnership (HUP) highlights strategies for points to sustaining long-term partnerships.

The Hennepin-University Partnership (HUP)

Kathie Doty

In 2005, Hennepin County, the most populous county in Minnesota, and the University of Minnesota, agreed to work together to create a liaison position that would catalyze and support connections between the two entities around research and policy. Over the next two years, the relationship that was developed through the liaison and supported by leadership on both sides transitioned into a more formal partnership that was named the Hennepin-University Partnership (HUP). This partnership came about as organization leaders recognized the need for greater outreach and collaboration among large, influential institutions in order to address challenges facing the communities of which they are a part. In the past, time-limited summits, projects and other forms of collaborative work produced valued results, but the county and the university sought more sustained relationships and more strategic partnering on issues of importance to communities. In addition, both organizations wanted a more streamlined process for building, funding and sustaining this cross-sector work. The formalized structure involved a full-time director as well as legal and administrative support for the creation of a master cooperative agreement that embodies the partnership concept and streamlines the contracting process that accompanies most collaborations (see Appendix D).

The formalized structure came about due to the convergence of multiple factors. Foremost was the desire of both organizations to work together on a more regular basis to address societal challenges. Another important contextual factor was the climate at the university at the time, then led by President Robert Bruininks, whose priority areas of focus were education, families and children. At the outset, the partnership was enhanced as a result of the fact that two of the key organizational leaders involved also personally enjoyed working together.

The HUP offered the university a community engagement opportunity consistent with its land grant mission. The county understood the importance of taking advantage of the expertise of researchers right in its community—people who could help address the grand challenges being faced by the county and help find better solutions. In addition to facilitating a variety of peer-reviewed publications and faculty "career work," the HUP has spawned long-lasting, community-based structures around transit and public engagement, and has provided numerous real-world graduate student internship and research opportunities, many of which have led to full-time employment. Over ten years, HUP has facilitated more than 150 collaborative projects involving twelve different county departments and twenty-one different university departments or centers. As HUP celebrated its ten-year anniversary in 2015, both the county and the university publicly reaffirmed their intent to continue the work, seeing a variety of benefits and value to the relationship.

The equitable financial investment of both organizations was key to HUP's early success and reflects the underlying goal of mutual benefit. The university and the county each pay half of all program expenses, including the program director salary, costs for two part-time graduate students and other expenses needed to support the work. It is critical that collaborative work show value on both sides of the equation. HUP's annual survey results to date support this: Over 88 percent of participants either agree or strongly agree that they are satisfied with how their collaborative experience went, with equal proportions saying that the projects achieved goals (91.7 percent) and they were satisfied with the results of the project (94.4 percent). Nearly all respondents report a willingness to work with the other partner again in the future. To sustain this type of collaborative structure over time, it is very important for partners to ask themselves if they are serious about doing the work over time and whether or not they have a funding source. The idea that universities can provide consultant-like services for free is antiquated, and ultimately, much academic work is prioritized in relation to availability of funding. So having a committed source of funds is key.

There are multiple points of entry to receiving HUP services. At the HUP website (http://hup.umn.edu), there are five different points of entry to collaborative work: *Create a Work Order* (establishing a project with funding and parameters within the master cooperative agreement, see Appendix E); *Work with Students*; *Find Expertise* (under which links to both county and university contacts are offered); *Join the Online Community*; and *Tell Us about a Project* (offering existing or recently completed partners to update HUP about their work). The *Find Expertise* resource is particularly valuable, as it offers lists of interested participants on both the county and university sides by broad policy or subject area.

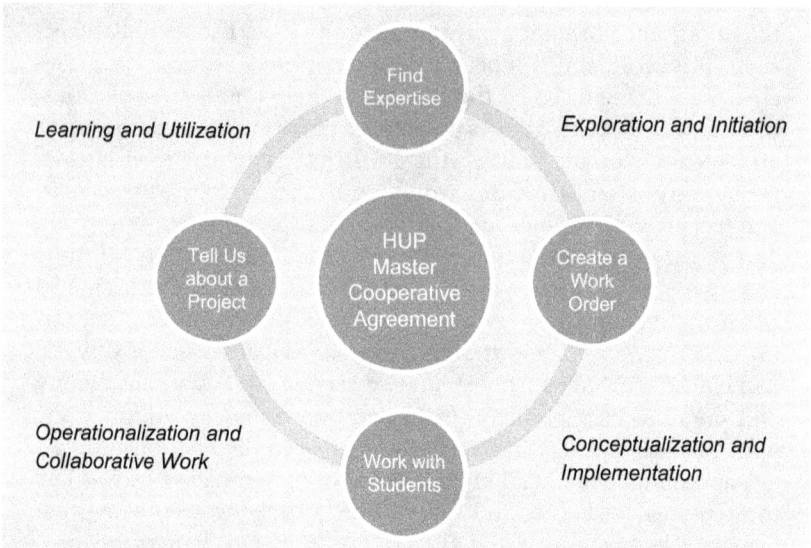

Figure 4.3 Hennepin-University Partnership Components and Collaboration Stages

Figure 4.3 shows a simple diagram of the HUP structure in relation to the broad collaboration stages.

As the diagram illustrates, those interested in entering into a partnership, from either the academic or county organization, may enter through any of these four "doorways." Because HUP catalogs collaborative work of all types, those who are already working on a county–university project are encouraged to share that work under *Tell Us about a Project*. When the county is interested in providing student work opportunities, they can inquire through the *Work with Students* area. For those early collaborators just starting out, they can obtain the fiscal supports to facilitate their work through the *Create a Work Order* area. And to help both county and university staff locate partners in the other organization, there is the *Find Expertise* area.

HUP has evolved to bring order to the establishment of working agreements, as well as to create conditions to monitor the outcomes of the collective work—something that was impossible prior to the creation of HUP when one-time projects sprang up independently. There were contextual factors in place that made the timing of the establishment of these more formalized partnership processes possible in Hennepin County. In addition to the 2005 priorities of University of Minnesota President Robert Bruininks, Hennepin County Commissioner Randy Johnson believed strongly in the value the university brought to communities in Hennepin County and the county as a whole. At the university, an administrative home was established for HUP at the Center for Urban and Regional Affairs (CURA) under Director Tom Scott, who likewise believed strongly in the importance of government and academia working together. The early success can be attributed in part to the strength of the administrative bonds between the university and the county, as well as Scott's familiarity with local government and his interest and understanding of local politics.

The director position was well supported by both Dr. Scott and the county staff leader, County Administrator Richard P. Johnson. These two individuals had a vision of what the partnership could be and believed in its value. It was a huge plus that Dr. Scott and Mr. Johnson also developed a mutual respect and strong working relationship at the outset of the partnership. This initial relationship between key leaders at Hennepin County and the university has been sustained as both of these leaders subsequently transitioned to retirement. David Hough succeeded Richard P. Johnson as Hennepin County Administrator, and Edward Goetz succeeded Tom Scott as Director of the Center for Urban Regional Affairs, and both have been exceptionally involved and supportive as the partnership continued to evolve. The fact that the partnership continues to be well supported after major changes in leadership is a testament to the organizational support that this partnership enjoys. This bodes well for the future and speaks to the tangible commitment of both Hennepin County and the University of Minnesota to genuine and sustained engagement.

Physical presence also matters, as the director's office is on the university campus in CURA, and attending county director administrative leadership meetings is part of regular director duties to ensure this person stays abreast of what the current challenges are.

Funding was critical to startup and sustenance, made possible through the strength of the commitment of the two original organizational leaders, President Bruininks and Chair Randy Johnson. Each agency committed 50 percent of the funding required for the director position, as well as the student staff, office space and some supplies. Funding is extremely important overall and, in particular, attempting to do this without funding just does not work. When anyone looks at their to-do list at the start of the day, they focus on the things where accountability is the greatest. What is not paid for is often perceived as less important.

The other key critical component to HUP's ability to thrive and continue is its perceived value. Both sides of the county–university collaboration must see the structure as valuable and producing measurable results; without this, it should simply not continue. Value is demonstrated in multiple ways, through real-world student experiences, publishable works and, importantly, changes in practices or policy that result from collaborations. Ensuring that both organizations and participants are informed of the outcomes of these collaborations is a key purpose of the regular events and celebrations of collaborative work that the HUP team plans each year. Although individual collaborators are aware of their own experiences, awareness of the long-term success is key to HUP's continuation.

Regular monitoring of HUP's contribution to the university and county organizations occurs through HUP's project-based survey process. Surveys are administered to partners in active collaborations at three time points in the work: at initiation, at a previously identified project mid-point and at the conclusion. The final survey in particular allows participants to engage in reflection on their experiences sharing their overall satisfaction levels, the work products that were generated, outcomes or benefits, unanticipated outcomes and whether they would engage in such a partnership again. Over the most recent six years of the ten-year history of HUP, roughly half of the partners completed all phases of the survey process representing nearly thirty unique projects. The following summary data illustrate some of the key contributions of the HUP work that produce the ongoing value of the project.

Mutual Benefit and Value

Diversity of Departments and Programs

The continuation of HUP partly rests upon broad knowledge of the project and the participation of multiple subsections of each organization. Figure 4.4 shows the broad array of county departments and university program and department areas engaged in collaborations from survey respondents in order of frequency reported.

It is noteworthy that the top seven to eight departments and programs are oriented around community, education, social or family policy areas. Consistent with the policy focus for this book, these are also high priorities for policymakers and academics who wish to work together around these issues.

Goals

Policymaking agencies and academic organizations have different reward systems and cultures. It is reasonable to expect that collaboration goals would also vary by sector. Figure 4.5 shows

County Department	University Department/Program
Human Services and Public Health	Humphrey School of Public Affairs
Library	Extension
Environmental Services	Epidemiology and Public Health
Housing, Community Works and Transportation	College of Design
Public Affairs	Writing Studies
Public Health, Maternal Health	Medical School, Pharmacy
Research, Planning & Development	School of Social Work
Taxpayer Services	Urban Outreach & Engagement
Sherriff	Facilities Management
Human Resources	Religious Studies
Corrections	Psychiatry
County Attorney	Post-Secondary Teaching & Learning
	Integrative Therapies/Healing
	Master Gardner (Extension)
	College of Science & Engineering
	Civil Engineering
	Center for Spirituality & Healing
	Center for Science, Technology & Public Policy
	Center for Early Education & Development
	Carlson School of Management
	Center for Advanced Studies in Child Welfare

Figure 4.4 HUP Participation by Department and Program
Source: Larson, 2014, p. 5.

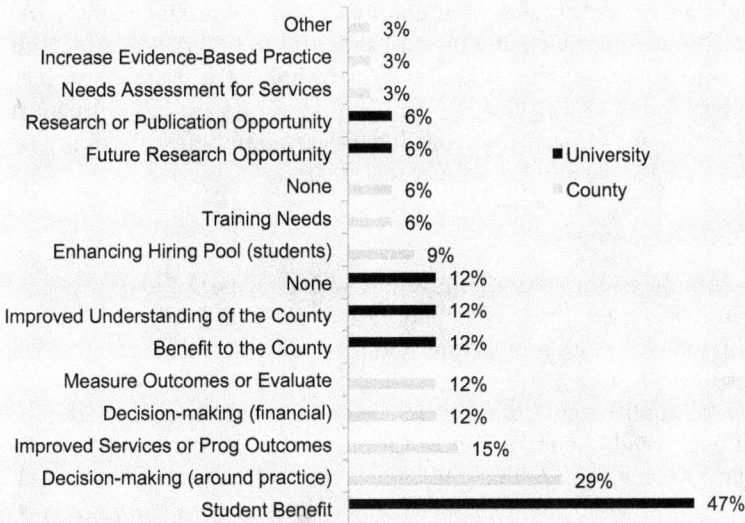

Other 3%
Increase Evidence-Based Practice 3%
Needs Assessment for Services 3%
Research or Publication Opportunity 6%
Future Research Opportunity 6%
None 6%
Training Needs 6%
Enhancing Hiring Pool (students) 9%
None 12%
Improved Understanding of the County 12%
Benefit to the County 12%
Measure Outcomes or Evaluate 12%
Decision-making (financial) 12%
Improved Services or Prog Outcomes 15%
Decision-making (around practice) 29%
Student Benefit 47%

■ University
County

Figure 4.5 Expectations and Goals
Source: Larson, 2014, pp. 6–8.

the goals and expectations of university and county partners for their collaborations combining survey response options and thematically coded, open-ended responses. These are the things that partners expect they will realize upon the completion of their work together.

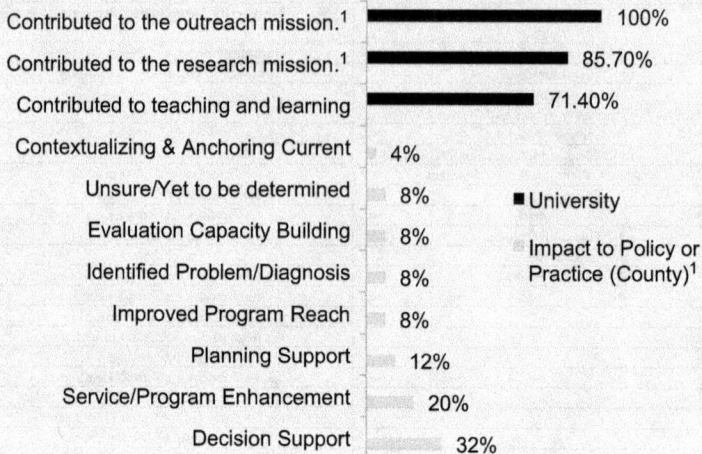

Figure 4.6 Results

Source: Larson, 2014, pp. 13–14.

[1] Combines Agree and Strongly Agree responses from survey question.

At a glance, it is clear that county expectations concerning partnership through HUP are around supports to decision-making and informing day-to-day practice. Nearly half of university partner expectations are around student experiences working with local government. Other benefits included learning about the county or providing service to the county.

Results and Impact

Again, the final survey results reflect both university and county perspectives on the fruits of collaborations in Figure 4.6, which combines survey response options and thematically coded, open-ended responses.

Accomplishments are key to sustaining collaborative relationships through the HUP. Figure 4.6 shows that there are very specific and practical results that the county sees coming from HUP work and interestingly, in some cases, the county is even waiting yet to see what transpires (i.e., "Unsure/yet to be determined"). The university overwhelmingly welcomes the work as contributing to the broad goals of the institution—particularly the outreach mission of the University of Minnesota.

Overall, a majority of HUP survey respondents also reported that they felt the collaboration in which they participated achieved its goals (91.7 percent Agree or Strongly Agree), they felt satisfied with the results of the project (94.4 percent Agree or Strongly Agree) and partners intended to continue collaborations in a variety of ways in the future. Whereas 39 percent stated that they intended to continue with the current work, 28 percent reported they would use the findings for their current practice or in their current program, and another 22 percent said they had new projects planned (Larson, 2014).

Not all researcher–policymaker collaborations can be established within or nurtured by a structure such as HUP, but there are a number of factors that have ensured HUP's success from which other organizations can benefit. It is critical to learn from experiences—both within and outside of HUP. In particular, having past consulting experience is a great benefit for directing HUP. In consulting, time must be spent up front helping customers understand and articulate what they need. During the proposal phase, it is common to provide one proposal and have a client respond with, "Well, no, actually, we want this other thing," and this leads to a gradual refinement and clarification of needs. To partner with another, one must be a good partner oneself. It is essential to be a good listener and be responsive but, above all, the organizational support is essential.

Ingredients for Sustaining HUP

Value

Demonstrating value to both sides of the county–university partnership has sustained Hennepin-University Partnership into its second decade. HUP is committed to monitoring the maintenance of these benefits over time, assessing participant experiences on a regular basis and using feedback from its participant surveys to inform new ways to engage and nurture partnerships.

Institutionalized Connection

Creating mechanisms to deal with the oftentimes cumbersome processes for managing the funding and staffing of partnerships that emerge organically was one of HUP's initial objectives. With these formal administrative structures in place, HUP could turn its attention to institutionalizing the relationships necessary for maintaining connectivity between the county and the university. After ten years, HUP has evolved and "become" an entity that transcends changes in leadership and staff. Also, because of its structure, which involves multiple county departments and multiple university disciplines, the possibilities for collaborative work seem nearly endless. HUP has celebrated its tenth anniversary and received another resounding endorsement for ongoing financial support from the county and the university. In addition, HUP received special recognition from the Association of Public and Land-Grant Universities (APLU) in June 2015 as a recipient of the W. K. Kellogg Foundation Community Engagement Scholarship Award. Putting knowledge to work through institutionalized collaborative relationships has ensured the vitality and ongoing contribution of HUP. These themes also resonate with the following case study, which features a partnership focused on educational outcomes.

Sustaining a Research Partnership to Improve Educational Outcomes

Carolyn J. Heinrich, Vanderbilt University and Annalee Good, University of Wisconsin-Madison

Introduction

For more than a decade, the U.S. Department of Education has been engaging in concerted efforts to increase the use of rigorous evidence generated by "scientifically-based research" for guiding program and practice improvement and improving student outcomes in K–12 education (Coalition for Evidence-Based Policy, 2002). A central focus of these efforts has been on developing tools or mechanisms for not only identifying evidence-based interventions (such as through the What Works Clearinghouse), but also in fostering partnerships to produce new, high-quality research evidence that is relevant to and viewed as credible by those in a position to apply it in practice (Bryk, Gomez, & Grunow, 2011). The Institute of Education Sciences (IES) has committed to developing partnerships between researchers and policymakers (or, in their terminology, between researchers and practitioners, i.e., those acting on the evidence to improve policy and practice) with expanded funding to support the evaluation of state and local education policies (2009), a new research–practice partnership grants program (2013) and, most recently, continuous improvement in education grants (2015) that recognize the value of research efforts that move beyond questions of "does it work?" to understand how policies, programs and practices can be adapted to accommodate local conditions and challenges in implementation.

The growing interest in developing and investing in research–practice partnerships in education coincided with (and was likely further spurred by) the vast increase in data collection and use associated with the implementation of the No Child Left Behind Act (NCLB) of

2001, the reauthorization of the Elementary and Secondary Schools Act (ESEA) that built on the Improving America's Schools Act of 1994 (Finnigan, Daly, & Che, 2013). NCLB expanded provisions for assessment and accountability (requiring more student testing and the setting of standards and targets for evaluating adequate yearly progress, AYP), while also mandating increasing levels of interventions for schools that were not making AYP, with the intent of compelling better performance and offering students additional educational options. Students in Title I schools that were identified for improvement could choose to transfer to a nonidentified school (a rarely used option) or sign up to receive free supplemental educational services (SES) in the form of out-of-school tutoring from a state-approved provider. The burden of implementing these mandated services and new testing and accountability regimens, with no additional federal funding, fell primarily to local educational agencies. For example, in offering students a choice in SES, school districts had to develop and manage contractual relationships with private providers (for-profit and not-for-profit) and hold them accountable for increasing student achievement (Heinrich, 2010).

The research partnership we introduce here originated within this NCLB context with an initial request from a school district, Milwaukee Public Schools (MPS), for assistance in evaluating its SES providers with the goal of increasing their effectiveness. The research relationship began in 2006 between MPS and the University of Wisconsin-Madison (our research team base), with funding from MPS. Then, with funding support from IES starting in 2009, it expanded to five other districts (Austin Independent School District, Chicago Public Schools, Dallas Independent School District, Minneapolis Public Schools and Los Angeles Unified School District) that were likewise in need of support for implementing and evaluating the effects of SES under NCLB. Although IES funding for the research ended in 2013, around the same time that most states had or were securing waivers from implementing NCLB provisions such as SES, the research partnership with MPS continues (along with two other school districts) with funding from other sources.

Although the research we present here might be described as a case study of a single research partnership, within this study we draw on our experiences with six different school districts and empirical analyses we conducted over nine years with large-scale, longitudinal data sets, as well as data collected through interviews with school district personnel and private service providers, focus groups with parents and observations of tutoring sessions. We aim to 1) highlight and explicate the structures and mechanisms that were developed over time to support and sustain this research partnership; 2) describe specific examples of the use of research evidence by the school district partners to change policy and practice and promote program improvement; and 3) present both qualitative and quantitative evidence that suggests a probable link between evidence-based changes made by the practice partners and student outcomes.

The Role of Research Partnerships in Informing Education Policy and Practice

The push for evidence-based policymaking has been growing for decades and has intensified with the Obama administration's commitment to a legislative agenda focused on research-based program models, in addition to stepped-up efforts to produce rigorous evidence on the effectiveness of new social programs and policy initiatives (Haskins & Margolis, 2015). Education policy has been a key focus of these efforts in the Obama administration, including through the implementation of smaller-scale, multisite randomized controlled trials (RCTs) for programs such as "Closing the Reading Gap" and large-scale initiatives such as Race to the Top and Investing in Innovation, with the goals to establishing a stronger link between evidence and funding and only fund programs that positively affect student learning.

A pivotal factor in the success of the evidence-based policymaking agenda will be the development and use of evidence not only at executive and legislative levels, but also at the point of service delivery or at the local level to inform policymaking and program implementation. Research partnerships in education have arisen largely in response to greater capacity on the part of local administrators and educators to understand the value and precepts of research, how they can help to develop it and how it can be applied to support policy and program improvement and increase educational outcomes. In turn, research partnerships are more likely to thrive where researchers strive to better understand how to be responsive to educators' needs and definitions of problems, provide timely and accessible findings and cultivate sustainable relationships with practitioner partners. One of the hallmarks of successful research partnerships is their focus on research and program innovations that are driven by local (e.g., district) needs, and therefore, they are more likely to be viewed as both useful to practice and more credible because the work takes place in local contexts and conditions (Coburn, Penuel, & Geil, 2013). Through their review of existing, emerging and evolving research-to-practice partnerships, Coburn et al. (2013, p. 2–3) have developed a definition of them, identifying the primary attributes that we think characterize well the research-to-practice partnership we have formed with MPS:

- "Long-term, open-ended commitments" (not formed around a single consulting agreement or grant)
- Focusing on "problems of practice, issues and questions that districts find pressing and important" and producing "original analyses to answer research questions posed by the district"
- Employing "intentional strategies" to support "sustained interaction that benefits both researchers and practitioners," where the "focus is jointly negotiated and responsibility for how the work unfolds is shared"

As indicated earlier, our research partnership did not begin as an open-ended commitment, but rather with a specific research agreement (to evaluate an NCLB intervention) that subsequently grew into a more expansive, long-term and collaborative effort. Although there are now grant opportunities explicitly intended to establish longer-term research collaborations, we surmise that many likely begin like ours, with a more modest scope or starting point for the research relationship that allows for important initial groundwork on which the larger efforts and intentional strategies can be built to grow and sustain the partnership.

Our research partnership also expanded beyond MPS to involve other large, urban school districts that were struggling with similar challenges in the implementation of NCLB. The objective of bringing in other school districts was to support the exchange of information and ideas and to learn from the variety of local policy efforts and program strategies that districts were implementing to provide opportunities for extra academic assistance for students (as required under NCLB). Thus, in addition to our longer-term research alliance with MPS, we have sought to simultaneously link our allied partner with a network of other districts to facilitate cross-site learning and the transfer of local knowledge and practice for adapting policies and supporting continuous program improvement.

Another feature that has been key to the effective functioning of our partnership/network is what Tseng (2012, p. 22) describes as a "two-way street" of "practice to research and back." In this approach to the joint work of our partnership, local policy and practice inform the scope and direction of research; the findings of the research in turn are integrated into local program development and implementation, and the research cycle continues iteratively, with learning continuing on the part of both the researchers and practitioners. This type of two-way collaboration requires both a long-term and flexible orientation to the nature of the research and interventions that will be undertaken, as well as continuous appraisal of the stakeholder interests, needs and expectations for the partnership efforts. Indeed, the stakeholders (from policymakers and parents to funders and local school board members) have evolved over time, in addition to federal, state and/or local legislation or policy directives that also influence the focus of our work. We turn now to further discussion of some of the mechanisms and structures that have been critical to supporting and sustaining our research partnership over time.

Research Partnership Infrastructure

Because maintaining relationships and a strong commitment to the work of a research partnership relies on the type of two-way communication that we described earlier, mechanisms for facilitating this type of ongoing exchange and an open line to understanding our practitioner partners' (and stakeholders') questions and concerns have been central to the infrastructure that we have built in this partnership. Although establishing contact and working with district personnel will be required of most research projects that rely on district data and access to school sites, we have taken additional steps to track, organize and support these research relationships as we form them. For example, we create and maintain organizational charts that clearly show the organizational roles and responsibilities of our practitioner partners and that, to the extent possible, align those roles across different district partners (e.g., research/ evaluation staff who aid us in securing district research approval and data-sharing agreements, school leadership and staff who oversee and support the implementation of programs or interventions we are studying and those who manage district database systems). Given that we are often working with multiple levels or layers of staff in school districts and that in many districts staff changes are relatively frequent (sometimes within as well as across school years), we stay in regular touch with our key contacts via email and phone to keep the charts and contact information up to date.

These concerted efforts to maintain ongoing contact with our district partners have been critical in handling the challenge of turnover in personnel that inevitably arises given the longer-term nature of most research-to-practice partnerships (Coburn et al., 2013). Whether it is a major change in leadership—such as a district superintendent—or the departure of a district data specialist, we have found that the disruptions to project work can be considerable. For example, in the case of a superintendent departure in one of our partnering districts, an intervention and all related research work of the partnership was put on hold for more than half a year. In addition, most school district personnel that are tasked with research-related responsibilities are balancing them with a heavy load of program and administrative obligations that typically take precedence over engagement in research. And their ability to commit time to research is shaped not only by time requirements of other obligations, but also by how those obligations are prioritized by other external forces (i.e., political, economic/budgetary, public or community sentiment, etc.). In our research on interventions implemented under NCLB, the fact that the intervention was federally mandated, consumed a significant portion of school district Title I funds and could benefit from research support in its implementation made it a higher priority for a research relationship. Still, as those external pressures lessened over time and school districts were gradually released from the requirements of NCLB through federal policy waivers, it was essential to make explicit the value of our joint research for informing district policy and practice, which we have done through multiple research products (discussed later).

Consistency in our own project staffing has also been a key facilitator of the ongoing, two-way research and programmatic exchanges with our district partners. We designate specific research staff as district site coordinators, who in addition to their research roles, support the development of trusted relationships and keep an ear to the ground on policy developments and program challenges that are important in ensuring that our research is responsive to district needs. Most of our project staff have prior work experience in school settings that goes a long way toward building rapport and facilitating ease of communications on programmatic and administrative issues. In fact, with our longest-running district partner, MPS, our research site coordinator has remained consistent throughout the ten years of the project, which parallels a similar longevity in the district's program and data management staff. In addition, we shared an "embedded" researcher for a number of years who worked at the district administration building (in programming and data management) and was available to readily interface with program administrative and research support staff on questions or issues needing immediate attention or technical assistance. That said, although our partnership with MPS has benefitted from consistency in core (research and district) staffing, we see the concrete contributions or added value of the research for the district as the critical element that keeps our district partners engaged, even when staff turnover (rather than consistency) is the norm, as in another district that we have partnered with for more than seven years.

The "added value" of our research is encapsulated in a range of research products that we jointly develop with our district partners and disseminate to our research stakeholders. We pursue an "improvement science" approach to our work, in which we collaborate in identifying policy and program areas for study and improvement, assessing the effects of program and policy changes that are made and then regularly communicating the results of the research so that they can be applied by our stakeholders (i.e., district partners, parents, community-based organizations, etc.). For example, Appendix F shows a research brief we developed based on our research in five school districts to help guide parents in making well-informed choices of providers of supplemental educational services for their children. The brief includes information on attributes of high-quality programs (as identified in our research) and provides additional guidance to parents of children with special needs; it was distributed in both English and Spanish. A second sample product, in Appendix G, is a memo to our MPS partner that reflects our efforts to be accessible and responsive to our partners for more informal requests for data analysis or research summaries and for strategizing around issues or needs that arise more spontaneously. In this particular situation, our district collaborator called us the same day she learned a district contract with an online provider had abruptly ended and asked for a summary of the "real" (i.e. peer reviewed, not industry generated) research on other online programs. We quickly adjusted our research schedule to focus on gathering this information for a rapid turnaround to the district. Although it required some shuffling of our research resources, we see this type of responsiveness to district research needs as critical to building trust and understanding the relevance of the research to the district. We also assisted the district in this case with developing research-relevant language for a request for proposals for a new online vendor.

We also strive to time our research dissemination and discussions of research findings and recommendations around key decision-making timeframes of our district partners (e.g., around the school year calendar and activities involved in planning and implementing interventions). For example, prior to the start of the school year, we conduct in-person district research briefings to facilitate a two-way discussion of the research findings and their implications for potential program modifications and other decision-making on the part of district staff engaged in program implementation. And to enable cross-district discussion of the research findings across differing contexts and the sharing of strategies for program improvement, we hold joint webinars with our district partners (either before the end of the school year or the start of the next school year) so that they can draw on the latest study findings in these discussions and use them to inform program planning for the coming school year. Head (2015, p. 8) describes these types of activities as "knowledge-brokering," in that they go beyond a simple report of the findings to creating mechanisms for "dialogue and coproduction of insights in new contexts" among the end users of this knowledge. In addition, as Nelson, Leffler, and Hansen (2009) found in their research, policymakers and practitioners often prefer a brief (e.g., one-to two-page) summary of findings or other important knowledge for decision-making, conveyed in nontechnical language and written with a given audience or stakeholder in mind. We have thus developed these types of research products as well and have made them publicly available, and some school districts have also posted our briefs and reports on their websites and/ or made them available to parents and other interested parties; see an example of this type of research brief in Appendix H. In light of this, we have also created direct channels of communication for the public (i.e., a toll-free study information line) and taken extra care through our dissemination efforts to ensure that the results (and their limitations) are well understood and used with appropriate caution by the various research stakeholders.

Finally, the long-term nature of the research partnership is also supported by the project data infrastructure or archives that have been developed at a single site to facilitate both researcher and practitioner access to instrumentation and data and the secure transfer of data shared or collected in the study over time. We jointly monitor data quality and integrity and work closely with district staff and data specialists on data collection to ensure the correct linking, use and protection of the study data (as required under data sharing agreements and institutional review board approvals at each partnering institution). It is important that the actual interface where secure data are transferred between the district and research team is not only clear, but technical assistance is readily available in the event that districts have questions. This shared approach to building and maintaining the data resources for the project appears to increase practitioners' trust of the data and their view of it as "local" and relevant to their work (Finnigan et al., 2013).

Producing Evidence to Inform Policy Decision-Making and Practice

In describing the production of evidence in our partnership, we focus primarily on one particular intervention—the Tutoring for You (T4U) program—that was developed and tested through our research partnership with one of our district partners, MPS. Through the T4U program, MPS provides free afterschool tutoring in math and literacy for elementary students in need of supplemental instructional opportunities. T4U grew out of a redesign of the SES tutoring program (mandated under NCLB), drawing on the research findings generated in our collaborative study of SES with five other school districts. Once the state of Wisconsin received a federal waiver for portions of NCLB in 2012, MPS no longer had to provide tutoring under the SES structure and constraints imposed by NCLB. For example, despite the fact that large numbers of diverse organizations with widely varying hourly rates, tutor qualifications, instructional strategies and curricula entered local markets to provide tutoring, school districts were not able to set requirements for tutors under NCLB, who did not have to meet "highly qualified" standards or have specific training (Heinrich, 2010).

Our long-term research collaboration with MPS and other partnering school districts has enabled us to combine quantitative and qualitative methods in data collection, analysis and dissemination, through multiple phases of program development, evaluation, revamping and more evaluation. During the period prior to state waivers from NCLB, we drew on administrative and test score data from six school districts over the 2007–2008 to 2011–2012 school years, and qualitative data collected during the 2009–2010 to 2011–2012 school years (including observations of full tutoring sessions, parent focus groups and interviews with district administrators and staff and tutoring providers) in conducting the research. The dissemination of research findings to the districts (in the briefings, webinars and other forums described earlier) informed tutoring program redesign and modifications in MPS that we subsequently evaluated in the post-NCLB phase of this research, covering the 2012–2013 to 2014–2015 school years. In the yearly analysis of these data, we employed a quasi-experimental strategy (value-added modeling with school fixed effects) to estimate the average SES and T4U tutoring program effects.

In addition to administrative and test score data from MPS, the qualitative data collection included observations of full tutoring sessions (both in-person sessions and archived online tutoring sessions), focus groups with parents and guardians of students eligible to receive T4U and document analysis of formal curriculum materials from providers, policy documents and district survey information. We used an iterative and constant comparative method in the qualitative analysis to develop and refine our understanding of patterns in tutoring practices and program changes across districts and providers. Throughout the analytic process we examined potential patterns in the instructional setting, program management and policy implementation. (Additional details on the samples, data and methods used in the quantitative and qualitative analyses are available from the authors upon request).

Use of Research Evidence from the Research-to-Practice Partnership

One very basic lever for influencing tutoring effectiveness is the intensity or number of hours of tutoring provided, yet previously, very few studies had measured student attendance in the form of contact time or intensity (Heinrich et al., 2014; Zimmer, Hamilton, & Christina, 2010). Some research suggested that reaching some minimum threshold of tutoring hours (i.e., approximately thirty to forty hours) could be critical to producing measurable effects on students' achievement (Jones, 2009; Lauer et al., 2006), although Deke, Dragoset, Bogen, and Gill (2012) concluded that the intensity of services was not significantly related to the estimated size of tutoring impacts in their study.

In our research-to-practice partnership, we were able to draw on both cross-site and within-district variation in hours of tutoring received, driven in part by district policy and administrative decisions, to better understand the relationship of hours of tutoring to student achievement outcomes. Initially, only in Chicago Public Schools (CPS) were students routinely reaching thresholds of thirty-five or more hours of tutoring, largely because of the lower rates charged per hour for tutoring by providers, and we consistently observed positive effects of tutoring on student achievement only in CPS (Heinrich et al., 2014). In addition, in both Dallas Independent School District (ISD) in 2009–2010 and Minneapolis Public Schools (in 2010–2011) we were able to take advantage of natural "policy experiments," in which limited-time policy or program changes directly increased the number of hours of tutoring that students received in those districts only in those years. In Dallas ISD, the district used federal stimulus funds in 2009–2010 to increase the allotted district expenditure per student and thereby boost the number of hours of tutoring students received. Average hours of tutoring increased from approximately twenty-two hours in 2008–2009 to thirty-five hours in 2009–2010, and positive effects of tutoring on student achievement were observed only in this school year (as tutoring hours fell by half again in the subsequent school years). In Minneapolis, the district introduced a new program in 2010–2011 for a subsample (approximately one-sixth) of tutoring participants that, as informed by evidence emerging in the partnership, compelled providers to deliver at least forty hours of tutoring. Students in this trial program received an average of more than thirty hours of tutoring (only for that year), and consistent with what we were observing in other sites in the study, we found positive program effects on the achievement of these students in that year. In interviews, district staff across our study sites lamented the NCLB provisions that constrained their ability to require more hours of tutoring from providers.

Drawing on this evidence from the research partnership and following new flexibility granted by federal waivers from NCLB that had precluded school districts from controlling tutoring provider hourly rates or setting minimum tutoring hours requirements, MPS established a maximum hourly rate of $35 per hour for tutoring providers beginning in the 2012–2013 school year, the first year of the T4U program. Under SES, tutoring providers in MPS had been charging anywhere from $55 to $108 per hour; however, MPS knew from our work and discussions with CPS and other district partners that some of the same providers offering tutoring in MPS were providing tutoring services to CPS students at as much as less than half the rate charged in MPS and Minneapolis. This provided additional justification for MPS to establish a maximum rate that was one-half to one-third of what some tutoring providers had been charging in the district. As a result, MPS has seen a steady increase in the number of hours of tutoring students have received (on average), from 21.7 hours under SES in 2011–2012 to 33.7 hours under T4U in 2014–2015. Table 4.1 summarizes this and other policy and program changes made by MPS in launching the T4U program that were based on evidence generated in the research partnership.

In addition, our qualitative observations of students in SES tutoring sessions frequently showed differences between the advertised time of tutoring sessions and the actual instructional time (Heinrich et al., 2014). Irrespective of format, students tended to receive less instructional time than what was advertised by providers, although tutoring completed in the student's home most closely matched advertised time (less than three minutes' difference on average), whereas that provided in the school and community setting was often considerably less than average advertised time (nineteen to twenty-five minutes less on average). Under T4U, MPS set a minimum threshold of forty hours of tutoring per student, a maximum session length of one hour of tutoring and a maximum 5:1 student-to-tutor ratio, while also stepping up district monitoring of tutoring sessions with on-site (school) coordinator reviews and observations (announced or unannounced). The district stipulated that the results of these reviews and desktop audits could be shared with the public and/or the state educational agency, the Wisconsin Department of Public Instruction. An MPS district administrator described some of these important research-based changes in an interview during the summer of 2012:

> Some of our [SES] providers offered as little as 9 hours [of tutoring] and some offered, you know, about 27 hours. And according to your research . . . the nominal 40 hours is required, but we couldn't require these private companies to offer services, you know, more than the DPI application. The other thing that it will allow us to do is to set the number of hours per day and per week that students can be tutored. And before the waiver, some of the providers tutored our students two nights, three nights at two hours each tutoring session.

Table 4.1 MPS Tutoring 4 You "T4U" Evidence-Based Program Redesign

2011–2012 *under SES*	2012–2013 *under T4U*
Hours of service	**Hours of service**
9–26	>40
Class size	**Class size**
1:1–10:1+	1:1–5:1
Grade Level	**Grade Level**
K–5/K–12	K–5 to K–12 (only Grade 2 in 2014–2015)
Service Delivery Model	**Service Delivery Model**
In home, in community, online, school	School, online (synchronous)
Math or literacy; can combine in one session	Either math or literacy for the year
Hours per session	**Hours per session**
2 hours 2 × 3 per week	1 hour 2 × 3 per week
Enrollment	**Enrollment**
Providers canvas schools and community	Schools conduct process
Providers service a variety of schools	Providers assigned to one to two schools (reduced to two total providers in 2014–2015)
	No provider marketing; MPS identifies and recruits
	Parent/guardian must complete the registration

Table 4.1 (Continued)

2011–2012 under SES	2012–2013 under T4U
Hourly rate	**Hourly rate**
$55.00 to $108.00 per child in session 1:1–10:1+	$35 per hour rate per session 1:1 to 5:1
ELL	**ELL**
Services provided in native language and/or English	Services in native language if low Lau level and English
Materials not in native language	Materials provided in native language if low LAU level
Special Education	**Special Education**
Services lacked differentiation	Services appropriate to IEP
Tutor Qualifications	**Tutor Qualifications**
No DPI guidelines	Certified teacher in subject are tutored
CBC requirements	Match elementary tutor to math or literacy area
Target Population	**Target Population**
Free and Reduced Lunch (FRL), School Identified for Improvement (SIFI) schools, all students at site, priority to minimal and basic	Focus schools to address gaps Minimal/basic
	No services for proficient or advanced students
Monitoring	**Monitoring**
DPI, principal, coordinators, SES office	Fidelity of implementation "walks" Site coordinator, desktop audits
	Provider site visits
	Tutoring observations, file review, review of findings meeting
	On-site reviews may be announced or unannounced; findings may be shared with the public and/or the Wisconsin Department of Public Instruction
	Parent survey
Curriculum	**Curriculum**
DPI-approved curriculum	District-aligned supplemental reading or math curriculum
Site Coordinator	**Site Coordinator**
MPS not mandatory	Position exists at school level but no additional compensation (2012–2013)
Termination	**Termination**
Terminate for cause Right to cure Individual student services	Terminate for failure to achieve desired student progress listed in learning plan

These observations were echoed in a group interview with Wisconsin DPI administrators in 2012:

> And it seems like Milwaukee . . . it does seem like they use a lot of the research that you had gotten in terms of the per-pupil amount, seems to be a little more reasonable. They have some more criteria in there in terms of qualification.

By the 2013–2014 school year, the median number of hours of tutoring received had reached forty hours, and the tutor-to-student ratio in all observations of sessions was no larger than 1:3. In addition, the difference between advertised and instructional time (as recorded in observations during the 2013–2014 school year) had been reduced to less than five minutes.

The research partnership qualitative research also revealed considerable *intra-provider* variation in both instruction and in curriculum materials, deriving from a variety of formal (website or materials directly from provider administrators) and informal sources (tutors' own resources or students' work from day school) used in sessions (in addition to variation across providers). The result was that the "in-use" curriculum was at times inconsistent with the formal curriculum, which is problematic given that providers were marketing to parents based on their formal (approved) curriculum. In addition, there often was a lack of alignment between day school and tutoring curriculum and instructional strategies, which can hinder the capabilities of the tutor to help meet the student's instructional needs. Furthermore, few providers were staffed with tutors who had adequate instructional backgrounds or training to support students with special educational needs and/or English as a second language, and some tutoring providers did not have access to school records or staff with knowledge about students' needs to adapt instruction for these students. Accordingly, we found across all of our district research partners that tutoring services were less effective for students who were English language learners or had special needs (Heinrich et al., 2014). In the T4U program, MPS now requires all providers to use curriculum directly aligned to the district day school curriculum with overarching goals and drill-down goals for students with special needs. T4U providers are required to provide appropriate services for students with special needs and English learners (unlike under SES), and MPS requires information sharing (Individual Educational Plans or IEPs) between the schools and the tutors to ensure that they are meeting the needs of students with disabilities. Additionally, when sufficient staff are available, tutors are now required to be certified teachers (another restriction that school districts were not allowed to impose under NCLB). Tutors hired by the two contracted providers in 2013–2014 and 2014–2015 were required to have teaching certification, which we confirmed in observed sessions.

Finally, MPS made two other major program design changes in the first two years of the T4U program that were intended to reduce program management challenges and improve student outcomes, although these were less directly connected to any particular piece of evidence generated in the partnership. First, thirteen of the fourteen tutoring providers under SES returned to the school district in 2012–2013 to offer T4U services (despite the dramatic reduction in hourly rates paid for tutoring), but rather than allowing providers to compete for student "market shares," MPS assigned providers to one to two schools in the district, which led to a considerably more even distribution of students across the providers (who were prohibited from conducting marketing campaigns and directly enrolling students in their programs). In fact, some providers during the 2012–2013 school year expressed in interviews a preference for this system, as it allowed them to focus more on programming and staffing than on recruitment and enrollment. Second, in the 2013–2014 and subsequent years of T4U, the district contracted with only two tutoring providers via an RFP process: one that delivered services in online tutoring sessions and the other that operated solely in face-to-face formats. These two providers were found to have positive impact on reading test scores, and in fact, were among the most effective in increasing students' math test scores. Thus, nearly every change that MPS made in its district tutoring program, T4U, was based on evidence generated through five years of collaborative, improvement science-oriented research and the dialogue and co-production of insights that it facilitated with our district research partners.

Implications of Evidence-Based Program Changes for Student Outcomes

One of the goals of this study was to move beyond descriptive documentation of the potential benefits of research-to-practice partnerships to present empirical (quantitative and qualitative) evidence linking the work of this partnership to improvements in students' educational outcomes. Using MPS student record data with value-added models, we estimated the associations between student participation in T4U and changes in their math and reading achievement, comparing them with the estimated effects of participation in SES (before the evidence-based changes were made in the T4U program).

In the first year of the T4U program (2012–2013), we estimated both average program effects and effects sizes for each of the thirteen tutoring providers in both math and reading. Whereas in the prior school year (2011–2012), only one tutoring provider had been identified as effective in increasing students' math achievement and another one as effective in increasing students' reading achievement, in the following year (2012–2013), all but two of the thirteen tutoring providers were effective in increasing student achievement in at least one of these subjects (see Figures 4.1 and 4.2 that present provider-specific effects). In the subsequent school years (2013–2014 and 2014–2015) when only two providers were delivering T4U services, we saw additional gains in students' math and reading achievement, as shown in Figures 4.3 and 4.4, which compare average gains in student achievement across all four school years (SES in 2011–2012 and 2012–2015 for T4U). Standard error bars on the effect estimates shown in Figures 4.3 and 4.4 indicate that although there was no statistically significant effect of tutoring on student achievement (in reading or math) during 2011–2012 (before T4U), all of the estimated effects of T4U on student math and reading achievement are positive and statistically significant in the subsequent years.

These observed improvements in student test scores are corroborated by improved student engagement in the observation of tutoring sessions, especially by 2013–2014. Although we cannot make any broad claims based on data from ten sessions observed in 2013–2014, we did find overall positive and consistent student engagement across both online and in-person formats (with the exception of when technical difficulties occurred in online sessions). In addition, students were asked to actively apply skills and knowledge by an engaged tutor in small group settings, as opposed to many examples of large group "homework help" sessions or worksheet drills observed previously. Similarly, caregivers of students in T4U across two focus groups in the spring of 2014 felt positive about the T4U experience and believed tutoring positively influenced students' skills, as well as their confidence level in school. For example, one parent remarked, "[my student] is very smart but he needs the little cues, the little redirection, and he likes to have that reinforcement." Another parent in a different focus group expressed similar feelings, "[my student] won't forget the things that he has learned, I mean he's learned so much so far, it's like he has come a long way. So I like it." Please see Figures 4.7 through 4.10 for performance data on the T4U programs.

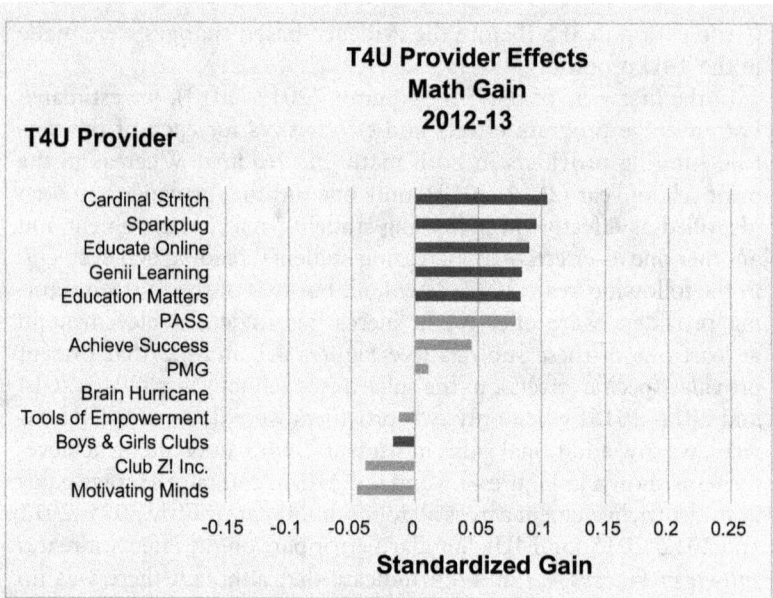

Figure 4.7 Estimated Effects of T4U Providers on Student Math Achievement, 2012–2013

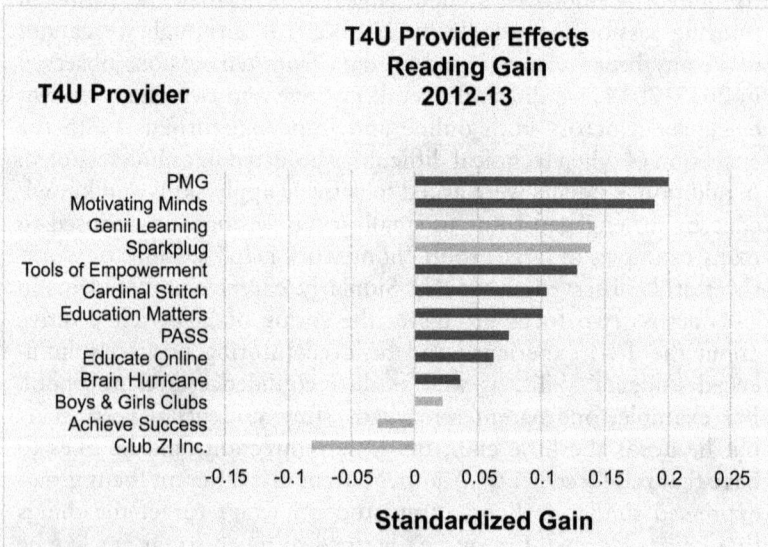

Figure 4.8 Estimated Effects of T4U Providers on Student Reading Achievement, 2012–2013

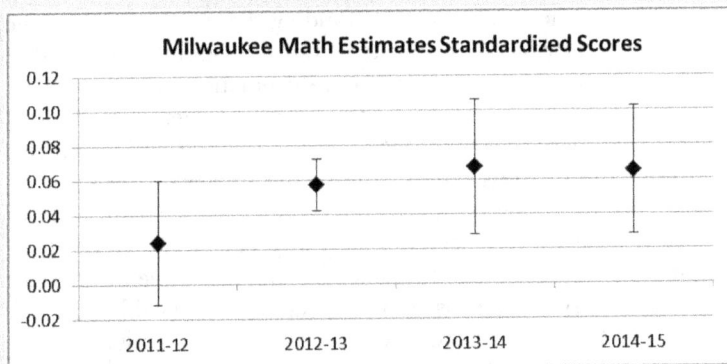

Figure 4.9 Estimated T4U Effects on Student Math Achievement, 2011–2015

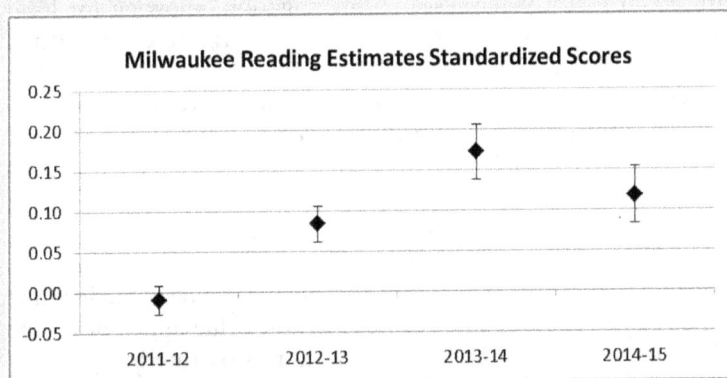

Figure 4.10 Estimated T4U Effects on Student Reading Achievement, 2011–2015

Lessons and Conclusions

The art of creating and cultivating research partnerships is not a component of a typical undergraduate or graduate research program of study; thus, researchers, practitioners and policymakers are likely to "learn the ropes" of how to do this on the job (or in the context of field research). In the case of the partnership we developed with MPS, we did not start out with a "grand plan" of how to make this long-term, two-way research-to-practice relationship work, nor did we have the infrastructure or large-scale funding in place to "grow" it from the beginning. We began with a small-scale, district-funded study and then built the structures for communication and collaboration over time, including the trust and respect that undergird them. The external funding that subsequently came in to support the research was critical for ongoing staff support that allowed for a deepening of the research-to-practice relationships. At the same time, the funding was not specifically targeted or awarded for creating the partnership scaffolding. The "deal maker" in this case—that transformed the relationship from a one-time research opportunity to a long-term collaboration—was the realization of *mutual benefits* from the collaborative approach to conducting the research that emerged. For the practitioners, this came in the form of more relevant, rigorous and immediately applicable research products, whereas the academic partners saw the fruits of more discerning and impactful research results that were put back into practice to improve student outcomes.

Another key lesson that we draw from our experience is the importance of a flexible (as well as long-term) orientation to the nature and focus of the research investigation, allowing for local policy and program priorities to help shape the research agenda and the scope of the work over time. Some of the infrastructure that we developed, such as the end-of-year/summer research briefings, enabled us to get into an iterative research-to-practice/policy cycle, where research findings are integrated into local policy and program development and implementation, and the learning is ongoing on the part of both the researchers and practitioners/policymakers. This is, in effect, a "deal maker" for the ongoing success of the partnership. In addition, the fact that our research funders, the Institute of Education Sciences and a private donor, value and support the infrastructure we have created to sustain this partnership has been critical to its success. This has allowed us to move beyond our original research questions and take the research in new directions that reflect the changing policy landscape and education context and that support district efforts aimed at continuous policy and program improvements.

And as noted earlier, seeing visible program successes emerge from the work of the research partnership is also a major boon to sustaining the relationship. Because the sharing of research results and discussion of their implications for policy and practice were two-way and ongoing in this partnership with MPS, there were many opportunities to apply the results and to assess the effects of the changes made to policy and practice. In due course, as shown here, we were able to observe strong associations between the evidence-based program and policy changes implemented and the end goal of increasing student achievement. The two-way commitment to this partnership, bolstered by the excitement of seeing a link between our work and student outcomes, is now sufficiently strong that we have found ways to continue the work during periods where there has been a gap in funding support. We are currently working with MPS on new avenues of research investigation and think in terms of five-year horizons for our collaboration, recognizing that although the full details of the scope, foci and funding are yet to be determined, the commitment among the partners is solidly in place to make it happen.

Although we see this research partnership as having produced many benefits for the partners and other education stakeholders, there are several questions that we would recommend other parties consider before pursuing this type of research collaboration. First, how can researchers invest time and resources in developing research products that are not typically "rewarded" in the academic profession (e.g., counted in a tenure case file)? Do you have the will and capacity (time) to cultivate relationships and trust with practitioners in order to understand and be responsive to their research needs, which inevitably take you off campus and into the field? In addition, are you willing to reorient your own research interests or agenda to find the productive middle ground for building a fruitful collaboration? Academics earlier in their careers (even if they have achieved tenure) should ask whether they can afford a major time commitment and the flexibility in their research pursuits that may be required, or whether it is in their long-term career interests to do so. Lastly, how can partnerships mark their successes in ways that benefit both individually (i.e., press releases, academic journals) and jointly (e.g., combined presentations at national conferences)?

Policymakers and practitioners face similar challenges in making longer-term commitments to research collaboration in terms of the time required to fold research responsibilities into a typically heavy load of regular programmatic and administrative responsibilities. Furthermore, they may also take some risks in pursuing research investigations when they are asked to be open to publicly disseminating the findings, even if the outcomes are not favorable. The risks and challenges may compound over a longer-term partnership where greater time and resources are invested and expectations are accordingly built up for positive outcomes and benefits for stakeholders. In this regard, they should ask whether they are open to learning and accepting disappointing results, without closing the door on the partnership when that happens. With time, what we learn from policy or program disappointments can be used to develop improved policies and implementation of programs that can lead to better outcomes, as we experienced in our work with MPS.

Sustaining Partnership

Mutual Benefit

Similar to HUP, the partnership between the university and school districts described by Heinrich and Good is a structure created to facilitate the policy research occurring between distinct organizations. Also a strong theme across both partnerships is the critical importance of mutual benefit. For Heinrich and Good, this takes many forms, such as the collaborative manner in which research topics are identified, the ways in which research findings are disseminated and applied in school systems and the practice learning that then informs future research. They describe this as an "iterative research" model that cultivates the cycle and ensures mutual benefits to both systems.

Learning

This case also illustrates the importance of cross-sector learning. Heinrich and Good emphasize the need for both the university research partner and policymakers (in this case, school districts) to be willing to set aside and commit the time and to possess the will to learn about, learn from and invest in working with one another. Part of this collegiality includes sensitivity to work calendars (e.g., the school year) and when key decisions are made. The importance of mutual learning is noteworthy. This attitude of mutual respect is a manifestation of the partnership's value of all partners bringing knowledge essential to partnerships and the "listening and learning" that are key to any successful policymaker–researcher relationship (Langworthy & Larson, forthcoming).

Key Takeaways

This chapter on sustaining partnerships highlights three successful, long-standing researcher–policymaker partnerships. Taken together, the broad lessons they offer highlight being attuned to and taking advantage of key contextual conditions to develop a robust partnership, making financial and structural commitments to ensure partnerships work and last and cultivating trust by engaging in open communication and "ego-free" learning across sectors. These partnerships work and last because each partner (or set of partners) is committed to listening and learning from the other and to being responsive. This is manifested in tangible ways, such as the involvement of legislators and executive branch state staff in the planning of the Family Impact Seminar topics, the institutional cross-connections constructed to support HUP and the maintenance of organizational role and responsibility knowledge among members of Heinrich and Good's research-to-practice partnership, among others.

What looms large across all three case studies is the importance of identifying, measuring and cultivating mutual benefit and value. All of the organizations profiled here are committed to and have mechanisms in place for assessing whether their work continues to produce value to *both* sides of the partnership. Approaching this objectively is essential, and as Kathie Doty states, "If there is no mutual value, we should not be doing it" when it comes to maintaining the funding for HUP.

In addition to these lessons, these successful collaborators offer tools to help others in their pursuit of similar work. The HUP offers extensive information on its website that is available publicly. Those interested in building a similarly structured partnership are likely to find all elements of the site valuable. We also include the HUP master cooperative agreement as Appendix D. For those who are not yet ready to formalize a cross-agency structure in exactly this way, simply exploring HUP's materials will offer insight about one approach to take; examining specific tools and documents may be of particular interest. In particular, visitors to the site might explore the latest *Example Collaboration* profiled. Or, in addition to examining the master cooperative agreement in the appendix, visitors may find connecting to the project via social media or subscribing to the HUP newsletter to be of use. Similarly, Heinrich and Good share three examples of the policy briefs their project has issued to describe work from their partnership and details of the methods used in the analysis they describe in this case.

Beyond these specific case studies, the field of social work offers valuable guidance about partnerships not unlike those we feature here. The National Association of Social Workers released its 2014 action brief, *Creating and Sustaining Effective & Outcome-oriented Child Welfare University-Research Agency Partnerships*. The important values realized from these partnerships that align well with the HUP case study shared here include supporting student field placements, linking agencies to university resources, unity of purpose and perhaps most importantly, addressing the structural barriers to partnership such as bidding and contracting processes and costs (NASW, 2014, pp. 3–4.) Additional attributes of successful partnerships are also noted.

A more comprehensive resource on policymaker–university partnership is offered by the Alliance of Regional Collaboratives for Climate Adaptation (ARCCA) at http://www.arccacalifornia.org/toolkit/element9/. This online toolkit provides a complete guide to partnerships with local universities. Section 2, Getting Organized, provides tips for making connections to local governments, developing governance structures and securing funding. Although the resources under element 9, *Engage and build partnerships with local universities*, are focused on climate change research and initiatives, they contain case studies and other important resources that outline important attributes of university partnerships. Element 10, *Develop initial work plan*, contains additional case study examples for establishing initial plans for collaborative research work.

Finally, The Good Project, hosted by the Harvard Graduate School of Education and a partnership across multiple academics and experts, offers a guide to partnership called *The Good Collaboration Toolkit: An approach to building, carrying out, and sustaining good collaboration* (The Good Project, 2013). The toolkit contains tips and activities that users can undertake to explore, create and maintain partnership. It is presented in distinct sections: *Identify and Evaluate, Engage with Potential Collaborators, Nurture Relationships with Active Collaborators* and *Debrief and Reflect*. Each activity is briefly laid out and described, most in no more than two pages, making them easily digestible. One important activity to support sustaining a partnership, for instance, is titled "Passion and Engagement: Is it still there?" intended to help collaborative partners, individually and as a group, reflect on the accomplishments of the partnership, the level of ongoing commitment and interest and if interest has lagged, what might be done to reignite interest and engagement (The Good Project, 2013, p. 57). As the HUP survey results illustrate, collaborative partners must perceive value in ongoing involvement and the contribution toward broader goals in the interest of cultivating a willingness to work with that partner again in the future.

References

ARCCA California. (2016). *Regional adaptation collaborative toolkit*. Online resource. Retrieved on February 2, 2016 from: http://www.arccacalifornia.org/toolkit/.

Bellah, R.N., Madsen, R., Sullivan, W.M., Swidler, A., & Tipton, S.M. (1996). *Habits of the heart of the heart: Individualism and commitment in American life*. Berkeley: University of California Press. (Original work published 1985).

Bogenschneider, K. (2014). *Family policy matters: How policymaking affects families and what professionals can do* (3rd ed.). New York, NY: Routledge Books, Taylor and Francis Group.

Bogenschneider, K. (2015). Invited commentary: The research evidence policymakers need to build better public policy for children of incarcerated parents. In J. Poelhmann-Tynan (Ed.), *Children's contact with incarcerated parents: Implications for policy and intervention* (pp. 93–113) in Advances in Child and Family Policy and Practice. Washington, DC: American Psychological Association.

Bogenschneider, K., & Corbett, T. (2010a). *Evidence-based policymaking: Insights from policy minded researchers and research-minded policymakers*. New York, NY: Taylor & Francis Group.

Bogenschneider, K., & Corbett, T. (2010b). Family policy: Becoming a field of inquiry and subfield of social policy. *Journal of Marriage and Family, 72*, 783–803.

Bogenschneider, K., Little, O.M., & Johnson, K. (2013). Policymakers' use of social science research: Looking within and across policy actors. *Journal of Marriage and Family, 75*, 263–275.

Bogenschneider, K., Little, O.M., Ooms, T., Benning, S., Cadigan, K., & Corbett, T. (2012). The family impact lens: A family-focused, evidence-informed approach to policy and practice. *Family Relations, 61*, 514–531.

Browne, W.P. (1999). Studying interests and policy from the inside. *Policy Studies Journal, 27,* 67–75.

Bryk, A., Gomez, L., & Grunow, A. (2011). Getting ideas into action: Building networked improvement communities in education. In M. Hallinan (Ed.), *Frontiers in sociology of education* (pp. 127–162). Netherlands: Springer.

Coalition for Evidence-Based Policy. (2002). *Bringing evidence-driven progress to education: A recommended strategy for the U.S. Department of Education.* Retrieved from: http://coalition4evidence.org/wp-content/uploads/2012/12/Evid-based_educ_strategy_for_ED.pdf.

Coburn, C.E., Penuel, W.R., & Geil, K.E. (2013). *Research-practice partnerships at the district level: A strategy for leveraging research for educational improvement in school districts.* New York, NY: William T. Grant Foundation.

Deke, J., Dragoset, L., Bogen, K., & Gill, B. (2012). *Impacts of Title I supplemental educational services on student achievement (NCEE 2012–4053).* Washington, DC: National Center for Education Evaluation and Regional Assistance, Institute of Education Sciences, U.S. Department of Education.

Drabble, L., Lemon, K., D'Andrade, A., Donoviel, B., & Le, J. (2013). Child welfare partnership for research and training: A title IV-E university/community collaborative research model. *Journal of Public Child Welfare, 7,* 411–429.

Finnigan, K.S., Daly, A.J., & Che, J. (2013). Systemwide reform in districts under pressure. *Journal of Educational Administration, 51*(4), 476–497.

Friese, B., & Bogenschneider, K. (2009). The voice of experience: How social scientists bring research to bear on family policymaking. *Family Relations, 58,* 229–243.

The Good Project. (2013). *The good collaboration toolkit: An approach to building, sustaining, and carrying out successful collaboration.* Online document. Retrieved online on February 2, 2016 from: http://www.thegoodproject.org/collaborationtoolkit/the-good-collaboration-toolkit-checklist/.

Haskins, R., & Margolis, G. (2015). *Show me the evidence: Obama's fight for rigor and results in social policy.* Washington, DC: The Brookings Institution.

Head, B.W. (2015). Toward more "evidence-informed" policy making? *Public Administration Review, 76*(3), 472–484.

Heckman, J. (1990). Social science research and policy: Review essay. *Journal of Human Resources, 25*(2), 297–304.

Heinrich, C.J. (2010). Third-party governance under No Child Left Behind: Accountability and performance management challenges in supplemental educational services provision. *Journal of Public Administration Research and Theory, 20*(1), 59–80.

Heinrich, C.J., Burch, P., Good, A., Acosta, R., Cheng, H., Dillender, M., Kirshbaum, C., Nisar, H., & Stewart, M.S. (2014). Improving the implementation and effectiveness of out-of-school-time tutoring. *Journal of Policy Analysis and Management, 33*(2), 471–494.

Hines, D.A., & Bogenschneider, K. (2013). Introduction to the special issue: Communicating research to policymakers—Briefing report chapters from the Massachusetts Family Impact Seminars on Youth at Risk. *New England Journal of Public Policy, 25*(1), 1–3.

Jaynes, S. (2014). Using principles of practice-based evidence research to teach evidence-based practice in social work. *Journal of Evidence-Based Social Work, 11,* 222–235.

Jones, C. (2009). *The 2009 Supplemental Educational Services program: Year 4 summative evaluation.* Chicago, IL: Chicago Public Schools Office of Extended Learning Opportunities and Office Research, Evaluation, and Accountability.

Jones, J.M., & Sherr, M.E. (2014). The role of relationships in connecting social work research and evidence-based practice. *Journal of Evidence-Based Social Work, 11,* 139–147.

Kellogg Commission. (1999). *Returning to our roots: The engaged institution.* Washington, DC: National Association of State Universities and Land-Grant Colleges.

Kingdon, J.W. (2003). *Agendas, alternatives, and public policies* (2nd ed.). New York, NY: Longman.

Kraus, B. (2013). *Peace through seminar.* Guest blog. FightingBob.com.

Larson, A.M., & Langworthy, S.E. Learning to listen and listening to learn: Recursive information flow to build relationships and improve practice. *Child Welfare, 94*(3), in press.

Larson, A. (2014). *Hennepin University Partnership: Participant perspectives on a formalized academic-public agency collaboration structure.* Unpublished report. Saint Paul, MN: Hamline University.

Lauer, P., Akiba, M., Wilkerson, S., Apthorp, H., Snow, D., & Martin-Glenn, M. (2006). Out-of-school-time programs: A meta-analysis of effects for at-risk students. *Review of Educational Research, 76*(2), 275–313.

National Association of Social Workers. (2014). *Creating & sustaining effective & outcome oriented child welfare university-agency research partnerships.* Action brief. Washington, DC: Social Work Policy Institute.

Nelson, S.R., Leffler, J.C., & Hansen, B.A. (2009). *Toward a research agenda for understanding and improving use of research evidence.* Portland, OR: Northwest Regional Educational Laboratory.

Roosevelt, T. (1912). [Address]. *Address given before the Convention of the National Progressive Party in Chicago, IL.* Retrieved on June 17, 2009, from: http://www.ssa.gov/history/trspeech.html.

Simmons, C.W. (1996). *State and local information needs: The California Family Impact Seminar model.* Presented at the annual meeting of the Association for Public Policy Analysis and Management Research Conference, Washington, DC.

Stark, J. (1995). The Wisconsin Idea: The University's service to the State. In *State of Wisconsin 1995–1996 Blue Book* (pp. 101–179). Madison, WI: Wisconsin Legislative Reference Bureau.

Tseng, V. (2012). The uses of research in policy and practice. *Social Policy Report, 26*(2), 1–16.

Zimmer, R., Hamilton, L., & Christina, R. (2010). After-school tutoring in the context of No Child Left Behind: Effectiveness of two programs in the Pittsburgh Public Schools (PPS). *Economics of Education Review, 29*(1), 18–28.

5 Utilizing Research
An Intended Consequence

The Research–Policy Gap

The disconnect between the research and policy realms has been widely studied and documented for decades. It is well established that policymakers' use of research is typically minimal and that researchers usually do not make an effort to use policymakers' insights to inform their research. Recently, there has been increased attention to the reasons for this gap and how to mitigate and narrow it. This deepening interest stems in part from recognition that using research for a positive impact on policymaking is an area with great promise, one that both researchers and policymakers can contribute to and benefit from. As discussed further in this chapter, and as cases throughout this book illustrate, intentional researcher–policymaker partnerships are a promising and increasingly tested approach to developing and furthering sustained collaboration and impact. This is particularly true given the current landscape within the public sector, one where policymakers demand "evidence-based policy" and "data-driven decision making" from themselves, from those whom they fund and from those whom their policies affect.

To address the research–policy gap through partnerships requires an understanding of why the gaps exist. It is telling that researchers from multiple disciplines have examined the gaps' sources, which include differences with respect to the incentive structures for researchers and policymakers, the timeframes for accomplishing their work, mechanisms for sharing information, their professional training and the measures for determining whether they have succeeded. Choi et al. (2005) offer an insightful discussion of the possibility of partnerships as a mechanism for addressing many of these structural and cultural differences. The strategies put forth include changes to infrastructure as well as to the content of the interaction between researchers and policymakers. With regard to infrastructure, the possibilities presented include charging specific people with facilitating the bridging work between the sectors and incentivizing partnerships. The challenge of incentives is widely acknowledged, particularly with respect to a lack of incentives for academic researchers to engage with policymakers; doing so has traditionally been seen as detracting from the more lauded work of research and publishing. The content strategies put forth address this in part by encouraging the consideration of policymaker engagement and other activities often considered inconsequential as substantive components of research.

Although studies lend credibility to the concerns about research–policy gaps, even without the benefit of research, one can appreciate why the gaps exist. One need only reflect on how researchers and policymakers might answer the following five questions differently. In these examples, we have in mind a policymaker or staff person in the legislative branch:

> *What are you trying to accomplish?* Policymaker: action; Researcher: publish an article.
>
> *What is your training?* Policymaker: lawyer, insurance broker, farmer, engineer; Researcher: a PhD in economics, psychology, public policy.
>
> *What determines whether you succeed?* Policymaker: if my legislation passes and if we get the funding in the budget; Researcher: if my article is published and if I get tenure.
>
> *What is the typical timeframe for achieving that success?* Policymaker: it can be as little as a day; Researcher: at least two years.
>
> *Who are your closest work partners?* Policymaker: my fellow legislators, lobbyists; Researcher: colleagues at universities and at research think tanks.

Although these examples are overly simplistic, they highlight some of the fundamental differences between the sectors. The answers to these questions, coupled with what research has revealed, confirm that there are good reasons for the wide gap between these professional worlds. Their structures, processes, timeframes and other characteristics are fundamentally at odds when it comes to policymakers being able to take advantage of research when they need it and in a form which they can use. Some have recommended strategies for reducing these structural differences (Denis, Lehoux, Hivon, & Champagne, 2003), but we find it unrealistic to set a goal of changing long-standing institutions, their cultures and practices. We believe it is significantly more feasible to identify the ways that researchers and policymakers can partner *in the context of* the well-established differences between them.

Bridging the Gap?

Never has there been a better time to pursue research–policy partnerships. This is particularly true when it comes to increasing the use of research in policy and the use of policymaker insight to strengthen research. As participants in both sectors have developed a more complete and nuanced understanding about their respective differences, they also have developed new knowledge about how to leverage each other's strengths. This in turn has been immensely beneficial for narrowing the research–policy gap overall. *Data-driven, evidence-informed, research-based, evidence-based.* These terms have become ubiquitous in policy and practice contexts. They represent calls for the use of research in policymaking, which in order to succeed, let alone to be meaningful and sustainable, requires a narrowing of the research–policy gap. The emergence of more in-depth findings about research utilization in policy environments sets an ideal stage for researcher–policymaker partnerships. Among the many indicators of this trend, in 2009, the National Research Council of the National Academy of Sciences established a Committee on the Use of Social Science Knowledge in Public Policy. As the committee's final report states,

> This new committee decided to propose a framework for research on how policy makers make use of scientific knowledge and how the results of that research might lead to improved policy making and improved preparation of students in policy schools for careers in the policy world.
>
> (National Academy of Sciences, 2012)

One of the first manifestations of the acknowledgement of the research–policy gap, combined with the increasing desire (at least stated) for using research in the policy realm, was a massive increase in both the quantity of research disseminated to policymakers and with the array of entities carrying out research dissemination efforts. Websites provided detailed lists of organizations' "resources." Clearinghouses of research highlighting "best" or "promising" practices emerged with regularity (e.g., the U.S. Department of Education's What Works Clearinghouse and the now-concluded Promising Practices Network). The Internet provided a new mechanism for and a huge boost to these efforts. Search online for "research dissemination" and a seemingly endless array of guidance documents appear. Thankfully, some work in this area has pointed out the "passive" nature of much of this dissemination in favor of more transactional strategies for research utilization (Moore, Todd, & Redman, 2009). In their *Evidence Check Review*, Moore (2009) and her co-authors model what research suggests: they present the strategies in accessible, user-friendly language that although grounded in research, does not bombard the intended user with unfamiliar jargon that reinforces the structural and substantive differences between the sectors described earlier. Kirst (2000) is to thank for even earlier contributions to helping researchers connect their work with the policy realm.

In tandem with this surge in dissemination, university researchers, think tanks, interest groups, advocacy organizations and other entities that do "policy-relevant" work increasingly invest in communications and public relations apparatuses. Websites display headings such as "for policymakers" and "engagement" and feature policy briefs and other materials purportedly produced with policymakers in mind. (In the context of this discussion, it is noteworthy that some "briefs" are dozens of pages long.) Yet although many researchers and their institutions have invested in such dissemination efforts, too many of them have had a "throw the spaghetti against the wall and see if it sticks" mentality. A more accurate analogy might be "throw the spaghetti against the wall" with little, if any, attention to whether it sticks.

Though there has been progress to ensure that dissemination is more targeted, the process often remains one-directional instead of two-way and multitransactional. Moreover, research disseminators' efforts often devote minimal, if any, resources to learning directly from policymakers about their research needs, the timing of the research and the form in which the research is provided.

It is therefore no wonder that efforts to assess policymakers' use of research evidence reveal that the use is low. However, the fact that such examinations exist at all is encouraging. Entities that are investing considerable resources in such efforts include the W. T. Grant Foundation, the UK-based journal *Evidence and Policy* and the Frameworks Institute. Less studied and well known is that most researchers expend little effort to *use* policymaker input to inform their research. From bridging research and policy broadly to research utilization in particular, the cross-sector connecting that occurs often has been either an afterthought or a requirement, as discussed in Chapter 2 of this book on partnership motivations and Chapter 6 on investing in partnerships.

What Research Utilization Is and Why It Matters

To set the stage for the two partnership cases in this chapter, it is helpful to clarify what research utilization is and why it matters. Doing so quickly leads to related questions about evidence-based policy, what it means, what counts as evidence and who gets to decide. There is an important and growing literature on the emergence and rise of evidence-based policy. In the context of researcher–policymaker partnerships, however, our emphasis is on understanding what research use means and what circumstances and conditions facilitate it.

There are multiple ways of articulating the meaning of research utilization in policy, as well as multiple types of use. The use can occur at any phase of the policymaking process. Simply put, research utilization occurs when research plays a role in one or more aspects of a policymaking process. The role of research ranges from informing to influencing to determining policy, as well as affirming prior policy decisions (Lindblom & Cohen, 1979). Research use might occur during the conception, development, implementation or evaluation of policy. A role of partnerships in research utilization is to increase *strategic* use. Without a partnership, researchers typically conclude their work on an issue once findings and evidence exist. With a partnership, researchers can fundamentally change their role with regard to policy impact. Likewise, absent a partnership, policymakers who express a desire and need for research often have access only to the final research product in the form of a scholarly journal. A partnership with researchers, however, can fundamentally change the role of the policymaker with regard to evidence-based decision-making. For both, one might characterize the shift as moving from the production of research to its application.

There is scant literature on the types of partnerships that we are focusing on here, partnerships throughout which both researchers and policymakers are party to the research endeavor. We distinguish this from the literature on translational research, which, along with other resources on researcher–policymaker partnerships, is concerned mainly with knowledge translation, translational research, research brokering and so on (Clark & Kelly, 2005; Rigby, 2005). Translational work is important for bridging research and policy but does not have significant implications for the research *use*. A key distinction between researcher–policymaker partnerships and translational research is the two-way nature of partnerships and the one-way nature of much translational research. Translational research typically focuses on "increasing the use of research" in policy and practice (Stevens, Liabo, Frost, & Roberts, 2005), yet translation conveys a goal of getting "them" (usually the policymakers) to understand "us" (usually the researchers).

Relevant literature focuses on translating research for policy and identifying the "best translators" (Tseng, 2013). Other work focuses on "getting them the facts" and on the roles of individuals who serve as intermediaries in the absence of established partnerships between research and policy or research and practice (Dobbins et al., 2009; Lomas, 2007). Though we are supportive of these goals, the translational approach precludes opportunities for the shared learning and mutual benefits that the partnership approach affords. Furthermore, although it is promising that researchers increasingly want their work "translated" for policy purposes, translation does not equate to use.

Ideally, an increased desire for policymakers' real-world application of research occurs in conjunction with inviting and respecting insights from the policymakers who would do the using. One step closer to the mutually established and beneficial partnerships featured in this book are what Ginsberg, Lewis, Zackheim, and Casebeer (2007) call "interaction approaches to research translation." These focus on direct connections between researchers and policymakers as opposed to using intermediaries. Both the broker and the interaction mechanisms for translation can be worthwhile, particularly if there is a lack of willingness or skills for developing partnerships. But jointly developed and executed partnerships are preferable for multiple reasons, including their potential for lasting impact and sustainability.

Partnerships' Positive Impact on Research Use

Ongoing efforts to increase knowledge and understanding of when and why policymakers do and do not use research are yielding still more encouraging developments. Key among them is recognition of the importance of researcher–policymaker partnerships and the fact that when they work well, the partnerships respond to the needs of both sectors and employ conditions and strategies for ensuring that research use is effective. In sum, there is evidence that researcher–policymaker partnerships increase the use of research (Walter, Davies, & Nutley, 2003).

The two partnerships featured in this chapter exemplify the need for and values of using research in policymaking. The partnerships not only make the case for research use in policy, but also demonstrate strategies for ensuring that the use occurs. The first example is that of The Pew Charitable Trusts and the MacArthur Foundation working both as funders of and implementation partners with legislative and executive branches of state governments. This case reminds us of those in Chapter 2 that feature motivations for researcher–policymaker partnerships and show funders in the roles of both investor and expert. The second partnership case about research use tells the story of a high-level state official striving to bring evidence to bear on decision-making in a policy environment that did not initially welcome the research or the close involvement of researchers.

The New Mexico–Results First Partnership: Lessons from a Long-Term, Evidence-Based Policymaking Collaboration

Gary VanLandingham and Darcy White

In 2011, the New Mexico Legislative Finance Committee (LFC) held a hearing to discuss the state's poor outcomes for child well-being. The committee's staff researched this problem and reported that a high percentage of these children were academically behind on their first day of school, and evaluations showed that the state's child care and Head Start programs were not delivering improved educational outcomes for this population. Legislators concluded that investments in early childhood programs could help close this gap, but noted that the state had very limited resources to fund such interventions. As noted by LFC staff, "Members knew that agencies and advocates would come forward with a long list of programs seeking funding. They wanted to know which programs would represent the best investment of taxpayer dollars" (Sallee, personal communication, July 24, 2015). The LFC directed its staff to investigate cost-efficient programs that would improve outcomes for the state's children. More broadly, the committee sought innovative tools that would enable it to better assess the long-term implications of the state's budget choices across all social policy areas.

Soon after this meeting, LFC staff attended a national conference and heard a presentation about a new initiative that was seeking to partner with states to advance evidence-based policymaking. The Pew-MacArthur Results First Initiative (Results First), a joint project of The Pew Charitable Trusts and the John D. and Catherine T. MacArthur Foundation, began working with states earlier in 2011 to help them assess the long-term benefits and costs of investments in a wide range of social policy programs. Because Results First held the potential to help meet the legislature's information needs, the LFC's leadership invited Results First to form a partnership with New Mexico. This long-term partnership between practitioners and researchers, which began in the fall of 2011 and has continued through 2015, has been successful in:

- Building the capacity within New Mexico to customize and use highly sophisticated analytical tools, including a cutting-edge benefit–cost model
- Enabling LFC staff to incorporate analyses based on these tools into a series of reports that have assessed the long-term benefits and costs of alternative adult and juvenile justice, child welfare, mental health and substance abuse and early childhood programs
- Informing legislative appropriations decisions that have directed $92.2 million to early childhood and criminal justice programs that are projected to deliver over $373 million in long-term returns for New Mexico residents
- Beginning to extend this partnership into relevant executive branch agencies, with the goal of building enterprise-wide support for evidence-based policymaking

This case study describes Results First and discusses how the New Mexico–Results First partnership originated, the roles of the partners and its progress over time. It also discusses the achievements of the partnership, the challenges it has experienced and the changes in strategy that have been made to address these situations. The chapter concludes by identifying lessons learned that can benefit other entities pursuing long-term collaborative partnerships between practitioners and researchers.

Results First Background

Results First was created and is co-funded by The Pew Charitable Trusts, a nonpartisan, nonprofit organization, and the John D. and Catherine T. MacArthur Foundation, one of the nation's largest foundations. The two entities formed Results First after noting how states had struggled to deal with unprecedented budget gaps during the Great Recession. These shortfalls, which collectively exceeded $500 billion (National Conference of State Legislatures, 2011, 2012), required state leaders to make difficult decisions on how to allocate their limited resources among competing demands. Policymakers wanted to make strategic choices about what to cut, but most found that their states lacked information about the outcomes their individual programs achieved. As a result, most states resorted to across-the-board cuts that hindered their most effective programs while preserving those programs that generated poor outcomes for residents.

Pew and MacArthur had noted that Washington State was using an alternative approach that relied on rigorous evidence of program outcomes to inform its budget decisions. This process, focused on "what works," is based on a benefit–cost model developed by the Washington State Institute for Public Policy (WSIPP). WSIPP conducts comprehensive reviews of high-quality outcome evaluations (to date it has examined over 28,000 studies) to identify interventions that have been shown to achieve desired outcomes such as reducing criminal recidivism and improving high school graduation rates. WSIPP uses the results of its meta-analysis to calculate the predicted impact of these interventions on a variety of outcomes of interest, such as improved health or reduced crime. The benefit–cost model applies these effect sizes to state-specific cost and population data to estimate the return on investment that each program would generate if implemented in a state. The model can be used to analyze a wide range of programs in the adult criminal justice, juvenile justice, child welfare, pre-K to 12 education, mental health and substance abuse and public health policy areas. WSIPP publishes the results of its analyses on its public website using a user-friendly *Consumer Reports–type* format that lists and ranks programs by their projected return on investment.[1] The state legislature has used these results since the mid-1990s to inform its budget and policy decisions.

The Results First Initiative seeks to build the capacity of other states to replicate Washington State's success with this approach of evidence-based policymaking. It is thus a unique example of knowledge transfer between research and practice in that the initiative provides tools that capture "what works" information in a broad range of social policy areas. These tools include the benefit–cost model as well as a "clearinghouse of clearinghouses" that aggregates the program evidence ratings issued by eight national research clearinghouses.[2] Results First also provides training and technical assistance to help its partner governments implement and customize these tools, and policy and communications support to help build knowledge and support for the approach among policymakers in these jurisdictions. As of June 2016, Results First was operating in twenty-two states and seven counties.

Partner Roles

As noted earlier, the primary partners in the New Mexico–Results First collaboration are the state's LFC and the Results First team, who are staff of The Pew Charitable Trusts. The LFC is the New Mexico legislature's nonpartisan fiscal and management arm and has the jurisdiction and capacity to work across all state policy areas. It has a staff of forty persons who perform several roles, including analyzing budget issues, conducting evaluations of state agencies and programs and issuing an annual comprehensive statewide policy analysis report that identifies key issues of legislative concern and recommendations for addressing these issues. The LFC also develops an independent set of budget recommendations that legislators receive in addition to the governor's budget recommendations. The unit has a nationwide reputation for the quality of its work, and it received the 2015 Excellence in Evaluation Award by the National Legislative Program Evaluation Society. LFC staff have a close working relationship with legislators and regularly present their findings and recommendations through reports and presentations in legislative hearings.

Results First is housed within The Pew Charitable Trusts and is staffed by eighteen persons, including a team of state policy associates who manage project activities in partner governments and a technical assistance team that provides training and analytical support to the partner jurisdictions and develops tools that supplement the benefit–cost model. The Results First team also includes research staff who conduct case studies and develop reports and academic publications on key elements of evidence-based policymaking. The Results First team is supported as needed by other Pew units such as communications staff.

Partnership Establishment

Implementing an evidence-based approach to policymaking requires a commitment of time, data and staff with requisite expertise, which are collectively necessary to ensure that the effort will generate high-quality and credible results (Cousins & Leithwood, 1986; Patton, 2008). Further, experience has shown that reform initiatives often fail to achieve their intended objectives due to insufficient meaningful engagement by the entities that are directly and indirectly affected by it (Miller & Oliver, 2015). As a capacity-building initiative, government officials and staff lead the Results First work in their respective jurisdictions to ensure ongoing commitment to evidence-based policymaking. Results First does not require that a state commit a minimum length of time to the partnership because, as with any initiative or project, success with the work is contingent on state partners committing resources (discussed later) to integrate the Results First approach into their budget and policy processes.

To avoid the pitfalls mentioned earlier, Results First and the LFC carried out a due diligence process before entering into the partnership. Results First and the LFC conducted a series of conference calls, webinars and site visits to gauge each other's ability and willingness to commit to the partnership. As with all partner states, Results First sought to ensure that the LFC was willing and able to lead the process by dedicating needed resources to the effort, including staff with requisite data, statistical and fiscal analysis skills to operate the benefit–cost analysis model. It also sought to ensure that these staff had access to the state-specific cost and population data needed to customize the model. The LFC wanted to confirm that Results First was committed to providing training and ongoing consultation to support its implementation of the benefit–cost model and was willing to let the state own the process. Both parties verified that the partnership would have the enduring support of the state's legislative leadership, which they saw as essential for sustaining commitment to engraining the Results First approach into their budget and policy processes.

As it does with other partner states, Results First required the LFC to secure a letter of invitation, signed by the LFC chairman and vice-chairman, approving LFC's participation in the partnership. The letter specifically authorized LFC staff to engage with Results First, develop expertise in the benefit–cost model and regularly work with Results First staff to discuss how to appropriately answer policy questions frequently posed by state officials about the approach—all of which are critical to successfully engaging in evidence-based policymaking.

Partnership Implementation

The formal partnership between Results First and New Mexico began in the fall of 2011. Upon receipt of the letter of invitation from LFC leadership, Results First began regular site visits to the

state to provide training to LFC staff on benefit–cost analysis con-
cepts and develop a detailed plan for implementing and customiz-
ing the benefit–cost model. This plan identified key data elements,
the analytical steps required to obtain and analyze these data, staff
assignments and timeframes for these tasks.

At Results First's suggestion, the LFC decided to begin its work
by implementing the adult criminal justice component of the
benefit–cost model. Most participating jurisdictions begin their
work in this policy area, which is a major expense category in state
budgets. Also, a significant portion of the benefits from investments in areas such as child welfare, substance abuse and mental
health and education are directly related to long-term reductions in
criminal justice offending by service recipients. Early in the planning process, Results First and LFC staff determined that many
of the required data elements for implementing the criminal justice component would need to be obtained from the New Mexico
Sentencing Commission, which analyzes the state's criminal justice
data. Accordingly, Results First and LFC staff met with and secured
the support of the commission's leadership and staff, which had the
effect of extending the partnership to include this organization. The
LFC took responsibility for housing and operating the benefit–cost
model, with the Sentencing Commission agreeing to provide criminal justice system data. The LFC's deputy director for Program
Evaluation was given responsibility to lead the overall implementation effort, with senior staff within the unit working with Sentencing Commission staff to conduct data and fiscal analyses.

It took LFC and Sentencing Commission staff approximately
eight months to implement the criminal justice component of the
benefit–cost model. As part of its standard services to partner states
as they populate and implement the model, Results First staff vis-
ited the state approximately once every six weeks for multiday site
visits and also provided training via webinars as needed. Results
First and LFC staff also held biweekly conference calls to discuss
progress, problem-solve, address technical implementation questions and discuss options for educating key stakeholders about the
partnership. This outreach, common across all Results First partner
states, began early in the process and specifically targeted high-level
officials needed to garner support to initiate the partnership; it
included briefings for legislators and executive branch officials, as
well as formal presentations to legislative committees and the Sentencing Commission.

Upon completion of the criminal justice component of the
benefit–cost model in mid-2012, the LFC began to implement
additional policy area components of the model. This expansion
continued throughout 2013 and 2014, with Results First providing

technical assistance through the same mechanisms discussed earlier. Although the LFC team needed to obtain some information from the state agencies that administered the state's juvenile justice, mental health, substance abuse and education programs to implement these components of the model, it did not form partnerships with these agencies as it had with the Sentencing Commission because these components of the benefit–cost model required substantially less agency-specific data than the criminal justice component. In mid-2014, New Mexico became the first Results First partner state to fully implement all components of the benefit–cost model. LFC's work with the benefit–cost model is ongoing; however, Results First periodically releases updates to the benefit–cost model as new research, programs and policy areas are incorporated into its ongoing development.[3]

Partnership Outcomes

The New Mexico–Results First partnership has enabled state policymakers to use data and evidence much more effectively to inform their policy and management decisions. Significant achievements include enabling the LFC to incorporate sophisticated economic analysis into the policy and evaluation reports that it provides to the legislature and informing legislative decisions to appropriate over $90 million to evidence-based programs that are projected to achieve high returns on the investment of taxpayer dollars. The partnership has also given state agencies new tools to strengthen their program and budget management.

Since 2011, the LFC has incorporated benefit–cost analyses in a series of evaluation reports on state programs and agencies. Two types of analysis are particularly notable. First, the LFC has used the benefit–cost model to calculate the long-term return on investment that the state could achieve through funding alternative evidence-based programs. As shown in Table 5.1, the LFC has generally reported these results using a *Consumer Reports–type* format that enables readers to quickly compare programs by their predicted benefits and costs.

Programs to Improve Education Outcomes

Second, the LFC has used the benefit–cost model to report "the cost of doing nothing"—the long-term fiscal impact of current trends in the state. For example, the LFC calculated that 44.6 percent of released prison inmates commit new offenses and are returned to prison within three years. Using its benefit–cost model, it calculated that each recidivism occurrence costs the state approximately

Table 5.1 Example of New Mexico Consumer Reports–Style Benefit–Cost Analysis Report*

Program	Benefits to Participants	Benefits to Taxpayers	Other Beneficiaries	Other Indirect Benefits	Total Benefits	Costs	Benefits-Costs Net Present Value (NPV)	Benefits/ Costs Ratio	Percent of Time NPV Is Greater Than Zero NPV > 0
Nurse Family Partnerships	$9,974	$9,866	$8,946	$0	$29,789	($2,967)	$25,822	$9.70	89%
Head Start	$11,329	$7,167	$7,186	($3,139)	$22,452	(8,564)	$13,888	$2.62	89%
Parents as Teachers	$2,282	$1,282	$997	$0	$4,561	($2,966)	$1,595	$1.54	68%
Other Home Visiting Programs	$2,210	$1,035	$1,173	$0	$4,561	($2,966)	$1,595	$1.54	68%
Pre-K	$1,618	$690	$801	$0	$3,110	($2,900)	$210	$1.07	48%
Model Early Childhood Programs	$15,143	$10,168	$11,050	$0	$36,361	($34,332)	$2,028	$1.06	53%
4-Star	$1,602	$683	$806	$0	$3,092	($6,532)	(3,441)	$0.47	30%
Early Head Start	($602)	$2,844	$132	$0	$2,375	($12,042)	($9,667)	$0.20	28%
5-Star	($351)	($150)	($172)	$0	($673)	($6,864)	$7,537	($0.10)	6%
Even Start	($572)	($244)	($276)	$0	($1,093)				
3-Star	($973)	($415)	($479)	$0	($1,868)	($6,120)	($7,988)	($0.31)	17%
2-Star	(1,640)	($699)	($812)	$0	($3,151)	(5,269)	(8,420)	($0.60)	3%
Registered Homes	($3,0988)	(1,322)	(11,535)	$0	($2,904)	($5,9955)	($2,904)	($2.06)	0%

* New Mexico Legislative Finance Committee (2014). *Evidence-Based Early Education Programs to Improve Education Outcomes.*

$50,300, including taxpayer costs (to arrest, adjudicate and incarcerate the offender) and societal costs (incurred by the victims of the criminal offenses). The LFC reported that if these trends continue, the offenders released from prison in 2011 will cost the state $360 million over the next 15 years in taxpayer dollars (New Mexico Legislative Finance Committee, 2012), but noted that the state could avoid over $8.3 million in taxpayer costs and over $40 million in societal costs if it were able to reduce the recidivism rate by 10 percent through investments in evidence-based correctional education and treatment programs. The LFC conducted similar analyses of the costs of child maltreatment and high school dropouts in the state and noted that such analyses gained the attention of legislators about the importance of addressing such problems. The LFC issued instructions to its staff to incorporate these and similar benefit–cost findings into their budget analyses and recommendations.

To date, the New Mexico legislature has used these analyses to inform its decisions to appropriate $104.4 million in funding to evidence-based programs that were predicted to generate $410.7 million in long-term returns on investments for state residents. These included funding for early education, criminal justice and behavioral health programs. The LFC has made benefit–cost analysis an ongoing part of its internal processes, which the partnership has attributed to their ongoing success. As noted by LFC's deputy director, "Legislators see our model analyses as part of what the LFC does. It supplements our performance-based budgeting work and is engrained in the LFC work" (Sallee, personal communication, July 24, 2015).

The New Mexico Corrections Department is also using the approach to strengthen its program management and help meet its ambitious recidivism reduction goals. In response to a finding from a 2012 LFC report that 75 percent of the department's institutional corrections programs lacked rigorous evidence of effectiveness, the department's leadership established recidivism reduction as one of its key strategic goals and began working with Results First to gain a better understanding of the programs that it administers and identify alternative programs that will produce better returns on their investment (New Mexico Corrections Department, 2013). This work, led by a new Office of Recidivism and Reduction, includes conducting an in-depth review of its drug treatment and education programs and developing strategies for increasing its use of evidence-based programs. An early outcome of this effort was the finding that the department's primary institutional drug treatment program was ineffectively implemented. Whereas a program that lacks fidelity to its original model is typically reimplemented in this situation, the department decided to replace this program with an alternative evidence-based intervention that was predicted to generate positive long-term benefits.

In 2015, the New Mexico legislature sought to further increase the use of the Results First approach by additional executive branch agencies, but this action proved to be unsuccessful. The legislature passed House Bill 108, which, among other provisions, created a statutory definition of evidence-based programs and mandated that behavioral health programs that met this definition be given priority by executive branch agencies for funding in designated investment zones. Similarly, the legislature passed Senate Bill 297, which amended the state's Accountability in Government Act to define levels of evidence and require agencies, as part of the state's performance-based budgeting procedures, to conduct annual program inventories in order to identify programs' effectiveness and benefit–cost impact and to prioritize evidence-based, research-based and promising programs in agency budget requests. However, the governor vetoed House Bill 108 and the Senate Bill was not voted on. Executive branch officials indicated that although the governor supported the use of evidence-based programs, she opposed other provisions that she found unduly restrictive of executive branch prerogatives.

Following these outcomes, Results First staff met with the Corrections Department secretary to discuss the value of using rigorous evidence to inform budget and policy choices and offered their assistance. The secretary expressed his support for evidence-based policymaking and subsequently directed staff to begin developing a comprehensive inventory of its education and treatment programs. The department also has adopted a new administrative policy (CD-010100) that commits the agency to conducting an annual program inventory and requires that at least 70 percent of its program funds be allocated to evidence-based programs. This demonstrates that flexibility and outreach are important to developing and maintaining long-term partnerships, as is careful consideration of the political environment in which policies are adopted and implemented.

Key Challenges and Midcourse Corrections

Although the New Mexico–Results First partnership has been highly successful, it has encountered challenges since its establishment that have required changes in strategy. These challenges have primarily involved the necessity to extend the partnership to new entities as the scope of the work has expanded over time.

As noted earlier, the partnership was initially established between Results First and the LFC, although it was extended to include the New Mexico Sentencing Commission when it became apparent that the commission's cooperation was essential to obtaining the data and analysis needed to implement the adult criminal justice component of the model. This arrangement was effective in achieving successful implementation of the benefit–cost model and helping policymakers identify opportunities for cost-effective investments; however, early impact was limited to legislative decision-making as the key executive stakeholder—the New Mexico Corrections Department—was not equally involved. This lack of involvement spurred tensions between the department's leadership and the LFC, due in part to differences between the legislative and executive branches over budget policy and department concerns that it had not been adequately consulted before the LFC began issuing reports that were highly critical of its intervention programs. These tensions made the department wary of the partnership's purpose and hesitant to support the initiative and continue responding to LFC requests for data. It also became apparent that executive branch support was critical to Results First's success because the New Mexico legislature appropriates funding in lump sums, rather than through detailed program-level line items, and state agencies have substantial discretion when allocating funding to treatment interventions. Thus, without the executive branch's collaboration, the state legislature had little assurance that the funds appropriated for evidence-based criminal justice treatment interventions would, in fact, be spent on such programs.

This recognition led to a change in strategy for the partnership beginning in 2014. Results First's lead staff in the state (Holand, personal communication, August 5, 2015) said

> As a change agent, we should have communicated more regularly and acted more collaboratively with other branches from the beginning. Because we had worked with the legislature for so long, we have had to work harder at building trust with the executive branch.

Accordingly, Results First and the New Mexico Sentencing Commission increased outreach to the department's leadership to build trust and engage them in the partnership. This included multiple meetings with the department's senior staff and inviting these officials to the project's annual convening of participating Results First states. This outreach culminated in establishing a memorandum of understanding (MOU) in 2014 between the LFC, the Sentencing

Commission and the department that set forth the purpose of the partnership and responsibilities of each party, as well as the roles and responsibilities of Results First staff (see Appendix I). After this MOU was established, Results First began to work directly with department staff to help them compile a comprehensive inventory of the treatment and education programs operated by the department's institutions and assess the level of evidence that existed regarding each program's effectiveness. These steps expanded the New Mexico–Results First partnership to include the Corrections Department, and Results First is planning to further extend the partnership to other executive branch agencies that will begin similar inventory and assessment tasks in the future.

The Sentencing Commission has also worked to broaden awareness and support for the New Mexico–Results First partnership among other criminal justice stakeholders in the state. The Sentencing Commission is well positioned to do so as its membership includes a wide variety of important stakeholders, including representatives of the judiciary, prosecutors, public defenders and law enforcement agencies. The commission has held several hearings on the Results First approach, and its staff frequently discuss the partnership with representatives from its member agencies, resulting in stronger support for the effort and evidence-based policymaking in the state. As a Results First staff noted,

> There is no one entity in a state that makes unilateral decisions about the direction of criminal justice policy. In our role as a change agent, our relationship with New Mexico has become more meaningful as it has grown from working with just one branch to groups of stakeholders across the branches with different perspectives, roles, and authority to develop, execute, and uphold policy.
> (Holand, personal communication, August 5, 2015)

To reflect this lesson learned, Results First has changed its overall procedures for working with government partners. Before beginning to work in new partner states, Results First now contracts with government relations firms to provide strategic assessments of state's political landscape, and it frequently uses in-state firms to help manage relationships with key stakeholders. Results First also now seeks letters of commitment from the leadership of both the executive and legislative branches before accepting new states into the initiative.

The LFC and the Results First project team recognize the need to educate and obtain support from a wide range of internal and external entities that are involved in New Mexico's political process. Essentially, Results First's goal is to help states transform their operations by adopting an evidence-based policymaking approach, which requires changes to budgeting and policy systems that are generally recognized as being highly incremental (Lindblom & Cohen, 1979; Rosenbloom, Kravchuk, & Clerkin, 2009; Ryu, 2011; Wildavsky & Caiden, 2004). To support this shift in New Mexico, the LFC and Results First have begun working to generate public interest and support for evidence-based policymaking and the Results First approach through outreach to the media and the business community. These efforts have been successful and have resulted in the Albuquerque Chamber of Commerce sending a letter of support to the governor and several media stories that have discussed the New Mexico–Results First partnership.

Lessons Learned

The successes achieved and challenges encountered by the New Mexico–Results First partnership have generated key lessons that can be used by other entities seeking to establish ongoing knowledge utilization partnerships. These include the following: 1) it is important to secure broad policymaker buy-in at the beginning of a partnership and to maintain and strengthen this support over time; 2) partnerships should develop and implement an outreach and communications strategy throughout the life of the initiative that includes all relevant stakeholders and practitioners; 3) partnerships should develop agreements governing the access and use of data; 4) all partners should recognize that partnership initiatives such as building an evidence-based policymaking culture take time; 5) partnerships should identify and use policy levers to institutionalize partnership outcomes, such as evidence-based policymaking; and 6) partnerships should consider all elements of the policy process.

Secure and Build Broad Policymaker Support from the Beginning

For a knowledge utilization partnership to achieve and maintain long-term success, the parties implementing the process need to secure buy-in from a broad range of stakeholders from the beginning of the effort and take steps to maintain and build policymaker support over time (Bansal, Bertels, Ewart, MacConnachie, & O'Brien, 2012). The New Mexico–Results First partnership initially focused its efforts only on gaining policymaker support from the state legislature, primarily through the LFC. Although this focus was successful in enabling the legislature to direct $104.4 million in funding to programs that were predicted to generate substantial returns on investment, it became evident that this limited scope of engagement hindered the partnership's ability to embed evidence-based policy-making into the state's decision-making processes. This was particularly important, as state agencies have substantial discretion in allocating funding to individual programs.

For this reason, Results First has revised its partnership-building strategy to incorporate political assessments of potential partner states. These assessments, which are connected by lobbying firms within each state and typically take four to six weeks to conduct, use a series of state-specific questions developed by Pew staff to analyze the political landscape of the state, including appraisals of its political climate, key potential champions and power brokers across policy areas, and the likelihood of success in achieving meaningful budget impacts using the Results First approach. Results First staff use the assessment to develop a comprehensive engagement strategy for both the executive and legislative branches of the state, identify key stakeholders and specify outreach steps needed to build buy-in and support among these persons. Results First also now requires signed letters of commitment from the leadership of both branches before entering into a partnership with a state. Although this assessment process takes more time, Results First staff have found that it generates substantial benefits, including a more comprehensive understanding of a state's political landscape and enhanced multi-branch commitments to the process, resulting in partnerships that are more collaborative and more successful in achieving implementation of the benefit–cost model and use of the results to inform budget decisions that produce meaningful long-term impact.

To build ongoing support from key stakeholders, Results First has also revised its strategy to form two coordinating bodies in partner states: a technical workgroup and a policy workgroup. The technical workgroup includes program, fiscal and data analysts who are responsible for collecting and analyzing the information needed to implement the benefit–cost model and generating reports that present the results of these analyses. The policy workgroup includes executive and legislative branch officials who are responsible for guiding the work of the technical group, identifying key policy questions for analysis and serving as champions promoting use of the results to inform policy and budget decisions. The policy workgroup typically consists of high-level government officials and agency staff who work to provide services to the public and sometimes participate in technical workgroups to facilitate data collection and analysis. Given the unique structural and political dynamics of each state, Results First encourages multistakeholder workgroups, but leaves it up to states to decide who should participate in each.

The two workgroups help build understanding and support in using rigorous evidence to inform policy and budget decisions among a broad set of stakeholders. The workgroups also help set clearly defined roles and responsibilities for the partnership, which is critical to the parties understanding each other's intent and expectations (Pew-MacArthur Results First Initiative, 2014a). These workgroups also reflect Results First's goal of building state ownership of the process, which is critical to the partnership's success. As noted by Results First's lead staff in New Mexico,

> [The state] has to have the leading role in promoting the use of evidence—the underlying mechanism for this change being the flow of money—and using analysis results to inform budget and policy decisions. We support the state's use of our tools, but their choices are their own.
>
> (Holand, personal communication, August 5, 2015)

Develop and Implement an Ongoing Outreach and Communications Strategy

A key step in attaining the buy-in necessary for a successful research–practitioner partnership is creating and carrying out a comprehensive outreach and communications strategy that includes all relevant stakeholders and practitioners. Given the incremental nature of public budget processes, it is essential to educate a broad range of stakeholders and practitioners about the benefits of using rigorous evidence to inform policy and budget decisions in order to overcome this inertia. Accordingly, the New Mexico–Results First partnership has developed and implemented an ongoing communication plan, which includes outreach to key legislators and committees, executive branch officials, the business community, advocacy groups and the media.

The partnership has also learned that it is important to frame the initiative as a means to improve policy outcomes rather than to point fingers for poor outcomes. As noted by Results First's lead staff,

> It's easy to read the results of benefit-cost analysis as "the agency has been making bad choices for years and is wasting taxpayer money." Shifting the focus away from the past and toward the future allows change to be a collaborative process between the legislature and agencies, and that's the communication strategy we aim to develop.
>
> (Holand, personal communication, August 5, 2015)

Develop Agreements Governing Access and Use of Data

Another critical aspect of successful researcher–practitioner partnerships is securing agreements on data access and use. Getting multiple entities to collaborate in producing and using evidence and evaluation findings can be challenging, particularly when these stakeholders have limited proficiency in using data, limited trust and concerns about potential repercussions that could arise if the data show that programs are not working (Sutcliffe & Court, 2006). The New Mexico Corrections Department's negative reaction to the LFC's reports on its programs and its subsequent reluctance to provide data illustrate the importance of this issue.

To address this concern, partnerships should develop formal agreements at the beginning of their collaboration. These agreements should specify the goals of the partnership, the data to be shared, the analyses to be undertaken, the timeframe for these tasks and the roles and responsibilities of each partner. The agreements should also specify how analysis results will be shared and the level of feedback each entity will be able to provide before reports are produced for outside audiences. These agreements, once established, can be critical to securing agency commitment to providing needed data and support for the overall effort. Results First now discusses the use of agency data as part of their partnership-building strategy with all participating states.

Recognize that Building Partnership Initiatives Takes Time

The New Mexico–Results First partnership has learned that government innovations such as Results First often take several years before they become standard practice. This is particularly true with innovations such as evidence-based policymaking, which must not only gain the support of policymakers, but also overcome the political and ideological considerations, constituent needs and timing constraints that can trump evidence in policy and budget choices (Bardach, 2003; Bogenschneider & Corbett, 2010; Garri, 2007; Jennings & Hall, 2012; Kothari, MacLean, & Edwards, 2009; Patton, 2008; Pew-MacArthur Results First Initiative, 2013; Rogoff, 1990).

The New Mexico–Results First partnership has been in place for four years, but continues to work to address these challenges and build an evidence-based policymaking culture in the state. The partnership has identified two elements that are essential to supporting this change: 1) developing a shared long-term commitment to the initiative; and 2) maintaining ongoing communication with a broad range of stakeholders and ensuring that the evidence provided to policymakers is clear, relevant and timely.

First, developing a shared long-term commitment to a research–practitioner partnership is essential to making the use of research a part of standard practice (Nutley, Walter, & Davies, 2003). As noted earlier, one of the advantages that the Results First partnership has enjoyed in New Mexico is that the LFC had already made a commitment to using evidence to improve state outcomes, and it has viewed Results First as a complementary effort to its existing activities. This has made it easier to sustain legislative support for ongoing expansion of the partnership's work into new policy areas. When speaking to policymakers about the Results First approach, LFC staff describe it as a complementary tool that can help support existing statewide efforts, such as performance-based budgeting, which also focus on improving how the state does business and invests its tax dollars. As the LFC deputy director stated, "We have found that steering the discussion around helping policymakers make better decisions is more effective than talking about benefit-cost analysis" (Sallee, personal communication, July 24, 2015). Results First in turn has made a long-term commitment to assisting New Mexico in its ongoing work, in part because the state serves as an exemplar to other jurisdictions that are considering joining the initiative. Both LFC and Results First are now working to gain similar long-term support among the state's executive branch agencies.

Second, maintaining ongoing communication with policymakers is critical to gaining long-term support for a research–practitioner partnership (Bryson, Crosby, & Stone, 2015; Koschmann, Kuhn, & Pfarrer, 2012). This includes providing regular briefings to key stakeholders such as legislators and agency directors to build their understanding and interest in using evidence and ensuring that the evidence delivered is clear, relevant and timely (Innvaer, Vist, Trommald, & Oxman, 2002; Institute of Education Sciences, 2011; Nutley et al., 2003). This is particularly important given the partnership's goal of improving budget and policy decisions. State policymaking operates in highly compressed time periods, so analysis results need to be available when key decisions are being made (Bardach, 2003; Bogenschneider & Corbett, 2010; Kothari et al., 2009; Patton, 2008). This information also needs to be provided in user-friendly formats, such as the *Consumer Reports–style* tables, to enable policymakers to quickly understand the information (Bogenschneider & Corbett, 2010).

Identify and Use Policy Levers to Institutionalize Partnership Outcomes

Maintaining policymaker attention and support for any initiative can be difficult given the distractions inherent in the political process (Kingdon, 1995). Also, for change initiatives like Results First, the incremental nature of the budget system can make it difficult to ensure that partnership efforts have a lasting impact on how limited tax dollars are allocated.

To address these challenges, Results First has worked with its partner states to identify policy levers that can help their governments institutionalize Results First and evidence-based policymaking without active ongoing policymaker involvement (Pew-MacArthur Results First Initiative, 2015). These include establishing formal definitions of evidence of program effectiveness, enacted in law in some Results First partner states, to create a common vocabulary and understanding among stakeholders. These definitions typically recognize several tiers of evidence, ranging from randomized control trial results to rigorous comparison group studies to outcome data. Some states have also taken an additional step and have mandated that agencies give funding preference to evidence-based programs shown effective through randomized control trials (for example, Washington Juvenile Offender Sentencing Standards Rev. Code Wash. [ARCW] § 13.40.0357). Similarly, some states have passed laws or issued budget guidelines that require state agencies to report inventories of their currently funded programs, which are then analyzed to determine the level of evidence that exists of each program's effectiveness (Mississippi Performance Budget and Strategic Planning Act of, 1994).

Such mechanisms can be effective in creating ongoing systems that institutionalize the Results First approach, and similar efforts may be effective for other researcher–practitioner partnerships. But, as learned in New Mexico, it is critical to obtain broad stakeholder buy-in (in New Mexico's case, from both the legislature and governor) to make such policy levers successful in engraining the initiative into the state's culture.

Consider All Elements of the Policy Process

Finally, it is important to consider the full implications of the goals sought by partnership initiatives. For the New Mexico–Results First partners, it has become clear that getting policymakers to allocate funding to evidence-based programs is only one of many steps that are needed to achieve the desired improved outcomes for state residents (Pew-MacArthur Results First Initiative, 2014b). State agencies are reporting difficulty in scaling up evidence-based programs, and these interventions will not achieve desired outcomes unless they are well managed and implemented with fidelity to their designs. It will also be important for the state to regularly measure and report on program outcomes and to use monitoring data to support program improvements. Results First and the LFC are currently discussing steps that could be taken to address these challenges, which may include bringing in additional partners with expertise in these areas. Researcher–practitioner partnerships need to carefully assess all the actions that will be needed to achieve their goals, recognizing that this will be a dynamic process and strategies may need to change over time.

Conclusion

The New Mexico–Results First partnership has shown that it is possible to establish effective long-term researcher–practitioner partnerships and for such partnerships to achieve significant outcomes. However, such partnerships are likely to experience multiple challenges that will require strategy changes over time. Several lessons can be learned from the New Mexico–Results First partnership that may be useful to other partnership initiatives. Specifically, partnerships should secure broad policymaker buy-in at the beginning of an initiative and work to maintain and strengthen this support over time; develop and implement a robust outreach and communications strategy to secure the support of key stakeholders over the duration of the initiative; develop agreements among key participants governing the access and use of data; recognize that it will take time to achieve partnership goals, particularly major outcomes such as establishing a culture of evidence-based policy-making; identify and implement policy levers that institutionalize activities critical to achieving partnership goals; and consider all elements of the governmental processes that must be addressed in order to achieve partnership goals.

The Results First partnership is highly methodical both in terms of its overall approach and with regard to the specifics of implementation. Particularly strategic about Results First is the extent to which it addresses a current, known policy problem while simultaneously helping to build the policy partner's capacity to use research. As the case describes, the desire to use research for making policy decisions has led to capacity building in other agencies and policy areas in the New Mexico capitol and beyond. With regard to the specifics of implementation, the partnership included careful planning, a deliberate due diligence phase, and formal letters from state leadership delineating the partners' commitments. The partnership reminds us of the two cases featured in Chapter 3. Both of those cases likewise involved key players co-developing a partnership that was mindful of potential challenges and took initiative to address them.

Given how intentional and deliberate Results First has been in New Mexico and its other partnership states, it is all the more interesting that the New Mexico partnership came about by chance. As the case describes, the catalyst for the partnership was a conference at which staff of the New Mexico LFC heard a Results First presentation. This fortunate and serendipitous circumstance drives home the importance of creating opportunities for researchers and policymakers simply to "be in the same room." These opportunities are increasing but still are not nearly frequent enough, especially given the potential they have to spur partnerships such as that of Results First and New Mexico.

Results First illustrates not only the possibilities for how researchers and policymakers can partner with the goal of research use in specific policy areas, but also how a policymaking entity can develop skills that position it to use research for the long term on a wide range of topics. The Results First model has contributed to skills development and to the adoption of project management approaches that reach beyond the focus of the initial partnership. Moreover, by being able to point to a connection between what the research shows and budget implications, the partnership builds into its model a recognition of policymakers' constant need to focus on funding.

Finally, the Results First partnership openly points out tensions and challenges that surfaced in the early phase of the partnership and the ensuing corrections and strategy change. Being willing to highlight and address challenges are themselves attributes of successful partnerships. Many cases in this book share those positive characteristics, serving as a reminder that success and impact are not proxies for perfection.

In this spirit, we find it worthwhile to highlight three of the six lessons articulated in the Results First case. First is the decision to consistently involve the expertise of government relations firms before embarking on a partnership. The role of the firm is to educate Results First about the state's political landscape, which can provide critical insight in advance of launching a partnership and once it is underway. Second is that the partnership included communications and outreach components. That Results First and New Mexico recognized the value of making these formal components is consistent with how many of the cases throughout the book recognize communication as a tenet of partnership success. Third is the lesson to consider all elements of the policy process. This may seem automatic given that policymakers are part of the partnership; however, it underscores the complexities of policymaking and the array and diversity of stakeholders that may be involved in any policymaking process.

Each of the six lessons is valuable; however, we believe that these three set the partnership apart from many others. Our observations suggest that they represent areas that researcher and policymaker partners are often not aware of and therefore are not equipped to incorporate for a partnership's benefit. Moreover, the three lessons are noticeably absent in the literature on researcher–policymaker partnerships.

As is true across the cases in this book, the two in this chapter have similarities as well as important differences. That the cases overlap in some ways and differ significantly in others is useful for illustrating that research utilization can stem from multiple types of conditions involving researchers and policymakers. The second case in this chapter is that of Minnesota's legislative bipartisan Early Childhood Caucus. In contrast to the intentionality and structured approach of the New Mexico partnership, the Minnesota Early Childhood Caucus partnership, although also successful, evolved less formally and more organically.

Minnesota's Legislative Bipartisan Early Childhood Caucus

Karen Cadigan, PhD; Mary Nienow, MSW; and the Honorable Nora Slawik

Introduction

This is the story of Minnesota's legislative bipartisan Early Childhood Caucus (ECC), which was active from 2003–2010, and the role that the University of Minnesota played in its formation. In this partnership, the intent was initially to support the supply side of evidence- based policymaking by connecting policymakers to the sciences about early childhood. That is, to facilitate getting research that already existed to policymakers who were making decisions about access to, quality of and funding for parent education, child care, Head Start and public and private preschool. As it turned out, the university role also played a large part in supporting the demand side of supplying evidence by creating structures, events and social reinforcers for legislators to acquire, interpret and use evidence. In contemporary understanding of the role of connecting research and policy, this demand side is less understood and written about, making this a particularly unique case study. The story of the ECC includes supply and demand, research and researchers, policy and policymakers, advocates and funders, community forums and constituents, politics, an election and a life-size fiberglass cow.

The lessons called out here may be especially useful to researchers who want to infuse science into policymaking. These learnings are informed by and reflect Tseng's and others' (e.g., Nutley, Walter, & Davies, 2007; Tseng, 2013) descriptions of the supply and demands for evidence in policy contexts, Kingdon's policy windows (1995), Bogenschneider and Corbett's (2010) community dissonance theory and Finnigan and Daly's (2014) descriptions of research use in social networks, including the critical role of trust.

Supply and Demand in State Policymaking

States, the "laboratories of democracy," as Justice Louis Brandeis once described them (New State Ice Co. v. Liebmann, 1932), are especially important points of focus because state policies affect and are affected by local and federal policies. In this way, state policy spans and connects the broadest and narrowest of policy spheres; state policies act as an intermediary between both local and federal action.

In the state context, as in other policymaking spheres, the focus on connecting research with policy is often about how to improve the supply of research, making it more consumable (e.g., policy briefs), relevant (e.g., focused on a particular local issues) and timely (e.g., being responsive to policymakers requests). Tseng (2013, p. 3) has posited that "the hope for evidence-based policy and practice will unravel—another fad tried and failed" without scientists and scholars gaining a better understanding not only of how to supply research, but also illuminating how the demand side works. Simply put, the supply side comes from those who produce or package research and the demand side comes from those who use it in decision-making.

The study of evidence-based policy has more work to fully understand the demand side of research-informed policy, but we know it has to do with social networks and relationships. We also know that these networks and relationships of policymakers are in a context that is very different from that in which researchers live and work. The decades-old two-communities theory (Caplan, 1979) initially highlighted these different worlds between knowledge producers and knowledge users and noted the divide as a barrier to research utilization. The two-communities theory was expanded to note differences not only between the cultures of policymakers and researchers but practitioners as well (e.g., Shonkoff, 2000). This paradigm has been expanded on further as the community dissonance theory (Bogenschneider et al., 2013). Whereas Caplan and others note that differences among policymakers and researchers are based on structural (e.g., hard to change) factors of the institutions and professions in which they work, the community dissonance theory attributes human behavioral factors to at least some of the reason for the underutilization of research in policy. The good news about people's behavioral factors affecting research use is that changing conditions can in turn change human behavior, potentially creating pathways to strengthen evidence-based policymaking. The Early Childhood Caucus structure and branding from the outset was sensitive to the realities of the policymaking community and approached the task of connecting research and policy as one of being of service and value to legislators *without any particular legislative outcome in mind.*

An example of the cultural difference between the communities of researchers and policymakers is that researchers can and are expected to take time in decision-making to be methodical and accurate. Legislators, however, are pressed for time and have to make policymaking decisions very fast, using shortcuts about what information they use and what information they believe. This is a reality for decision-making bounded by the realities of time and workload and leads to relying on those they trust—their own party, already known colleagues, lobbyists or advocates who represent positions with which they already feel comfortable. Likewise, they use heuristics, shortcuts of a type, about what they do not believe, or information they do not trust that is also based on people who are, or are perceived to be, "on the other side." Knowing this, the Early Childhood Caucus structure and staffing were highly sensitive to actually being and being perceived as trustworthy by both Democrats and Republicans, which will be described next.

University Avenue: Connecting State Policy to a Public Land Grant University

> *"Connecting Research to Practice Should Be More of a Two-Way Street than is Implied in Research-to-Practice Approaches."*
>
> Tseng (2013, p. 5)

University Avenue is a four-lane corridor that stretches from the Minnesota state capitol, in St. Paul (the smaller of the Twin Cities) less than ten miles to the campus of the University of Minnesota in Minneapolis. This span of road includes new and old urban eateries, student housing, office buildings, most recently a light rail line and is, in fact, a two-way street.

On the demand side of University Avenue sits Minnesota's state legislature. Like most state legislative bodies it is part-time, with the 201 members of the Senate and House in session from January to May during budget-setting years, and typically February to May in the alternate, nonbudget years. When the Early Childhood Caucus was conceived in 2003, Minnesota's state government was divided.

The governor and House of Representatives were both Republican controlled, and the Senate majority was the Democrat Farmer Labor party, as it had been for the previous thirty years. There was not much demand, especially bipartisan demand, for research on early childhood education.

On the supply side just down the road from the capitol is the University of Minnesota. "The U" was founded in 1851, seven years before Minnesota was even admitted to the Union. It is one of United States' public land grant universities, supported partly by land donated from the federal government. Public land grant universities have a special role in expanding higher education beyond the privileged few, educating many people to be productive citizens and members of the workforce. When President Lincoln proclaimed the land grant system by signing the Morrill Act in 1862, he stated, "The land-grant university system is being built on behalf of the people, who have invested in these public universities their hopes, their support, and their confidence" (Morrill Act, 1862).

The U has one of the country's top-ranked graduate programs in child development, is a Research 1 University and has one of the nation's oldest research–to–policy and practice centers in the Center for Early Education and Development (CEED), founded in 1968. Some of the best-known theories, practices and assessments in child development, teaching and learning come from these grounds, these minds. There is no shortage of supply for research at this end of University Avenue.

If any community could connect state policy to contemporary research on early childhood, the Twin Cities should be it. After all, both of these institutions and their people are charged with making the world a better place. People and ideas could easily travel in straight lines along this University Avenue route to ask and answer questions. How hard could it be?

How It Began: A Policy Window and an Unexpected Messenger

In 2003, the seventh branch of the Federal Reserve Bank, itself just blocks off University Avenue in Minneapolis, released a paper on the economic value of educating at-risk young children (Rolnick & Grunewald, 2003). This economic frame was different from the long-used moral arguments on the importance of quality early childhood experiences for those who could not afford to pay out of pocket. Importantly, the paper's lead author was Dr. Art Rolnick, then the Fed's research director and an expert of Civil War–era banking practices. He was not a known messenger nor by any means an advocate for public investment into child care and preschool for the poor. His lack of special interest affiliation made all the difference in getting a broader group of decision-makers, including the business community, interested in early education as an economic development issue.

Dr. Rolnick said of his intent on the paper's impact:

> We were interested in what was already out there on early education but to look at it through a different lens. We figured there'd be a good return but we were surprised, frankly, at how high it was. Then, I was done. I figured I'd go back to what I was doing. It wasn't like I had an agenda per se and I had no intention of getting into the policy space.
>
> (Rolnick, personal communication, 2016)

In our experience, Dr. Rolnick's perspective is common. Researchers do not consider or factor in possibilities for "getting" their work "into" the policy space. In discussions with colleagues, we have learned that some want to engage in the policy realm but simply do not know how as it was not part of their training or what they were subsequently hired to do.

Yet seemingly resulting from just one piece of research, suddenly early childhood was being talked about in circles beyond the usual suspects. Existing advocates and supportive policymakers grabbed tight to this "new" research, showing that for every dollar invested in high-dosage, quality early childhood programs for low-income children the public could stand to see an $8 benefit. This attention opened a policy window that had not previously existed, first in Minnesota and later throughout the country (Cadigan, 2013). The Federal Reserve research showed how early education investments yield a return that far exceeds the return on most public projects that are considered economic development and captured the attention of all four caucuses: House and Senate, Democrats and Republicans.

A Legislative Vehicle

As a result of the Federal Reserve paper, more conversations by a broader group of public and thought leaders were taking place on the role and importance of early childhood development. However, there was no early childhood committee in either legislative body. Representative Nora Slawik was the initial brain child of the idea of an Early Childhood Caucus, having read about the Illinois bipartisan women's caucus and how they voted together on bills at times, thus lending legislative influence beyond the current structures of party or legislative body. Ideally the Early Childhood Caucus could develop into a group with the outcome of voting together. In fact one of the ECC leaders' retreats did result in a bipartisan group of legislators agreeing to support an early childhood Quality Rating and Improvement System.

Some held the view that a caucus would be a way to organize a group of legislators who were interested in early childhood without having to wait for legislative leadership (Republicans at the time) to deem it committee worthy. A legislative structure was particularly important because many factors influence a legislator's opinion, including political parties, staff, advocacy groups and constituents. An especially important influence is peers—other legislators who are needed for votes to pass bills and create momentum around issues. Although legislators are great multitaskers, they do not have time to attend all meetings, read all bills, sit in on testimony and absorb all relevant background information on issues such as early childhood financing. To inform themselves about what to decide and how to vote, legislators trust and rely on the opinions of their colleagues.

And so the Minnesota bipartisan legislative Early Childhood Caucus was formed in 2003 by representatives Nora Slawik (D) and Jim Rhodes (R) and senators Claire Robling (R) and Becky Lourey (D). The purpose of the caucus was to shape policies that affect Minnesota's youngest children, their families and caregivers. The caucus did this by educating legislators, creating dialogue, building consensus and providing direction for legislative action. The caucus was open to all members of the Minnesota legislature and grew increasingly in numbers over the years it existed.

Staffing and Structure

In the beginning there was no budget for nonpartisan staffing, making the first step of creating the Early Childhood Caucus attaining resources for organization and administration. The advocacy group Ready4K was supportive of the Early Childhood Caucus idea, but legislators thought the best staffing model would be to employ an honest broker, someone not clearly identified with an advocacy body or affiliated with a particular political party. Ready4K was an important group, and the executive director Todd Otis helped recruit the leaders for the first Early Childhood Caucus. However, there is the perception by legislators that advocacy groups are paid to influence members, and they do not necessarily hold the credibility of an academic institution with an unbiased view. In addition, the mission of the ECC and its staff along the way was to inform legislators. The mission of Ready4K was specifically to shape *policy* in the ways its board determined, and, as is typical in advocacy groups, informing legislators was part of the overall goal, not the end goal. This difference is an important one as it puts legislators as the clients to be served or as the players to be influenced. Both are legitimate perspectives, but for the nonpartisan trust building, it was critical for legislators to trust that the group's purpose was really to support them in making decisions, rather than tell them what to think or how to vote.

Legislators reached out to the Center for Early Education and Development (CEED) at the University of Minnesota where a graduate program in early childhood and public policy was under development. That program's director, Dr. Scott McConnell, had a graduate student (the first author) looking for a policy internship, and so the ECC staffing model was born. An unpaid intern who worked for university credits with direct connections to the research world would travel University Avenue in both directions, learning about the research interests and decision-making needs of legislators at the capitol and bring back relevant information from the vast supply at the U. One legislator reports that

> It was important to have the University staff involved because they brought disciplined research practice into the legislative arena. As academics, they shared the research and informed knowledge of early education through the lens of federal and state policy affecting young children. This included sharing historical, legal, economic and political context that led to key policy decisions.
>
> In particular, researchers shared three prominent studies of early education with the legislators, including those from the Perry Preschool in Michigan, the Abecedarian Project in North Carolina and the Chicago Child-Parent Centers that demonstrated that a high quality early learning program targeted to help children from disadvantaged environments can help children make gains, with benefits extending well into adulthood. Benefits include lower social costs, such as lower crime costs; and high school achievement, educational attainment and earnings.

This student staffing model stuck for the first few years, and giving legislators access to graduate student interns from the University of Minnesota allowed for a relationship "hinge," a direct link between the demand for, and supply of, evidence to inform policy between the policymakers and research on early development. This model of a nonpartisan outsider worked so well that after a few years, local funders, including The Sheltering Arms Foundation and the Greater Twin Cities United Way, came together to support a paid nonpartisan staff position for the ECC. The funders provided resources, but the ECC co-chairs were involved in hiring the staff person and opted for a consultant named Lisa Venable who had particular consulting experience in conflict resolution and bringing individuals toward common ground.

Four co-chairs from each political party caucus, one Senate Democrat, one Senate Republican, one House Republican and one House Democrat, always led the ECC. These leaders were initially informally chosen by the first co-chairs and later were appointed each session by the respective caucus leadership. Having equity in representation across political parties and legislative bodies added a critical structural value and took significant staff time for wrangling schedules and priorities of the four co-leaders. Getting each of the four caucus leaders to pay enough attention to decide on this soft appointment sometimes took much time, but again the focus was on being of service to the legislators as a group and on being absolutely bipartisan. It was necessary for the ECC staff to spend time emailing, phone calling and waiting outside offices and floor sessions to connect with legislative leadership.

The difference between a committee and a caucus was important here. Committees are formal, open to the public and recorded. Leadership positions in committees are appointed by the party in the majority, and political grandstanding has been known to occur. A caucus is less formal, does not have to be open to the public and stakes are not as high because bills are not being presented and passed. In a caucus, legislators may be able to relate to each other better out of the public eye, to ask questions and to be freer to brainstorm. Many legislators commented about how the "gift ban" had affected their ability to connect across bodies and parties in an informal setting. That is to say that because advocacy groups and the like could not host or sponsor buffet dinners on site for legislators anymore, members had lost an important social time when they would gather informally. One moment highlighting the camaraderie of the caucus came after a research presentation on the impact maternal education levels have on child outcomes. A senate Republican and Democrat discussed and agreed a stronger focus on education, rather than work requirements, was needed for women welfare recipients with young children.

Building a Brand, Building Demand

In its first years, the ECC work was to build a brand that was seen as truly bipartisan and to provide meaningful information and connections to legislators so the caucus was relevant to their work.

The membership at the end of the first year was twenty-two, with a carefully attended to and balanced group of eleven Democrats and eleven Republicans. By the end of its arc in 2008, the ECC membership roster was at 107, more than half of the legislators had signed on as members and many used that label in their campaign and office literature. Whenever someone signed on, the ECC staff would work to recruit a member from the opposite party, and the legislative co-chairs asked for party members in both bodies they thought would be interested. A logo depicting children and a capitol building was developed, the membership list was shared broadly and the group began to become known as an entity.

That first year, the caucus hosted the kickoff of what became an annual early childhood read-a-thon in the capitol rotunda. This is a good example of how the staffing time was used not just to share research but to create conditions where legislators would ask for or at least be open to research. Significant time went into these read-a-thon events that in and of themselves did not provide research but did get legislators interested in early childhood and the ECC and reinforced their participation and interest. It took someone to organize schedules, line up groups of children, schedule legislators to read, get community partners, solicit book donations and set the capitol rotunda up with a rocking chair, reading lamp and carpet squares and get press to attend. The first event brought in hundreds of local preschoolers, was co-hosted by the Minnesota Library Association, the Minnesota Children's Museum (complete with Clifford the big, red dog) and included book donations from a local publisher. There were more legislators who wanted a time to read to preschoolers than there were slots, and the caucus members got first dibs for this great activity and photo op. This signature event helped get word out about the caucus to both the community and to legislators so that constituents could ask their elected officials, "Are you part of the Early Childhood Caucus?" By the end of that first legislative session ECC membership had gone from twenty-two to seventy legislators.

Connecting, Convening and Constituents

During the 2003 and 2004 legislative sessions, the caucus held informational meetings for members with speakers presenting a variety of viewpoints on public policy and the role of early childhood. These topics of interest were generated by a survey of the members themselves. Rather than ad hoc providing information and speakers by what was available on the supply side, the ECC staff conducted interviews and surveyed legislators to learn about the demand side from them. This is an essential point. Legislators themselves directed the topics. Researchers did not decide what was important and then try to push in information. These speakers were also approved by the bipartisan four co-chairs. These approved speakers included university-based researchers, state-level program directors and the occasional national speaker (Jack Shonkoff, author of the then newly published *From Neurons to Neighborhoods*, and Pete Churchwell, CEO of the Public Service Company of Oklahoma and leader of the business community that led the charge for universal pre-K in that state). For every year thereafter, the topics discussed were based on legislator survey data. This was conducted by a paper survey sent out from the ECC chairs to the members. ECC staff followed up and prompted and prodded to get responses. ECC staff continuously reminded legislators that these ideas came from their peers, not from outside groups. Meetings were held in committee rooms in the evening so that they were convenient to legislators. Pizza was ordered and brought in as a further attraction, and legislators pitched in to pay for it so as not to even look like there was violation of the gift ban.

During the 2004 session, there was conversation with the early childhood practice and advocacy community about the ECC legislators holding community forums around the state that would highlight some interesting cross-sector early childhood programming and allow legislators to be in contact with their constituents on their own turf on early education issues. The Sheltering Arms Foundation, a local foundation, provided a $5,000 grant to the advocacy group Ready4K, who in turn contracted with the ECC graduate student to organize these forums. For ease of administration, however, these funds went through an advocacy group, and Ready4K's staff helped significantly with turnout and local organizing. The bipartisan leaders and nonpartisan ECC staff person were at the front of the decisions and events and planned forums for thirteen communities across Minnesota from August to October. This was also election season as the Minnesota House was up for re-election in November that year. There was conversation among interested parties—community leaders, advocates, legislators, program directors, university staff—about the pros and cons of having bipartisan events during election season. Finally, at one roundtable meeting where it looked like the idea might be scrapped altogether because some organizers were concerned that issue forums could turn to political grandstanding, former Minnesota congressman and Minneapolis mayor Don Fraser added his succinct contribution to the hour-long discussion: "It's my view that getting people together to talk about issues is always a good idea" (Cadigan, Karen. Summer

2003. Notes taken at the public meeting of Ready4K, St. Paul, MN). Within weeks the first community forum took place.

The structure of the bipartisan community forums included having one sitting member from each party on the panel (what we started calling the Noah's ark model, two by two) so there was always at least one Democrat and one Republican. There were always as many local legislators on the panel as possible, and an influential but not overtly partisan local citizen moderated. Holding to the two-party representation for legislators proved challenging in districts where all of the elected officials were members of one political party or the other. In those cases, the ECC staff, with support of the four ECC co-chairs, would recruit an opposite party member from legislative leadership or a relevant committee to participate. Moderators were often local superintendents or chamber of commerce leaders, and locations included school buildings, higher education campuses, public libraries and city council chambers. Legislators were prepped for the forums by giving them a handful of facts and figures straight from the research so they would have an opportunity to show off their knowledge in front of constituents. These community forums were held in a similar style for the next few years with funding from local philanthropy but staffing by the University of Minnesota team.

Building Social Connections

To further build connections and conversation and to more deeply develop the demand for research information, an ECC legislative leaders' retreat was developed. Convening legislators for any significant amount of time during session is a challenging task not for the faint of heart. This retreat and the other similar annual retreats that followed only worked because they took into account the realities of time and schedule that affect policymakers' ability to be anywhere reliably during session (e.g., it was scheduled at a day and time known to have no committee hearings or floor sessions, and we worked to get leadership not to call meetings). Barriers were removed and rewards were in place for attendance. For example, the locations that were walking distance from the capitol were somewhat special and fancy (over the years both the Minnesota Children's Museum and the Minnesota History Center were used), food was available (within gift law limits), attendance was "by invitation only" via an actual paper invitation so as to note they were part of select group and as invited legislators RSVP'd we would inform others of who would be there. For example, once a committee chair planned to attend, we would reinvite those on the committee that their chair would be in attendance. If the majority leader said she would attend, we would be sure to let the minority leader's office know. Access to high-profile community members also proved reinforcing. For example, letting legislators know that Art Rolnick was a speaker or that the executive director or board members of the Children's Museum would be giving a welcome was a noted attraction. Press briefings were released both ahead of time, noting who was expected to be in attendance, and afterward, noting who was actually in attendance. Constituents could then prompt and thank their legislators for attending. Finally, there was a group photo taken of the legislators that was given to them as a follow-up and thank you. The very first retreat group had splendid camaraderie such that they instigated getting their group photo taken around the life-size cow statue that resided for a time in the Children's Museum board room. Years later, those framed pictures of legislators with the cow can still be seen in capitol offices displayed with other memorabilia.

Challenges

The ECC interns and later paid staff came to be seen as people with access to decision-makers. At times there were questions about the appropriateness of having relationships with state legislators but not as a lobbyist. Sometimes this was a bit accusatory. We are not registered lobbyists and are not actively supporting or blocking a particular bill. The only thing we advocate for, some would say, is the use of research in policymaking. One important guideline was that for a public university there is clarity that allows for staff and students to be in relationship with legislators and share information without being a lobbyist, because these activities were not asking for resources for the U itself.

At times it was a challenge to keep the caucus meetings closed to the public, which was an important tenant for the caucus so legislators could talk freely among themselves. In the beginning, some legislators invited constituents to attend or word would get out to the public about the location and meeting time. We never banned public members from attending, but the expression of the importance of the legislators having the time to be in conversation out of the public eye nearly always meant that citizens bowed out.

Holding firm on the insistence of being bipartisan was also difficult. This was especially true during the community forums in election season, where a charged political contest was underway. In one case, the ECC graduate student staffer had the awkward responsibility of asking a Democrat running for office to stop his input, which was an accusation to one of the panel members (the sitting Republican legislator), of running an untruthful radio ad (unrelated to early education). It detracted from the spirit of the event, and several community attendees were very off put by this political and nonissue-based focus, including a few who got up and left.

Multiple legislators were not fans of hosting anything with sitting legislators from the other party in districts where they hoped to unseat those same members in the upcoming election. In one email, a member of the minority party at the time inquired about the ECC hosting a community meeting where both sitting legislators were members of the majority party at the time: "I still have no idea why we are helping x and y get re-elected. These are two seats we actually have a chance at unless this kind of stuff keeps up. Do you understand the politics of this at all?" There were many, many exchanges and reminders by the ECC staff and by the legislative co-chairs that the purpose of the caucus was to inform decision-making with research and provide decision-makers with settings to do that in a more thoughtful, less political way than had been done previously.

Impact and Success

Positive individual, structural and policy outcomes resulted from this university–legislative, researcher–policymaker (and philanthropic community) partnership. Of course, other contextual pieces contributed to each of the following outcomes, but these areas are some that highlight the direct and indirect impacts of the ECC.

Individual Impacts

- Built capacity in the knowledge base of state policymakers and allowed equitable access to that knowledge that was not reliant on party or legislative body.
- Provided public opportunities for legislators to show their interest in and knowledge about early childhood issues, gaining them "credit" for doing so and allowing constituents to thank them.
- Provided local opportunities for legislators to show their interest in and knowledge about early childhood issues. This was especially important in Greater Minnesota.
- Increased number of legislators and university staff/faculty who had individual relationships with each other and could call upon each other.
- Provided policy context training for about a half-dozen graduate students in child development and related fields.

Structural Impacts

- Early childhood committees were formed in both houses.
- Legislators formed similar caucuses around food insecurity, cancer, mental health and other topics.
- A statewide Office of Early Learning was formed.

Policy and Funding Impacts

It is worth noting that the public policy impacts included funding, as described here.

- Early Learning Scholarships grew out of the legislators' support of Art Rolnick's work and the desire to increase access to high-quality early childhood programs for three- and four-year-olds with the highest needs in order to improve school readiness. Minnesota currently has $25 million per year invested into the Early Learning Scholarships, which has framed (and sometimes bumped into) the conversations about "universal" preschool.
- Tiered Quality Rating and Improvement System, now called Parent Aware, was one of the first issues that the ECC supported on a bipartisan, bicameral basis. It took some years and the federal Race to the Top Early Learning Challenge grant to make that a reality in Minnesota, but the seeds were planted during ECC activities.
- Provider use of Early Learning Scholarships is tied to Parent Aware, which is available on a voluntary basis to multisector early education settings across the state.
- Earning the $45 million Race to the Top Early Learning Challenge grant was rooted in the relationships, policy ideas and beginnings of an early childhood system from the seeds planted by the ECC.

Lessons Learned

Among the many lessons learned from this partnership experience, the five that follow here have much to offer researchers and policymakers at all levels of government and in both the legislative and executive branches.

> *Lesson one:* The messenger matters. Look beyond usual suspects for delivering information on a particular topic. Look for common ground among different messengers and bring

them together. Recruit messengers who are good at both the listening and talking sides of communication.

Lesson two: To be truly bipartisan, always include representation from both/all parties. Do whatever it takes to get input and guidance from both sides. Be aware of your own biases and beliefs and check them at the door. Be vigilant about even the perception of partisanship.

Lesson three: To find out about the demand side of research interest, ask the consumers. Do what it takes to get information from a balanced group. Help the policy consumers demand research and create pathways to provide it.

Lesson four: Actively build social networks between and among legislators. Provide opportunities for policymakers to have informal conversations, connect legislators across parties and bodies who have similar interests and be strategic about which policymakers are convened together for public forums or panel participation.

Lesson five: Use the right social reinforcers to get policymakers' attention. Provide opportunities for policymakers to be connected to their constituents, including photo opportunities and possible media events.

We have worked in policy, practice and research roles, and we are convinced that these lessons apply nearly universally when it comes to maximizing the chances of success for partnerships between policymakers and researchers. We are even more certain given that two of us have changed roles since the partnership started and yet we continue to draw on these lessons to inform our new realms and experiences with new potential partners facing new challenges.

The story of the Minnesota Early Childhood Caucus brings to light the diversity and complexity of factors and conditions that impede policymakers' use of research. The case of the ECC explains why many of those impediments exist and provides useful insights for mitigating them. The application of a supply–demand framework is particularly useful. If attended to, the framework can play an important role in urging individuals and organizations who are considering researcher–policymaker partnerships (or who are already in the midst of such a partnership effort) to do so with the supply–demand tension at the forefront. The ECC case suggests that research and policy partners ideally will recognize and respond to that tension prior to a partnership's development.

The case also provides a contribution through its confirmation of the critical importance of context when it comes to bridging research and policy. At the top of the list with regard to contextual considerations is the ever-present political lens through which elected officials must view their work (this lens is present among nonelected policy officials as well but is often less pervasive). Maintaining a political lens is a constant necessity in the policy realm, and as the ECC case illuminates, is best attended to directly. A further added value of the ECC case is its candid reflections on the partnership process, a process that started by chance and maintained its organic quality throughout, while formalizing components of the partnership when doing so was prudent. The attributes of the case noted here are three of many that it offers. They reinforce and complement those presented through the Results First case.

Key Takeaways

As with the partnerships featured throughout this book, the Early Childhood Caucus and Results First cases share similarities and differences, reinforcing the notion that partnerships require certain conditions to succeed but that those conditions will not be consistent across partnerships. Both partnerships shared the goal of more and better utilization of research by policymakers who faced specific challenges and needed to make specific decisions. In each case, research played a role before the decision-making phase. This is consistent with some of the learnings discussed earlier in that the bidirectional and transactional *partnerships*, not one-directional acts of dissemination or translation, are what led to the use of research.

The Results First and Early Childhood Caucus partnerships involved leaders at the state government level seeking external research expertise to help solve particular policy problems. Results First adapted its existing partnership model to the New Mexico context, whereas the Minnesota Early Childhood Caucus developed a model based on the knowledge and experience of specific partners. Results First involved multiple staff at large, established institutions. The ECC got off the ground thanks to the leadership of a few people who represented supply and demand, research and policy. They formed the foundation of a partnership, which then spread to other individuals in areas of their respective organizations and beyond. Ultimately, the ECC became a collaborative effort supported by a mix of policymakers, researchers and practitioners. This cross-sector interaction and partnership was critical to the caucus's impact and success.

Both of the partnerships featured in this chapter exemplify the potential of research utilization that stems from collaboration early in the research process of a partnership as opposed to after the research is complete. A significant difference, however, is the level of planning involved. The existence of Results First in New Mexico depended on agreement to certain roles and responsibilities before launching the partnership. In the case of the ECC by contrast, although there was strategic and thoughtful planning along the way, there were no preconditions that determined whether the partnership could go forward.

Another area ripe for comparison between the two partnerships is that of financial investment. In the case of Results First, potential partners learned at the outset that funding was available to support the partnership should the partners agree to the required conditions. In the case of the ECC, the promise of funding was not a consideration for moving forward. In fact, it was the formation of the partnership that its leaders saw as potential leverage for future funding for early childhood that contributed to their willingness to partner. Chapter 6 of this book considers the role of funders in researcher–policymaker partnerships. It highlights the positive impacts of the increased financial support that researcher–policymaker partnerships are experiencing nationwide and at all levels of government. Furthermore, and of particular relevance to research utilization, Chapter 6 notes the growing practice of tying funding to the use of research evidence. In that chapter, we feature a case of increased federal government investments in efforts that commit to being evidence based.

Notwithstanding the numerous distinctions between them, the Results First and Early Childhood Caucus cases provide all-important, tangible guidance for successful researcher–policymaker partnerships. They are reminders that an aspect of partnerships highly relevant to real-world impact but often overlooked is the extent to which decision-makers use the research evidence that the partnerships generate.

Notes

1 More information on the benefit–cost model and examples of WSIPP reports that present its results can be found at http://www.wsipp.wa.gov/ReportFile/1602/Wsipp_What-Works-and-What-Does-Not-Benefit-Cost-Findings-from-WSIPP_Report.pdf.
2 More information on the Results First Clearinghouse can be found at http://www.pewtrusts.org/en/research-and-analysis/issue-briefs/2014/09/results-first-clearinghouse-database.
3 Governments that establish partnerships with Results First vary in the scope of their activity, typically starting in one policy area and expanding into additional policy areas over time.

References

Bansal, P., Bertels, S., Ewart, T., MacConnachie, P., & O'Brien, J. (2012). Bridging the research-practice gap. *Academy of Management Perspectives, 26*(1), 73–92.
Bardach, E. (2003). Creating compendia of "best practice". *Journal of Policy Analysis and Management, 22*(4), 661–665.
Bogenschneider, K., & Corbett, T.J. (2010). *Evidence-based policy making: Insights from policy-minded researchers and research-minded policy makers.* New York: Taylor & Francis.

Bogenschneider, K., Little, O., Ooms, T., Benning, S., Cadigan, K., & Corbett, T. (2013). Building family-focused policy: The Family Impact Lens Toolkit. In K. Bogenschneider (Ed.), *Family policy matters: How policy-making affects families and what professionals can do* (3rd ed., pp. 262–293). London: Routledge.

Bryson, J.M., Crosby, B.C., & Stone, M. (2015). Designing and implementing cross-sector collaborations: Needed and challenging. *Public Administration Review, 75*(5), 647–663.

Cadigan, K. (2013). Commentary on the uses of research in policy and practice. *Social Policy Report, 26*(2), 17–19.

Caplan, N. (1979). The two communities theory and knowledge utilization. *American Behavioral Scientist, 22*, 459–470.

Choi, B.C.K., Pang, T., Lin, V., Puska, P., Sherman, G., Goddard, M., Ackland, M.J., Sainsbury, P., Stachenko, S., Morrison, H., & Clottey, C. (2005). Can scientists and policy makers work together? *Journal of Epidemiology & Community Health, 59*, 632–637.

Clark, G., & Kelly, L. (2005). *New directions for knowledge transfer and knowledge brokerage in Scotland.* Retrieved from: http://www.gov.scot/resource/doc/69582/0018002.pdf.

Cousins, J.B., & Leithwood, K.A. (1986). Current empirical research on evaluation utilization. *Review of Educational Research, 56*(3), 331–364.

Denis, J.L., Lehoux, P., Hivon, M., & Champagne, F. (2003). Creating a new articulation between research and practice through policy? The views and experiences of researchers and practitioners. *Journal of Health Services Research & Policy, 8*(4), 44–50.

Dobbins, M., Hanna, S.E., Ciliska, D., Manske, S., Cameron, R., Mercer, S.L., O'Mara, L., Decorby, K., & Robeson, P. (2009). A randomized controlled trial evaluating the impact of knowledge translation and exchange strategies. *Implementation Science, 4*, 61.

Finnigan, Kara S., & Alan J. Daly, Eds. (2014). *Using research evidence in education: From the schoolhouse door to Capitol Hill.* Springer: New York.

Garri, I. (2007). Political-short-termism: A possible explanation. *Public Choice, 45*(1–2), 197–211.

Ginsberg, L.R., Lewis, S., Zackheim, L., & Casebeer, A. (2007). Revisiting interaction in knowledge translation. *Interaction Science, 2*(34), 1–15.

Innvaer, S., Vist, G., Trommald, M., & Oxman, A. (2002). Health policy-makers' perceptions of their use of evidence: A systematic review. *Journal of Health Services Research and Policy, 7*(4), 239–244.

Institute of Education Sciences. (2011). *SLDS best practices brief: Stakeholder communication: Tips from the States.* Retrieved from: https://nces.ed.gov/programs/slds/pdf/best_practices.pdf.

Jennings, E.T., Jr., & Hall, J.L. (2012). Evidence-based practice and the use of information in state agency decision making. *Journal of Public Administration Research and Theory, 22*(2), 245–266.

Kingdon, J.W. (1995). *Agendas, alternatives, and public policies* (2nd ed.). New York: Longman.

Kirst, M. (2000). Bridging education research and education policymaking. *Oxford Review of Education, 26*(3–4), 379–391.

Koschmann, M.A., Kuhn, T.R., & Pfarrer, M.D. (2012). A communicative framework of value in cross-sector partnerships. *Academy of Management Review*, *37*(3), 332–354.

Kothari, A., MacLean, L., & Edwards, N. (2009). Increasing capacity for knowledge translation: Understanding how some researchers engage policy-makers. *Evidence and Policy*, *5*(1), 33–51.

Lindblom, C.E., & Cohen, D.K. (1979). *Usable knowledge: Social science and social problem Solving*. New Haven, CT: Yale University.

Lomas, J. (2007). The in-between world of knowledge brokering. *British Medical Journal*, *334*, 129–132.

Miller, D. & Oliver, M. (2015). *Engaging stakeholders for project success*. Program Management Institute. Retrieved from: http://www.pmi.org/~/media/PDF/learning/engaging-stakeholders-project-success.ashx.

Mississippi Performance Budget and Strategic Planning Act of 1994, Miss. Code Ann. § 27–103–159 (2014).

Moore, G., Todd, A., & Redman, S. (2009). *Strategies to increase the use of evidence from research in population health policy and programs: A rapid review*. Retrieved from: http://www.health.nsw.gov.au/research/Documents/10-strategies-to-increase-research-use.pdf.

Morrill Act (July 2nd 1862) Public Law 37–108, 07/02/1862; Enrolled Acts and Resolutions of Congress, 1789–1996; Record Group 11. Washington, DC: General Records of the United States Government, National Archives.

National Academy of Sciences. (2012). *Using science as evidence in public policy*. Retrieved from: http://documents.library.nsf.gov/edocs/Q183.3.A1-U85–2012-PDF-Using-Science-As-Evidence-In-Public-Policy.pdf.

National Conference of State Legislatures. (2011). *State budget update: Fall 2011*. Retrieved from: http://www.ncsl.org/portals/1/documents/fiscal/fallsbu2011final_freeversion.pdf.

National Conference of State Legislatures. (2012). *State budget update: Summer 2012*. Retrieved from: http://www.ncsl.org/portals/1/documents/fiscal/SummerSBU2012_Free.pdf.

New Mexico Corrections Department. (2013). *New Mexico Corrections Department strategic plan for fiscal years 2015 through 2018*. Retrieved from: http://cd.nm.gov/pio/docs/2014–2015_SP.pdf.

New Mexico Legislative Finance Committee. (2012). *Reducing recidivism, cutting costs and improving public safety in the incarceration and supervision of adult offenders*. Retrieved from: http://www.nmlegis.gov/lcs/handouts/CCJ%20072612%20LFC%20NMCD%20Report.pdf.

Nutley, S., Walter, I., & Davies, H.T.O. (2003). From knowing to doing: A framework for understanding the evidence-into-practice agenda. *Evaluation*, *9*(2), 125–148.

Nutley, S., Walter, I., & Davies, H.T.O. (2007). *Using evidence: How research can inform public services*. Bristol, UK: Policy Press.

Patton, M. (2008). *Utilization–focused evaluation* (4th ed). Los Angeles, CA: Sage.

Pew-MacArthur Results First Initiative. (2013). *States' use of cost-benefit analysis: Improving results for taxpayers*. Retrieved from: http://www.pewtrusts.org/~/media/legacy/uploadedfiles/pcs_assets/2013/pewresultsfirst50statereportpdf.pdf.

Pew-MacArthur Results First Initiative. (2014a). *Results first in your State.* Retrieved from: http://www.pewtrusts.org/~/media/assets/2013/results-first-in-your-state-brief.pdf?la=en.

Pew-MacArthur Results First Initiative. (2014b). *Evidence-based policymaking: A guide to effective government.* Retrieved from: http://www.pewtrusts.org/~/media/assets/2014/11/evidencebasedpolicymakingaguideforeffectivegovernment.pdf.

Pew-MacArthur Results First Initiative. (2015). *Legislating evidence-based policymaking: A look at state laws that support data-driven decision-making.* Retrieved from: http://www.pewtrusts.org/~/media/assets/2015/03/legislation resultsfirstbriefmarch2015.pdf.

Rigby, E. (2005). Linking research and policy on Capitol Hill: Insights from research brokers. *Evidence & Policy, 1*(2), 195–213.

Rogoff, K. (1990). Equilibrium political budget cycles. *The American Economic Review, 80*(1), 21–36.

Rolnick, A., & Grunewald, R. (2003). Early childhood development: Economic development with high public return. *Fed Gazette.* Retrieved from: https://www.minneapolisfed.org/publications/fedgazette/early-childhood-development-economic-development-with-a-high-public-return.

Rosenbloom, D.H., Kravchuk, R.S., & Clerkin, R.M. (2009). *Public administration: Understanding management, politics, and law in the public sector* (7th ed.). New York: McGraw-Hill.

Ryu, J.E. (2011). *Bounded bureaucracy and the budgetary process in the United States.* New Brunswick, NJ: Transaction Publishers.

Shonkoff, J. (2000). Science, policy and practice: Three cultures in search of a shared mission. *Child Development, 71*(1), 181–187.

Stevens, M., Liabo, K., Frost, S., & Roberts, H. (2005). Using research in practice: A research information service for social care practitioners', *Child and Family Social Work, 10*(1), 67–75.

Sutcliffe, S., & Court, J. (2006). *Toolkit for progressive policymakers in developing countries.* Retrieved from: http://www.odi.org/sites/odi.org.uk/files/odi-assets/publications-opinion-files/190.pdf.

Tseng, V. (2013). The uses of research in policy and practice. *Social Policy Report, 26*(2), 3–13.

Walter, I., Davies, H., & Nutley, S. (2003). Increasing research impact through partnerships: Evidence from outside health care. *Journal of Health Services Research and Policy, 8*, 58–61.

Washington Juvenile Offender Sentencing Standards, Rev. Code Wash. (ARCW) § 13.40.0357.

Wildavsky, A.B., & Caiden, N. (2004). *The new politics of the budgetary process* (5th ed.). New York: Pearson/Longman.

6 Investing in Research, Investing in Policy Outcomes

Welcome to the final chapter of *Researcher–Policymaker Collaboration: Strategies for Launching and Sustaining Successful Partnerships*. The earlier cases demonstrate that motivations for and key components of researcher–policymaker partnerships are not driven by funding alone. Funding and the likelihood of ongoing investment, however, often have a significant impact both on the emergence of partnerships and their sustainability.

In the preceding chapters, funding played a vital role in each of the researcher–policymaker partnerships described. Without start-up funding, for instance, the SanDERA work on creating an effective early warning system to identify San Diego Public School District students at risk of school failure could not have begun or been able to demonstrate its value. Without investment in Results First, the New Mexico Legislative Finance Committee would not have been able to pursue its research goals or devote the resources necessary to augment its internal capacity for evidence-based policy. Without ongoing funding, Minnesota's Hennepin-University Partnership could not support the diverse partnerships that provide mutual benefit to the county and the University of Minnesota and maintain the long-term relationship between the two institutions. Investments of various types and scopes play an important role in every case study that we feature, regardless of whether funding figured prominently in its retelling. Funding or the lack thereof—and investment more broadly—can make or break a partnership's long-term success, not only with regard to sustained commitment, but also to outcomes such as the utilization of research that stems from the partnerships, as discussed in Chapter 4.

As a number of these case studies show, researcher–policymaker partnerships take shape in a number of ways. Many materialize from the serendipity of two individuals from distinct sectors coming together who share a passion for the same social policy area and identify a problem that neither can adequately address alone. Oftentimes it is at this stage that an idea for collaborative work takes shape, followed by a search for funding to support the idea.

But what of the researcher–policymaker partnerships that are funded by a benefactor who specifies a collaborative relationship as a condition of the research work? What are the anticipated benefits and reasons for these requirements from the perspective of the funder? Do funders believe that these partnerships are a good investment, and are these working relationships expected to continue in the years to come as complex social problems continue to emerge? This chapter shares insights about funders and their priorities for researcher–policymaker partnerships. It also discusses funders' perspectives on these working relationships. The featured partnership in this chapter is that of the U.S. Office of Management and Budget leaders and the heads of nonprofit, nonpartisan policy research organizations, the Coalition for Evidence-Based Policy in particular. We begin with some context.

Trends

As noted in the preface and the chapter on the book's approach and structure, the trend of research partnerships in the United States has a history in medicine, agriculture, science, pharmaceuticals and the military. Some of the impetus for this stemmed from the mission of the land grant university system, established in part to support the needs of a rapidly reconstructing and growing post–Civil War nation. Compared with the hard sciences, the areas of social and education policy are relative latecomers to partnerships with academia. As a result, the literature on partnerships between policy and research largely reflects the sectors and disciplines that have been doing these partnerships the longest. Regardless of the sector or discipline, however, it is reasonable to expect that some of the motivations and anticipated benefits for such partnerships are the same.

In the last two decades, another trend has emerged, which has contributed significantly to a growth in both quality and quantity of researcher–policymaker partnerships. The evidence-based policy movement has fueled efforts to narrow the well-documented and widely acknowledged research–policy gap. A plethora of "what works" initiatives across levels of government and policy domains are driven in part by the increasingly attended to importance of using research to support policy decision-making. These "what works" efforts in turn have been fueled both by government and private sources of investment, and the "willingness to pay" for a greater chance of evidence-based outcomes shows no sign of waning.

Collaboration is increasingly a requirement of funding and a significant factor in obtaining support for research. A simple search of www. grants.gov confirms this, as it produces over 7,000 grant opportunities containing "collaboration" and "research" as key words. (Grants.gov is a resource for identifying and applying for federal grants. It is a partnership among federal agencies managed by the U.S. Department of Health and

Human Services.) Although a majority of all collaborative research grants are in medicine, defense and public health, a significant proportion are for the education or social policy areas (e.g., housing, public assistance and school dropout prevention) (Grants.gov, 2016).

Partnerships in the Hard Sciences

Federal and private institutions in the United States and globally invest billions of dollars every year to support innovations in the hard sciences. Academic researchers and private-sector companies collaborate with each other and with government agencies, constituting the "trifecta" of academia, corporations and government. This three-way partnership is considered by some to be a natural phenomenon, combining "great university innovators, experienced entrepreneurs, and adequate funding sources" (Ford, Shino, Sander, & Hardin, 2008, abstract).

Clark and Lloren's (2012) large-scale study of the partnership behavior of over 4,000 hard science[1] academic researchers showed that federal funding plays a critical role in the degree to which researchers collaborate with one another. The relationship is curvilinear, peaking when roughly 57 percent of a scientist's work is supported by government-funded grants or other forms of support (Clark & Lloren, 2012, p. 716). They and other scholars identify government support of collaborative research activities as a form of human capital investment necessary to respond to the needs of industry and changes in scientific inquiry. Specifically, adding to scientific knowledge requires specialization, and increased specialization of inquiry leads to discoveries in productivity, increased effectiveness and efficiencies (Clark & Lloren, 2012). The social sciences also reflect this specialization trend, as greater accountability for the results of public spending on services drives evidence-based models of service delivery. Clark and Lloren (2012) acknowledge differences in academic disciplines with respect to collaborative behaviors and norms. Although the research does not explore partnerships that occur between academia and other sectors (such as the policy sector), they acknowledge that funding alone is not sufficient to guarantee partnerships. Moreover, they note that removing other barriers may be equally and perhaps more effective in enhancing collaborative behavior. In particular, they identify addressing the "transaction costs" of partnerships as being key—an area on which the Hennepin-University Partnership has focused its efforts as described in Chapter 5.

Partnerships in Social Policy and Education

In its guidelines for managing federal interagency collaborative mechanisms, the U.S. Government Accountability Office (GAO, 2012) identifies flexibility in funding as critical. Again, although these guidelines apply to within-sector work among federal agencies, the lessons of funding are important across sectors as well. The GAO's survey of partnership experts showed that not only has the executive branch invested in structures to cultivate federal interagency partnership (e.g., the Joint Incentive Fund program portion of the National Defense Authorization Act requiring coordination between the Veterans Administration and the Department of Defense), but it has established broad initiatives to facilitate multiple agencies addressing shared issues (GAO, 2012). As examples, the National Strategies and Initiatives and Specially Created Interagency offices are two such mechanisms charged with addressing shared issues and challenges across federal departments (GAO, 2012, p. 5). Similarly, the Early Learning Interagency Policy Board (IPB) is a cross-department initiative of the Obama administration, spanning the federal departments of Health and Human Services and Education. It focuses on developing policy recommendations and improving program coordination. The IPB addresses federal coordination and encourages and supports local coordination in this policy area as well (U.S. Department of Education, 2016).

A timely social policy challenge facing the United States is the rapidly aging population and the anticipated effects of this aging upon multiple systems serving the elderly. Collaborative research aimed at improving medical practice, general geriatric care and other areas of policy for the elderly are priorities for multiple federal agencies, driven in large part by the Affordable Care Act (ACA). Zerzan and Rich (2014) identify multiple cross-sector initiatives that spring from the ACA in response to foundations filling in funding gaps in the wake of the Great Recession as federal and state governments had reduced capacity to fund research efforts. These research efforts are aimed at improving care, clinical practice and education.

Child care subsidy is yet another social policy area receiving federal funding for cross-sector partnerships. Child care subsidy is an economic support to low- and moderate-income families who are working toward or maintaining employment. The program has both child development and family economic stability objectives, and eligible families are typically receiving or have recently stopped receiving Temporary Assistance for Needy Families (TANF). As part of this effort, the federal Child Care Bureau of the Department of Health and Human Services began funding Child Care Research Partnership grants (CCRPs) in the mid-1990s to identify the policy and practice issues related to child care subsidy investments that produce positive results. These CCRPs mandated that one partner be a state agency responsible for administering the child care subsidy program through the Child Care and Development Fund and that at least one other partner be a research group. In most cases, these partners have been academic researchers (Office of Planning Research and Evaluation, Child Care Research Partnerships, 2015). One of the longest-running CCRPs is the Oregon partnership, with Oregon State University. The Oregon CCRP's mission statement succinctly presents its partnership goals as follows: "The mission of the Child Care Research Partnership is to ensure that basic information about childhood care and education in Oregon is current, accurate, and available on local, regional, and state levels and is accessible to all decision-makers." It goes on to describe the multisector partners involved, "The partnership brings together university-based researchers, state agency early learning staff, the network of child care resource and referral agencies, and child care practitioners" (Oregon Child Care Research Partnership, 2016).

Partnerships occur in other areas of social policy such as juvenile justice, public health and education. These partnerships have noticeably been increasing in number, and among other shared characteristics, they have in common the desire to improve public policy through meaningful, rigorous research.

Government Funding of Researcher–Policymaker Partnerships

Funders make researcher–policymaker partnerships a priority because of the multiple anticipated benefits. For some federal grants, collaborating with academics is a requirement of grant receipt yielding partnerships generally believed to produce better science, practice, products and public policies than efforts that lack partnership. At the same time, operational issues that reflect some of the structural and cultural differences between the research and policy realms discussed in earlier sections of the book present challenges to the ongoing success of some partnerships (Cousins & Simon, 1996).

Interestingly, the case study that we feature about investing in partnerships is a little known but highly important partnership between federal agencies and nonprofit research partners that emerged during a Republican presidential administration and continued with vigor and increased investment during a Democratic administration. The primary partners are the U.S. Office of Management and Budget and the nonprofit Coalition for Evidence-Based Policy. It offers a valuable perspective on the benefits of researcher–policymaker partnerships and reflects aspects of each of the other chapters.

U.S. Office of Management and Budget and the Coalition for Evidence-Based Policy

From Interviews with Jon Baron and Kathy Stack

During the George W. Bush administration, as part of the President's Management Agenda, the White House and its Office of Management and Budget (OMB) championed the use of research evidence and rigorous evaluation in order to improve results achieved in federally funded programs nationwide. This work was led by Clay Johnson III, the deputy director for Management at the president's OMB, and Robert Shea, OMB's associate director, who oversaw government-wide performance improvement efforts. Beginning in 2006, the administration's cross-cutting initiative to improve science, technology, engineering and mathematics (STEM) education programs and a president's budget proposal to create a small home visiting initiative for low-income mothers provided important new opportunities to engage federal agencies and Congress in adopting rigorous evaluation standards.

The Bush administration had set the stage for these efforts a few years earlier, with the launch of the program assessment rating tool (PART), a tool for assessing the effectiveness of government programs. OMB required agencies to utilize PART in evaluating the effectiveness of their programs. PART was controversial. Many critics, including Democratic members of Congress, feared that PART represented another means to reduce government by setting such high standards for programs that few would be recommended for ongoing funding. Others were concerned that PART did not use objective, evidence-based criteria for assessing program effectiveness.

To address the concern about objective criteria for assessing effectiveness, Robert Shea worked with Jon Baron, president of the Coalition for Evidence-Based Policy, and his colleagues to develop guidance for the federal agencies on *What Constitutes Strong Evidence of Program Effectiveness*. In this guidance, which was issued in 2004 to help clarify the PART criteria, OMB for the first time identified well-conducted randomized controlled trials as the strongest method for evaluating program effectiveness and discussed which quasi-experimental methods are good alternatives in cases where randomized controlled trials are not feasible (Haskins & Baron, 2011).

The successful collaboration between OMB and the coalition on PART guidance made the coalition a natural partner in bringing evidence to bear on policy-specific initiatives led by OMB during the latter part of the Bush administration. The STEM education and home visiting initiatives described later laid a strong foundation for signature initiatives launched in the early years of the Obama administration with a strong focus on evidence and evaluation.

The Academic Competitiveness Council and the Formation of a Response Partnership

President Bush signed the Deficit Reduction Act (DRA) into law on February 8, 2006, which included a section establishing the Academic Competitiveness Council, an interagency council to be led by the secretary of education, Margaret Spellings, which included over a dozen federal agencies operating STEM education programs. The secretary sought OMB's assistance in providing leadership and coordination for the council, which Congress had charged with developing recommendations on how to improve the effectiveness and coordination of over 100 separate programs.

To this end, officials at federal agencies with STEM-focused education programs engaged in a yearlong assessment of their programs' "successes" and outcomes, identifying areas for improvement to current and future programs. Of greatest concern was the widely varied nature of the evaluation methods that each program and agency was using to assess program impact.

Working at OMB with Shea, Kathy Stack, Deputy Associate Director for Education, Income, Maintenance, and Labor, played a pivotal role in working to inventory the evaluation models used by agencies and programs. For Stack, a career civil servant, this high-level undertaking by OMB leadership provided an opportunity to improve the quality and rigor of evaluations inside government, which could only be achieved through a partnership with a neutral, authoritative outside organization. The organization was the Coalition for Evidence-Based Policy, which although a fairly young organization was highly regarded for its objectivity and expertise in advancing evidence-based reforms in government programs. A critical element for the success of this partnership was the political cover that OMB leadership provided to Stack and her colleagues, enabling them to pursue this informal collaboration. Strong commitment from OMB's senior leadership was critical to getting agency buy-in on an initiative that would subject programs and agencies to scrutiny, using rigorous measurement and evaluation standards that could threaten their funding levels.

Background: STEM Evaluations

Under the legislation creating the Academic Competitiveness Council (ACC), the Bush administration launched an interagency working group to assess STEM education programs across all federal agencies. OMB, education and other agency staff supporting the ACC first created an inventory of all federal STEM programs and gathered information about the monitoring techniques and evaluations each agency used to measure effectiveness. In addition, OMB and agency staff sought to determine duplication of programs and target populations being served to inform recommendations for better coordination and program integration. OMB also asked the agencies to submit examples of their most rigorous STEM education program evaluations for the coalition to review.

By mid-2006, eight federal agencies with the most robust evaluation capacity had submitted approximately 115 STEM education program evaluations for review. These included the National Science Foundation, the National Institutes of Health and the Departments of Education and Commerce, among others (Coalition for Evidence-Based Policy, 2006). The William T. Grant and Edna McConnell Clark foundations funded the coalition to carry out its review of these evaluations. Funding from these nonpartisan external sources was critical to supporting the neutrality of Baron and his colleagues and in enhancing the legitimacy of their work in the eyes of Congress. Receiving independent foundation support also allowed Baron and the coalition to focus on objective evidence criteria and to straddle a dichotomy of political thought regarding their findings. For instance, the desire to require that social services are backed by evidence often reflects a conservative ideology, whereas advocating for programs that are proven to work for low-income families is considered more liberal. The duality of the coalition's approach led to its reputation for being reliably neutral.

In the end, of those program evaluations that Baron and his colleagues reviewed, the coalition determined that only ten were sufficiently rigorous to produce reliable evidence about the program's effectiveness and that the majority of evaluations made claims about effectiveness based on evaluation methods that were not scientifically credible. These findings clearly illustrated the need for more reliable evaluation methods and helped provide a foundation for Stack and Baron to improve processes and evaluation across government programs. Their eventual objective included the establishment of a cross-agency process to embed evidence-based approaches into government programs so as to increase the programs' effectiveness in improving people's lives. Meanwhile, the partnership between the coalition and OMB helped spawn a new evidence-based initiative in a different policy area: early childhood.

Background: Nurse Home Visiting Program

In the summer of 2006, at approximately the same time as the ongoing STEM evaluation, David Olds, founder of the Nurse Family Partnership National Service Office, met with OMB, presenting key research findings from the Nurse Family Partnership (NFP) program. After Olds had a lengthy discussion with Stack and her colleagues, OMB decided to again partner with Baron and the coalition to design a new program model for scaling up evidence-based home visiting interventions, such as NFP. Stack recalls that Olds' program evaluation results stood in stark contrast to what other federally funded programs were able to present.

The NFP, a national nonprofit and multistate program, was founded by Olds in 2003 after decades of research on low-income urban children and families. Olds, a professor of pediatrics, psychiatry and preventative medicine at the University of Colorado Health Sciences Center, developed the NFP as a way to help disadvantaged first-time mothers become better parents and link them proactively to social services and support systems. NFP provides home visitation for low-income, at-risk, first-time mothers during pregnancy and the first two years of the child's life. Olds and his colleagues tested variations of this concept at several locations around the United States with nurses and with paraprofessionals. The evaluations of the various approaches to the home visiting program revealed that the original model, which required certified nurses, produced the strongest results. Researchers speculated that it was the perceived authority and trust of the nurses—and the pregnant mothers' concern about their health and that of their child—that yielded the best outcomes among first-time mothers.

The strength of the evidence of NFP's impacts formed the foundation upon which the coalition and OMB pushed for funding for the program. NFP was backed by the results of three well-conducted, randomized controlled trials (RCTs) that showed sizable effects in reducing maltreatment. These trials occurred in 1977, 1990, and 1994 in three different NFP locations (in three different states). At least two of the three RCTs showed the following impacts: improved prenatal health, fewer childhood injuries, fewer subsequent pregnancies, increased intervals between births, increased maternal employment and improved school readiness. Research on NFP is ongoing.

With the continued help of Baron and his colleagues at the coalition, Stack and others at OMB were able to advocate for creating a new $10 million initiative to provide seed capital to states to encourage them to scale up evidence-based nurse home visiting interventions, using the flexible federal funding they receive under federal block grants (e.g., Maternal and Child Health Block Grant, TANF, Social Service Block Grant). Their initial proposal would support evidence-based models that used trained nurses, a key element of the NFP program that had strong evidence to support it. Shea, a strong proponent of the work that the coalition was doing, trusted Baron's assessment of the home visiting program and advocated for it to presidential staffers. The initiative was included in the president's 2008 budget to Congress.

There was initial political resistance to the proposal from proponents of home visiting programs other than NFP—most of which did not have credible evidence, and several of which had been rigorously evaluated and found not to be effective. They believed that any new federal home visitation funding should be used to support a diverse array of programs, not just NFP. They worked with Congress to try to broaden the program's focus and reduce the evidentiary requirements.

Baron stepped in and played a pivotal role in helping congressional staff understand the uniquely strong evidence for NFP. At Baron's suggestion, congressional staff broadened the legislative language to allow other models to qualify for funding—even if they did not use nurses—but maintained the strong evidence criteria. In the final legislation, Congress directed that the federal funds be used "to support models that have been shown, in well-designed randomized controlled trials, to produce sizeable, sustained effects on important child outcomes such as abuse and neglect." Moreover, the strategy of using a small pot of discretionary funds to leverage larger formula funding streams was a key feature of the Obama administration's home visiting program, which has provided hundreds of millions per year to states as dedicated funding for home visiting program operations.

The Bush administration also underscored its strong support for rigorous evidentiary approaches. In a letter from OMB Deputy Director Clay Johnson III to Louisiana State Senator Mary Landrieu, Johnson emphasized that the nurse home visitation program was backed by rigorous evaluations and that "nurse home visitation for first-time mothers produces significant, long-term reductions in child abuse and neglect and improvements in several other crucial outcomes for both mothers and children" (C. Johnson and M. Landrieu, personal communication, June 13, 2007). Reflecting on the success of the nurse home visiting program, Stack recalls that it was Baron's ability to be a voice both internal and external to government that allowed the program to gain such traction. The end result of these combined efforts was the 2007 congressional enactment of a new $10 million allocation of funds for states that agreed to use the money to implement early childhood home visiting programs with strong evidence of effectiveness (Haskins & Baron, 2011).

This small $10 million initiative served as the blueprint for the significantly expanded federal home visiting program, proposed by President Obama and enacted in the Affordable Care Act in 2010, which now provides roughly $400 million annually to states to expand evidence-based home visiting services for low-income mothers. The Obama administration employed the same design principles in its "tiered evidence" grant programs in other policy areas, including

HHS' Teen Pregnancy Prevention program and Education's Investing in Innovation initiative. In addition, the original home visiting program design was the inspiration for a 2016 president's budget proposal at the U.S. Department of Education called "Leveraging What Works," which would award competitive grants to local school districts that present a plan for using their K–12 formula grants to scale up evidence-based practices.

Creating STEM Evaluation Standards

As it continued its STEM assessment evaluations, OMB realized that many of the programs that Congress and OMB were funding were not backed with evidentiary support of program effectiveness. Further, many of the programs' designers and advocates lacked the willingness to alter their methods to a common evaluation structure. Baron and Stack advocated for the greater use of rigorous evaluation methods and standards across STEM education programs. With the support of political leadership, including Johnson and Shea, Stack and Baron were able to organize workshops for skills building in program evaluation. One way that they approached this was hosting a two-hour tutorial for staff of all federal agencies who were involved in the evaluations. According to Stack, the majority of participants were not transformed by these workshops. However, the participants recognized how greatly their own evaluation approaches diverged from the evaluation standards in the OMB PART guidance and agreed on the importance of having more consistency across government programs. Backed by Baron's impartial instructional approach, OMB was able to gain support for a cross-cutting effort to develop stronger, more consistent STEM education evaluations across government.

For the next phase of this work, in 2008 OMB partnered with Russ Whitehurst of the Institute of Education Sciences (IES)—the research arm of the U.S. Department of Education—to prepare an official report for the White House National Science and Technology Council on the interagency STEM efforts. Whitehurst, then director of IES, worked with Joan Ferrini-Mundy, at the National Science Foundation, to assist OMB with a cross-agency call, inviting agencies to identify important STEM programs and propose evaluation plans to assess each program's impact. Approximately seventeen proposals from thirteen agencies were submitted. Afterwards, Whitehurst, Ferrini-Mundy and OMB led a seminar series with the goal of helping each agency improve their evaluation plans and adopt the most rigorous evaluation design feasible for the research questions being addressed. Initially, almost all of the proposals sub-mitted to OMB reflected "pre-post" models; following the seminar series, the majority had designed strong quasi-experimental evalua-tions or randomized controlled trials.

The Bush administration's focused effort to improve evaluations of STEM education programs, made possible through a partnership between OMB and the coalition, helped shape the 2010 Obama evaluation initiative to encourage agencies to design rigorous pro-gram evaluations across a range of policy domains (see https://www.whitehouse.gov/sites/default/files/omb/assets/memoranda_2010/m10–01.pdf). It also laid the groundwork for the Obama admin-istration to develop common evaluation guidelines that are now used across multiple federal agencies (see https://www.nsf.gov/pubs/2013/nsf13126/nsf13126.pdf and http://www.acf.hhs.gov/programs/opre/resource/the-administration-for-children-families-common-framework-for-research-and-evaluation).

Why These Partnerships Worked

By 2007, OMB and the coalition had carried out a series of trainings for federal agency leaders in rigorous evaluation and evidence-based approaches. Perhaps most significantly, these partnerships found success in large part due to the nonpartisan, nonthreatening nature of the coalition. Being independently funded by the William T. Grant Foundation, the Edna McConnell Clark Foundation and others, Baron and his colleagues were perceived as an objective, neutral party across government party lines.

Additionally, Baron attributes a great deal of the success of these partnerships to the careful precision with which the coalition con-ducted its evidence reviews, including the expertise with which they were able to evaluate both the STEM program methods and the NFP. In the case of the 115 STEM program evaluations, Baron highlighted that

> upon close inspection, the results were frequently overstated. That's more common than not, because almost all of the incen-tives for both the researchers and the program providers are to present positive findings and frame them in the most favorable possible light. For the researchers, positive findings are often a key to publication; for program providers, positive findings are usually essential to future funding.

In this way, legislators in the Senate and the House came to see Baron and the coalition as an objective, evidence-based third party rather than as an advocate for a particular program.

Both Stack and Baron highlight the importance of communication and translatability of the research. Baron highlights that he and his team shied away from using jargon both in training programs and in advocacy settings. "We always explained to people, in plain language, why that particular finding was credible or not credible so they could understand it for themselves," recalls Baron. Congressional staff came to see the coalition as a trusted and reliable source. For Shea and Stack, Baron was key for discussions across agencies, advocating for improved methods and standards. Because Baron had found such success working on the STEM evaluations, he was able to capitalize on this rapport to make a case for Olds' research and President Bush's home visiting initiative that was modeled on NFP's research-based approach.

The partnership between OMB and the coalition no longer exists but its legacy lives on. The Obama administration has continued to use and build upon the rigorous standards and metrics that OMB and the coalition promoted. Specifically, OMB leadership under the Obama administration, including Peter Orszag, Robert Gordon and Jeffrey Liebman, embraced the value of random-assignment evaluations (Haskins & Baron, 2011). Baron and Stack currently work at the Arnold Foundation serving as the Vice-President of Evidence-Based Policy and the Vice-President of Evidence-Based Innovation, respectively. In this new capacity, Baron focuses on funding rigorous research aimed at growing the body of evidence-based social programs that meet the same high-quality standards he established while at the coalition and on assisting policy officials to expand implementation of such programs. Stack works with government agencies and researchers to create partnerships that embed rigorous evaluation into program operations and strengthen processes and data infrastructure to help federal, state and local governments build evidence that is relevant to their own decision-making.

Key Takeaways

As the OMB–coalition case demonstrates, the federal government has supported cross-sector partnerships stemming from a desire to know what works and what is effective, driven by the need to invest wisely in increasingly scarce public dollars. Throughout the partnership, the wariness of some programs to accept criticism of their methods and models was successfully addressed by the coalition through its use of high-quality, rigorous methods for evaluating program effectiveness. The objectivity of the science was reinforced by the coalition's political neutrality and its nonpartisan funding sources. In the highly politicized environment where programs may be on the defensive with regard to proving their worth, it was essential to the success of the partnership that it perform its critique and make its recommendations from the most objective position possible. Doing so in any other way would likely have failed at convincing the programs to change.

To effectively share the findings of their analyses, the researchers in the partnership also needed to find ways to make the complexities of their work accessible to decision-makers. This required communicating in plain language and in a form that was digestible to nonresearchers and policy-makers while successfully conveying the key findings from the analyses.

In the context of evidence-based policy, a willingness to pay for what works and narrowing the research–policy gap, researcher–policymaker partnerships have gained traction as a mechanism for doing all three. Yet as the preceding cases reveal, successful partnerships are not likely to come about by chance. Furthermore, there is an inherent tension between, on one hand, the "required collaboration" that so many funders now include among criteria for receipt of funding and, on the other hand, allowing partnerships to develop more organically but often with funding to support them. Although the OMB–coalition partnership developed in large part absent funding, it crystalized when available funding helped catalyze and solidify the partners' joint work. This partnership case and the positive, complementary trend of increased investment in researcher–policymaker partnerships are reasons for optimism when it comes to future development of and support for collaboration and sustained partnerships between researchers and policymakers.

Note

1 Biology, computer science, mathematics, physics, earth and atmospheric science, chemistry, agriculture and all engineering fields.

References

Clark, B.Y., & Llorens, J.J. (2012). Investments in scientific research: Examining the funding threshold effects on scientific collaboration and variation by academic discipline. *The Policy Studies Journal, 40*(4), 698–731.

Coalition for Evidence-Based Policy. (2006). *A review of evaluations of federally-funded programs and projects in science, technology, engineering, and mathematics (STEM) education.* Internally circulated document.

Cousins, J.B., & Simon, M. (1996). The nature and impact of policy-induced partnerships between research and practice communities. *Educational Evaluation and Policy Analysis, 18*(3), 199–218.

Ford, B.K., Shino, K.J., Sander, E., & Hardin, M.J. (2008). BIR and STTR programs: The private sector, public sector and university trifecta. *Journal of Research Administration, 39*(1), 58–77.

Grants.gov. (2016). *Search of terms completed on June 14, 2016.*

Haskins, R., & Baron, J. (2011). *Building the connection between policy and evidence: The Obama evidence-based initiatives.* London, UK: NESTA.

National Science and Technology Council (2008). *Finding out what works: Agency efforts to strengthen the evaluation of federal science, technology, engineering and mathematics (STEM) education programs.* A Report of the National Science and Technology Council Subcommittee on Education (December 2008). Retrieved from: https://www.whitehouse.gov/files/documents/ostp/NSTC%20Reports/NSTC_Education_Report_Complete.pdf.

Office of Planning, Research & Evaluation. (2015). *Archive of Child Care Research Partnerships, 1995–2014.* Retrieved on January 15, 2016 from: http://www.acf.hhs.gov/programs/opre/research/project/child-care-research-partnerships.

Oregon Child Care Research Partnership. (2016). Retrieved on January 15, 2016 from: http://health.oregonstate.edu/sbhs/family-policy-program/occrp.

U.S. Department of Education. (2016). *Early Learning Interagency Policy Board.* July 20, 2016. Retrieved from: http://www2.ed.gov/about/inits/ed/earlylearning/partnerships.html.

U.S. General Accounting Office (GAO). (2012). *Managing for results. Key considerations for implementing interagency collaborative mechanisms.* GAO-12-1022. Government report.

Zerzan, J.T., & Rich, E.C. (2014). Advancing geriatrics research, education, and practice: Challenges after the great recession. *Journal of Gen Intern Med,* 29(6), 920–925.

7 The Bright Future of Researcher–Policymaker Partnerships

This book features ten researcher–policymaker partnerships in the education and social policy areas. The partnerships profiled are robust and dynamic. Many have lasted a decade or more because of personal dedication, institutional commitments and an increasing demand from multiple perspectives to bridge the work of the two realms for better outcomes. They have had success and sustainability because researchers and policymakers both enjoy mutual value; each recognizing the collective contributions of their work to the impact that both are striving to have. Moreover, collective contributions typically produce better policy, better practice and improved conditions in communities and the systems that support them. Successful researcher–policymaker partnerships are still rare enough to deserve documentation and recognition (and provide an important topic for a book on the subject).

But what does the future hold? We believe the future is bright for these partnerships. Among other reasons, there is visionary leadership, technological innovation and budgetary conditions that will continue to demand and facilitate new partnerships while supporting those that are already in place.

Federal Direction, National and Local Needs

Many of the cases in this book focus on evidence-based policy and practice desired by policymakers, funders or both. We are entering a period of time where national leadership is setting the stage for broad expectations for multiple areas of government to be increasingly attuned to evidence of what works in policy and practice. In Chapter 2, we learned about the importance of context as one of the essential ingredients for getting a partnership started. The recent passage in Congress of the Evidence-Based Policymaking Commission Act of 2016 (H.R. 1831) is a remarkable example of support for a new national context for researcher–policymaker partnerships. By its very existence, the commission is helping to set a national expectation of the types of cross-sector partnerships described in this book. Commission members are appointees from both houses of Congress and include representatives of the research and policy sectors. Congress passed the act with bipartisan authorship and support, led by Speaker of the House Paul Ryan (R-Wisconsin) and Senator Patty Murray (D-Washington). The legislation articulates the priorities of assessing the readiness of administrative data to support federal policymaking.

This is groundbreaking in that it is bipartisan in sponsorship as well as design and sets the expectation for multiple areas of government and services to collect data, ensure the quality of that data and use data to understand services and improve them. It also requires consideration of the feasibility of improving data infrastructure to inform program evaluation, produce cost–benefit analyses and support continuous improvement (Sec. 4., H.R. 1831, 2016). Commission members are charged with assessing the information environment and advising on related evidence-based policymaking efforts at the federal level. In particular, the legislation states that the commission will conduct a study of data that, among other charges, will "make recommendations on how best to incorporate outcomes measurement, institutionalize randomized controlled trials, and rigorous impact analysis into program design" (Sec 4., (a), 2016). Further explaining its purpose, the commission provided an overview document at its first meeting that stated, "Through the course of the Commission's work, members will study how data, research, and evaluation are currently used to build evidence, and how to strengthen the government's evidence-building efforts" (Commission on Evidence-Based Policymaking, Overview, July 2016).

Although data is not the focus of this book, several of the featured partnerships coalesced around data-related needs and reflect the critical role that reliable, rigorous data—or the lack thereof—play in policymaker decision-making. Further, data use was essential in many partnerships' success and mutual benefit for the partners. Without data, researchers would have been unable to test theories or understand the effectiveness of practices and policies. Without evidence stemming from data, policymakers were unable to know whether their policies were successful.

In keeping with this emphasis on building the federal government's ability to fund what works, in part by augmenting access to and usability of administrative data, President Obama's 2017 budget contains evidence-driven initiatives aimed at supporting policies that have measurable and positive effects. Specific examples include increases in evaluation funding for effective disabled worker programs and additional resources for evidence-based grant making that provide more resources for programs that have undergone more rigorous evaluations (Kamensky, 2016). It is increasingly clear that successfully carrying out such efforts requires serious and strong partnership between researchers and policymakers. In *Show Me the Evidence: Obama's Fight for Rigor and Relevance in Social Policy*, Haskins and Margolis document key tenets of the evidence-based policy movement and the critical roles played by researchers and policy-makers alike. Importantly, and as alluded to in our chapter on investing, the George W. Bush administration made initial and substantial strides in this regard. There is no question that leadership, technological innovation and increasing knowledge of "what works" all are contributing to researcher–policymaker partnerships and greater use of evidence in decision-making. Also at play is the "time of fiscal constraints," a mantra at all levels of government that shows no signs of waning. Although some might argue that tight budgets limit opportunities for pursuing new endeavors, we posit the opposite, particularly when those endeavors have the potential to lead to better use of research evidence for better policy outcomes.

Federal emphasis on evidence, data and partnerships reflects trends at more local levels of government as well, although the degree to which all local governments engage in robust measurement has been highly variable. At state and county levels, the need for more rigorous measurement of policy effects has been important, although many agencies continue to claim that they are "data rich and information poor." Since the 1990s and the computerization of human services and education programs, state and local governments have produced billions of bytes of data. The initial purposes of data from these systems were to create efficiencies and support federal and state reporting requirements. Only later did governments understand the other needs they might meet for planning, research and monitoring. Some local governments have taken advantage of this new information resource—if they could afford to. The challenges have been twofold: lack of time and sometimes technical skills required to use and analyze data (or acquire those skills), and the resources to integrate and make accessible the data products analysts need to complete robust explorations. Cutbacks to government budgets, staffing and the Great Recession have only exacerbated this lack of local analytical skill and staff. In spite of these challenges, numerous small-scale integrated data projects have been undertaken across the United States, but comparatively less well-resourced jurisdictions have only been able to look on with envy as their neighbors forge ahead to take advantage of the information produced by the integration of data from the public sector. As a result, a third area in which the federal government has facilitated collaboration in education and social policymaking is in supporting the construction of integrated state data systems.

Over the last decade, jointly funded grants from the federal departments of Health and Human Services and Education have supported states' efforts to maximize the use of administrative data. This infusion of federal funds has helped to level the playing field across states, increasing states' and local jurisdictions' opportunities for using their data more effectively. In 2002, American Recovery and Reinvestment Act (ARRA) dollars funded the first state-level Statewide Longitudinal Data Systems

(SLDSs). SLDS systems initially focused on linking K–12 with higher education data to examine the postsecondary outcomes of students, and a number of these systems involve researcher partners. With additional federal funding, some states integrated wage data from their employment and economic development departments to build upon what they learned about higher education outcomes, carrying it forward into understanding workforce economic outcomes. As of this writing, nearly all fifty states have SLDSs in place, and states such as Maryland, North Carolina and Texas benefit from university-based research partners.

Recognizing that states and local governments serve residents across the life span, the federal government has provided direction and funding for P20W systems, or integrated data systems that span a broad life cycle of service use and social and education policy. The next step in moving toward this P20W ideal has been to fund integrated data systems for the earliest years, or Early Childhood Integrated Data Systems (ECIDS). Because of the relative complexity of early childhood policy and programming, states must develop unique capacities to undertake these newer integrated data systems (Coffey, Granneman, Larson, & Howe, forthcoming). This latest investment also aligns with the energized early childhood policy priorities of many states and the Obama administration.

Characteristics of researcher–policymaker partnerships like those featured throughout this book are apparent in the P20W context, and ongoing information infrastructure development offers new opportunities for these partnerships. Researchers working with P20W projects have access to copious amounts of linked administrative data as well as the on-the-ground insights of practitioners who serve populations under study. State agencies working with researchers benefit from the literature review and methodological and statistical expertise offered by academic researchers. In combining talents, these collaborations produce dynamic, mutually valued relationships that benefit the communities in which they work (Gooden, Graham, & Martin, 2014). The importance of this new era of information creation and research for government cannot be overstated. Fantuzzo and Culhane (2015) note that integrated data systems are poised to help address some of the most pervasive dysfunctions in American government in their description of their concept of *actionable intelligence:*

> Actionable intelligence (AI) satisfies our need for both effective and ethical processes to produce information that can shape policy and improve practice. In stark contrast to the unilateral and unidirectional approach to public administration and research that is irrelevant and unresponsive to the voice of community partners, actionable intelligence is the result of a dynamic process that uses quality integrated data within a community to foster essential dialogue among relevant

contributors. Here *data* are not intelligence, but they are necessary to produce actionable intelligence.

(p. 11, original emphasis)

Access to Data and Use

Successful researcher–policymaker partnerships rest upon a supportive context and a number of "ingredients" as described in Chapter 1 and throughout the case studies in this book. Because the business of researcher–policymaker partnerships is so often about rigorously collecting and analyzing data and facilitating the use of research results in policymaking, two new ingredients to the future of a successful partnership recipe are increased access to data and new tools to make results not only accessible, but also engaging.

Access to data is increasing thanks to federal investments and the drive of many levels of government to use data and make better sense of it. Once states construct systems that integrate data, they must ensure the access to systems and facilitate effective use. In particular, Kathy Stack (see Chapter 6) has emphasized both the need for states to harness administrative data to boost knowledge about program performance and the need to focus on data use as a learning tool, not as a punitive measure through high-stakes monitoring (Center for Public Impact, 2016). Data use also figures prominently in the CASEL Washoe and SanDERA cases in Chapter 3. As that partnership and many of the others in this book illustrate, researchers and policymakers working together to understand program impacts can serve to eliminate the "gotcha" anxieties of policymakers who see evaluation mainly as a way to cut programs and budgets. Stack states that "bringing evaluation officers and data together, they (agencies) can learn from experience and get excited about the possibilities" (CPI, 2016).

The latest round of federal SLDS funding (2015) through the Institute of Education Sciences (IES) focused on data use. Partnerships with researchers were not explicitly required for these grants, but again, many states are choosing to include researcher partners in their plans of work. Even if researcher partners are not directly involved, the research on data use is vital to informing the work that grant recipient states are implementing to boost the data literacy of policymakers and the public. The latter in particular is essential to upholding the transparency values of government agencies, while also ensuring the maintenance of data privacy. The overarching philosophy behind this shift from funding systems to funding the work that boosts use of those systems is that without use, policymakers and the public cannot benefit from better data. Working with researcher partners or utilizing the knowledge that comes from research on information use in policymaking and program improvement will continue to be essential in these new grant activities.

In spite of the groundbreaking technology products such as integrated data systems and the researcher–policymaker partnerships that support them, data systems alone are not a panacea for what ails education and social policy. The presence of an integrated data system does not guarantee effective use of information, and an integrated data system co-managed by a researcher partner does not guarantee partnership. Conaway, Keesler, and Schwartz (2015) reinforce the effective researcher–policymaker partnership themes emerging from previous chapters of this book in their state perspective on SLDSs. They note that the barriers to collaboration and the ability to take full advantage of the benefits of SLDSs as a means to collaborate rest on the need to establish mutual value in the results of research (aligning the needs of the agency with the interests of the researcher), mutual understanding of and flexibility to accommodate the pace of information needs (finding ways to build internal analytical capacity for tight policy-making timelines) and asserting the state needs for knowledge to build a coherent portfolio of information on which to base decisions (by creating a research plan for state policymaking into which researcher requests must fit to be approved) (Conaway et al., 2015). Conaway et al. (2015) also point out rightly that in spite of their great promise, SLDSs do not contain all of the information considered most meaningful for comprehensive policy analysis. Qualitative factors such as student motivation, attitudes toward interventions or resilience factors are typically excluded from systems that were originally constructed to meet reporting requirements.

On the other hand, SLDSs can provide the quantitative resources to ensure the vitality of mixed-methods research now considered to be more comprehensively informative to public policy (Burke Johnson & Onwuegbuzie, 2004: Micari, Light, Calkins, & Streitwiser, 2007). Again, this opens up another opportunity for policymakers and researchers to partner as quantitative analysis and qualitative methods are combined to provide the rich and multifaceted perspectives needed to develop the best possible education and social policies.

New Ways to Communicate Research Knowledge

To make change and inform policy, knowledge must be used. In the chapter on utilizing research and throughout this book, contributors shared insights on the communication methods that were most likely to lead to policymakers' use of research findings. In Cadigan and colleagues' case study of Minnesota's Early Childhood Caucus, face-to-face meetings were key, as were short, easily digestible reports. In the Massachusetts Department of Elementary and Secondary Education partnership, Conaway describes the department's requirement of two-page summaries of completed academic research (Conaway et al., 2015). In each of these examples and others, complex research findings were made clear, concise and easy to understand for policymakers as well as the public.

New trends in methods to communicate complex information clearly and effectively offer opportunities to support the work of researcher–policymaker partnerships. Thanks to advances in technology (tablets and touchscreens that maximize screen space with no need for menus), high dpi printing (allowing for ultra-high resolution printing) and findings from communications science about how the human brain learns best, researchers' findings need no longer be limited to the journal article or the arid government white paper. Innovative communication methods and data visualization in particular have become essential components of making complex research findings accessible to multiple populations, including policymakers and the public. Visual rhetoric and data visualization are two related methods of making complex research information accessible to policymakers and others with limited time. Both methods take advantage of the human brain's tendency to process complex information (and recall it) more effectively if it is accompanied by images (Tufte, 2001). Examples of innovative, accessible depictions of complex research are only increasing. For example, in some graduate education programs, students who will one day become researchers or perhaps policymakers are learning to summarize thesis and dissertation findings in engaging and creative ways. An example of this is the London School of Economics, which has paired its social science graduate students with its graphic communications department since 2009 for its Visual Rhetoric: Collaborating for the Social Sciences program (Hilton, Tsirogianni, & Bauer, 2014).

Faster computing power has assured that we can create visualizations nearly as quickly as analysis itself, and many users, including policymakers and the public, can easily acquire data querying tools and skills to make their own explorations possible, particularly on websites built with easy querying capacity. These changes stand to make the twenty-first century an exciting time for information management and use in general, but public policymaking in particular will benefit. These trends bode well for effective collaborations on policy analysis and the need to produce clear and meaningful communications.

Future Research

If Wilson's (1998) prescient work was correct, humanity will need to learn to work across sectors and academic disciplines to solve the most challenging problems into the foreseeable future. This book offers ingredients that we believe, and the case authors have confirmed, are essential to successful and lasting researcher–policymaker partnerships. We also believe that we have helped to fill some of the gaps in knowledge in this area. In spite of this, we know that our understanding of these partnerships is incomplete. To continue the progress, we recommend further exploration in additional areas related to partnerships. It is clear to us that additional knowledge is needed about the effectiveness of different structures of partnerships (e.g., degrees of institutionalization of specific aspects of the partnership); the role of funding in the longevity of partnerships (e.g., are there ways partnerships become self-sustaining after receiving an initial infusion of funding?); differences in experiences of researcher–policymaker partnerships in other countries or international organizations such as the World Health Organization, NATO or others; and the lessons of successful researcher–policymaker partnerships about communicating about the value of the partnership itself (and not only the research findings that the partnership helps to generate).

One area we feel is particularly ripe for additional exploration is the relationship of culture and researcher–policymaker partnerships. "Culture" describes the norms, values and procedures for functioning in an organization or group such as decision-making processes and power structures. Navigating the differences between organizational cultures is key to any partnership, but particularly so for researchers and policymakers who work together on research efforts because we believe the attributes where they differ the most are also often those that have the most important implications for policy research.

We are not the first to recognize this. In fact, a number of the contributors in this book highlighted cultural differences but primarily through the strategies they shared to improve and maintain their working relationship with their partners. Communication was critically important to the SanDERA case in Chapter 3. In this example, entities were in frequent and regular communication about project progress. So, too, was this emphasized in the cases from Heinrich and Good in Chapter 4. Listening also was emphasized in the Heinrich and Good case in which each side made a good-faith effort to understand the perspectives of the other and take into account the typical timeframes and workflows that needed to be accounted for to make progress on research. The Hennepin-University Partnership (Chapter 4) likewise attends regularly to understanding and nurturing a sense of value in partnership by gathering feedback from partners, and in Chapter 6, the New Mexico–Results First partnership members communicated biweekly and held regular site visits. In each case, partners noted the importance of learning about the other partner's day-to-day world and communicating regularly. In most instances, this increased mutual understanding and respect, and the likelihood that true partnership could ensue, by members leaving "egos and titles at the door."

In Gooden et al.'s (2014) interviews with SLDS partners they identified informal and formal domains in which partners needed to focus their efforts to successfully collaborate. Formal structures included things like memoranda of understanding, payment structures for handling funding and technology and security rules around handling data. Informal factors included relationship building and the cultivation of trust, shared vision and leadership and communication and collaboration (Gooden et al.,

2014, p. 188). As shown by the cases in this book, the informal factors are typically addressed through each partner getting familiar with the culture and norms of the other. Listening and learning are essential.

Although this is easier said than done, we are confident that it is an area ripe for additional research and practical guidance and may be one of the more significant areas of future research. Specific aspects of the cultural differences between policymakers and researchers are informed by work that has been done in other disciplines and sectors. For example, the evolution of a sector, as can be observed from the early discussion of the establishment of the land grant university system in Chapter 1 can influence how the university system sees its role in the larger community and its work with other sectors. Within both the research and policy sectors, professional associations and even the dominant educational discipline and level of education can influence leadership style (Braxton & Hargens, 1996; Del Favero, 2001), willingness to share power (Kuhn, 1962, 1996; Ruscio, 1987), attitudes toward changes in practice such as adopting evidence-based models and decision-making practices (Jarvis-Selinger, Collins, & Pratt, 2007; Lopez & Russell, 2008). Given that history, professional association influence and education are significant parts of the policymaker and research sectors, they are likely salient attributes that inform how we understand culture when we undertake collaboration. Future research should take a closer look at multiple researcher–policymaker partnerships to closely examine the patterns of interaction and the elements of infrastructure that produce the best results and most lasting relationships when navigating cultural differences. We suspect that additional ingredients are essential to this important aspect of collaboration and look forward to those ingredients being added to our list. Most of all, we see researcher–policymaker partnerships as tangible manifestations of the need to bring together multiple sectors, talents and perspectives to solve some of the most challenging education and social policy problems.

References

Braxton, J.M., & Hargens, L.L. (1996). Variations among academic disciplines: Analytical frameworks and research. *Higher Education: Handbook of Theory and Research*, *11*, 1–45.

Burke Johnson, R., & Onwuegbuzie, A.J. (2004). Mixed methods research: A research paradigm whose time has come. *Educational Researcher*, *33*(7), 14–26.

Center for Public Impact. (2016). *An emphasis on evidence*. Retrieved on July 5, 2016 from: http://www.centreforpublicimpact.org/article/an-emphasis-on-evidence/.

Coffey, M., Granneman, K.L., Larson, A.M., & Howe, C. (forthcoming). Building state capacity to use longitudinal data systems. *American Review of Public Administration*.

Commission on Evidence-Based Policymaking. (2016). *Overview*. Washington, DC. Retrieved on August 5, 2016 from: http://www2.census.gov/about/linkage/meetings/2016–07–22/about-cep.pdf.

Conaway, C., Keesler, V., & Schwartz, N. (2015). What research do state education agencies really need? The promise and limitations of state longitudinal data systems. *Educational Evaluation and Policy Analysis, 37*(18), 16S–28S.

Del Favero, M. (2001). *The influence of academic discipline on administrative behaviors on academic deans.* Unpublished doctoral dissertation, Vanderbilt University, Nashville, TN.

Fantuzzo, J., & Culhane, D. (2015). *Actionable intelligence: Using integrated data systems to achieve a more effective, efficient, and ethical government.* New York, NY: Palgrave Macmillan.

Gooden, S.T., Graham, F.S., & Martin, K. (2014). Research partnerships at the state level: Bridging the academic-practitioner divide. *State & Local Government Review, 46*(3), 184–196.

Haskins, R., & Margolis, G. (2015). *Show me the evidence: Obama's fight for rigor and results in social policy.* Washington, DC: The Brookings Institution.

Hilton, T., Tsirogianni, S., & Bauer, M.W. (2014). *Visual rhetoric: Collaborating for social impact.* Report. University of the Arts London, London School of Economics.

Jarvis-Selinger, S., Collins, J.B., & Pratt, D.D. (2007). Do academic origins influence perspectives on teaching? *Teacher Education Quarterly, 34*(3), 67–81.

Kamensky, J. (2016). Obama's last budget scales up evidence agenda. *PA Times, 2*(2), 10–14.

Kuhn, T.S. (1962). *The structure of scientific revolutions.* Chicago: University of Chicago Press.

Kuhn, T.S. (1996). *The structure of scientific revolutions* (3rd ed.). Chicago: University of Chicago Press.

Lopez, V., & Russell, M. (2008). Examining the predictors of juvenile probation officers' rehabilitation orientation. *Journal of Criminal Justice, 36,* 381–388.

Micari, M., Light, G., Calkins, S., & Streitwiser, B. (2007). Assessment beyond performance: Phenomenography in education evaluation. *American Journal of Evaluation, 28*(4), 458–476.

Ruscio, K.P. (1987). Many sectors, many professions. In B.R. Clark (Ed.), *The academic profession: National, disciplinary, and institutional settings* (pp. 332–365). Los Angeles: University of California Press.

Tufte, E. (2001). *The visual display of quantitative information.* Cheshire, CT: Graphics Press, LLC.

United States Congress. (2015). *H.R. 1831, Evidence-based Policymaking Commission Act of 2016.* Retrieved on July 8, 2016 from: https://www.congress.gov/114/plaws/publ140/PLAW-114publ140.pdf.

Wilson, E.O. (1998). *Consilience: The unity of knowledge.* New York, NY: Alfred A. Knopf.

Appendix A

Juvenile Justice Reforms in HB86 and Ohio FY 2012–2013 State Budget (HB 153)

- Promotes research-informed practices with RECLAIM program and reallocation of institutional savings into evidence-based community programs.*
- Creates a uniform juvenile competency law.
- Increases judicial discretion in some instances and makes statutory changes to specific juvenile sentencing provisions, including a new limited waiver option.
- Creates an Interagency Mental Health Juvenile Task Force.

1. **HB 86 promotes researcher-informed practices.** Specifically in reference to how RECLAIM dollars should be spent, it adds new language that states: "Research-supported, outcome-based programs and services, to the extent available, shall be encouraged."
2. **HS 86 adopts a uniform juvenile competency code that applies to all delinquency proceedings using a juvenile-specific standard.** A juvenile is incompetent if, "due to mental illness, intellectual disability, or developmental disability, or otherwise due to or a lack of mental capacity, the child is presently incapable of understanding the nature and objective of proceedings against the child or of assisting in the child's defense." A child who is 14 or older who "is or otherwise found to be mentally ill, intellectually disabled, or developmentally disabled" is rebuttably presumed to "not have a lack of mental capacity" (for purposes of determining mental capacity only). The law provides significant detail on procedures for identifying experts, conducting competency evaluations, addressing youth found incompetent, etc.
3. **HS 86 extends juvenile court authority to allow for judicial release throughout a youth's term of commitment.** Under this reform, judges maintain jurisdiction to consider early-release opportunities throughout a youth's commitment, including juveniles serving mandatory sentences.

4. **HB 86 revises four of the existing mandatory sentencing specifications involving a firearm to allow for judicial discretion in instances where the youth was not the main actor.** Specifically, juvenile judges have more discretion in sentencing for youth accomplices (complicity) under certain conditions where the youth did not furnish, dispose of or otherwise use the weapon.

5. **HB 86 creates a narrow reverse waiver provision for youth automatically transferred to adult court (mandatory bindover) that would permit transfer back to juvenile court.** This reverse waiver procedure would only apply in those circumstances where a youth is convicted of an offense that would not have originally qualified as a mandatory bindover offense. The case would go back to juvenile court for juvenile sentencing or an amenability hearing to consider the appropriate sentence.

6. **HB 86 creates an Interagency Mental Health Juvenile Justice Task Force to address the challenges of delinquent youth who "suffer from serious mental illness or emotional and behavioral disorders."** The six-month task force has representation from the state Supreme Court, the governor's office, the House, the Senate, ODYS, ODMH, juvenile judges, public defenders, child development experts, prosecutors, academic institutions and others. It must submit a report with findings and recommendations to the Legislature by March 31, 2012.

Note

* The final state budget (HB 153) states: "For purposes of implementing juvenile sentencing reforms . . . the Department of Youth Services may use up to forty-five per cent of the unexpended, unencumbered balance of the portion of appropriation item 470401, RECLAIM Ohio, that is allocated to juvenile correctional facilities in each fiscal year to expand Targeted RECLAIM, the Behavioral Health Juvenile Justice Initiative, and other evidence-based community programs."

   HB 86 was signed by the governor on June 29, 2011, and is effective September 30, 2011.

   Source: Celeste, G. (2013). The bridge to somewhere: How research made its way into legislative juvenile justice reform in Ohio, a case study, p. 41.

Appendix B

Operating Guidelines for San Diego Education Research Alliance (SanDERA) at the University of California, San Diego

A SDUSD/UCSD Partnership   June 2015

SanDERA Operating Guidelines

The San Diego Education Research Alliance (SanDERA)—an independent research entity based at the University of California at San Diego (UCSD)—was established in May 2010 by the San Diego Unified School District (SDUSD) and the Department of Economics at UCSD. SanDERA formalizes and focuses the long-standing relationship between the district and university, supports the articulation of a shared research agenda linked to the district's strategic goals and provides a structure for conducting and coordinating ongoing research and sharing findings within the education community and beyond. The guidelines contained in this document are intended to promote effective, consistent and appropriate operating practices for SanDERA and its partners.

1.0   Introduction

1.1   Mission of SanDERA

The San Diego Education Research Alliance (SanDERA) at the University of California at San Diego (UCSD) conducts rigorous and relevant research that contributes to the development of education policy and informs, supports, and sustains high-quality educational opportunities for all students in San Diego and beyond.

1.2   Purpose of SanDERA

SanDERA formalizes and extends a long-standing university/district partnership established for the purpose of conducting education research for and about SDUSD. SanDERA, in collaboration with the district, identifies questions and issues of interest to the San Diego education community, conducts research studies that address those questions and issues, builds and maintains a longitudinal data archive to support ongoing research activities, and informs policy and practice by sharing research findings in San Diego and beyond.

1.3   SanDERA Function

Working with district leadership, SanDERA:

- identifies high-priority issues or problems on which to focus research,
- formalizes a research agenda with clear links to the district's mission, goals, and strategic plan,
- makes its research agenda public and shares progress and findings with the SDUSD Board of Education, district leadership, and the education, business, research, and parent communities,
- informs wider audiences by publishing and presenting findings through its own website, academic journals, and outside organizations, and
- is open to collaborating with other districts and research entities to study issues of common interest.

1.4   SanDERA Guiding Principles

1.4.1   Shared Research Agenda

The SanDERA Executive Committee, in consultation with senior district leadership and the Board of Advisors, establishes and maintains a research agenda that is aligned with the district's mission, goals, and strategic plan, is focused on high-priority issues of problems facing the district, and informs the work of educators and policymakers in San Diego and beyond.

1.4.2   Rigorous and Relevant Research

Research projects undertaken by SanDERA are methodologically sound, carefully conducted, and focused on significant issues or challenges faced by SDUSD and the broader education community.

1.4.3   Data Quality and Security

Both SanDERA and SDUSD staff make every effort to ensure that data used in the conduct of SanDERA research are current, correct, consistent, and appropriate—and immediately seek clarification or share concerns, if questions or problems arise. SanDERA understands that access to SDUSD data is both a privilege and a serious responsibility. Data security is a top priority for SanDERA, and a range of safeguards is in place to ensure that data under SanDERA's control are protected.

1.4.4 *Effective Communication between Partners*

SanDERA and SDUSD staff are committed to maintaining open lines of communication. Twice monthly meetings of the Executive Committee serve as SanDERA's primary communication mechanism with the district; periodic meetings with the SanDERA Board of Advisors and district leadership ensure that all parties are aware of SanDERA's ongoing research activities and findings.

1.4.5 *Trust*

The SanDERA partnership is built upon a foundation of trust and a common desire to engage in academic research that impacts the quality of public education in San Diego and beyond. SanDERA has a "no surprises" policy. That is, new research is not initiated prior to obtaining formal consent from SDUSD and district leadership is briefed on research findings prior to publication or presentation to the public.

1.4.6 *Dissemination of Research Findings*

Dissemination of research findings is a key component of SanDERA's mission. SanDERA shares all research findings with its Board of Advisors, as well as with SDUSD senior leadership. Findings are also shared with the broader San Diego community at public forums, and with the research community via publications, presentations, and the SanDERA website.

2.0   SanDERA Organization

SanDERA is a collaborative partnership between San Diego Unified School District (SDUSD) and the Department of Economics at the University of California at San Diego (UCSD), established for the purpose of conducting research that contributes to the development of education policy and informs educational practice in San Diego and beyond. The SanDERA organization consists of an Executive Committee, a Board of Advisors, staff based at UCSD, and external research partners.

2.1   *SanDERA Executive Committee*

The SanDERA Executive Board is a permanent body established through a Memorandum of Agreement (MOA) between SDUSD and UCSD (see Section 3.1). The function of the Executive Committee is to direct the work of SanDERA, as described in Section 2.1.2.

2.1.1   Membership

SanDERA's Executive Committee is composed of six members—three from SDUSD and three from UCSD. SDUSD members are the Director of the Office of Research and Development, the Director of Data Analysis and Reporting, and the Director of Instructional Data Support. UCSD members are SanDERA's Executive Director, Director, and Senior Statistician.

2.1.2   Responsibilities

SanDERA's Executive Committee is responsible for:

- working with district leadership and the Board of Advisors to develop and carry out SanDERA's research agenda,
- establishing the SanDERA Board of Advisors and convening biannual Board of Advisors meetings,
- overseeing ongoing research projects and related publications,
- ensuring data quality and security,
- maintaining effective communication with the SDUSD Board of Education, senior leadership, and the SanDERA Board of Advisors,
- disseminating research findings,
- collaborating with external research partners and funders to support SanDERA's research agenda, and
- coordinating the activities of SDUSD and UCSD staff.

2.1.3   Meeting Schedule

The SanDERA Executive Committee meets twice monthly.

2.2   SanDERA Board of Advisors

The SanDERA Board of Advisors, co-chaired by the Executive Director of SanDERA and the SDUSD Director of the Office of Research and Development, provides advice to the Executive Committee on SanDERA policies, practices, products, and publications.

2.2.1   Membership

The Board of Advisors is composed of up to 12 standing members—three university representatives, three district representatives, three parent/community representatives, and three members representing the San Diego business, foundation, and/or philanthropic community. Up to two ad hoc members may be temporarily added to the Board of Advisors if their areas of expertise or interest are aligned with specific research projects or their expertise is needed to address issues related to a particular study.

2.2.1.1 Six members of the Board of Advisors (university and district representatives) are *institutional* members. The entities listed below have perpetual membership on the Board of Advisors and the organizations themselves appoint persons to represent them. Although appointed by their organizations, these persons meet criteria for Board of Advisors membership. Institutional members include:

University Representatives

- University of California at San Diego (UCSD)
- San Diego State University (SDSU)
- San Diego Community College District (SDCCD)

District Representatives

- SDUSD Superintendent
- San Diego Education Association (SDEA)
- Administrators Association of San Diego (AASD)

2.2.1.2 Six members of the Board of Advisors (three parent/community members and three business, foundation, and/or philanthropic community members) are *individual* members. These individuals, who meet the criteria for Board of Advisors membership (see Section 2.2.2), represent a variety of parent, community, business, and/or philanthropic organizations interested in educational issues in San Diego. The individuals themselves—and not their employers or affiliate organizations—are members of the Board of Advisors. As a result, if individual members move from one organization to another, they maintain their membership as long as they continue to meet membership criteria. The exception to this is individuals who become employed by SDUSD or another institutional member, who are not eligible to remain on the Board of Advisors unless they are appointed as representatives of their organizations. Individual members serve staggered three-year terms.

2.2.1.3 BOARD OF ADVISORS SELECTION PROCESS

Institutional members (university and district representatives) of the Board of Advisors are appointed by their respective organizations, and do not have term limits. If an institutional member resigns from the Board of Advisors, his/her organization will appoint a replacement.

Individual members serve three-year terms on the Board of Advisors, and may be re-nominated and reappointed for an additional three-year term if they meet membership criteria. After a two-year hiatus, a member may be appointed to one additional term. If an individual member resigns from the Board of Advisors before his/her term of office has been completed, the SanDERA Executive Committee will appoint a replacement to serve out the remainder of his/her term. The Executive Committee may propose the new member (i.e., replacement member) as an individual member in his/her own right at the conclusion of the original member's term.

Each year, the Executive Committee compiles a list of proposed *individual* members for consideration at the spring Board of Advisors meeting. Newly appointed members (both institutional and individual) participate in an orientation session prior to the start of their Board of Advisors terms the following fall.

2.2.2   Criteria for Membership

Members have an interest in contributing to the field of education research—specifically the research being conducted by SanDERA—and a willingness to support SanDERA's mission, purpose, and guiding principles. Members represent a variety of perspectives on the challenges faced by schools and school districts, are affiliated with a range of organizations and institutions across San Diego, and are racially/ethnically diverse.

2.2.3   Attendance

Members are expected to attend (or send a designated alternate who meets membership criteria) all Board of Advisors meetings. If a member cannot attend a meeting, he/she is responsible for remaining informed via communication with his/her alternate.

2.2.4   Responsibilities

The Board of Advisors is responsible for:
- advising the Executive Committee on issues related to SanDERA's research agenda and ongoing research projects,
- providing early feedback on research products,
- supporting dissemination activities, including public forums, and
- informing colleagues and constituents about the work of SanDERA.

2.2.5   Meeting Schedule

The Board of Advisors meets two times each year, in the fall and in the spring.

2.3   SanDERA Staff

SanDERA staff, based in the Department of Economics at UCSD, includes an Executive Director, a Director, a Senior Statistician, and several doctoral students. The Executive Director and Director provide direct oversight of all SanDERA operations, research projects, products, and publications, ensure data quality and security, supervise SanDERA staff, secure funding for all SanDERA activities, and maintain effective working relationships with the SDUSD Board of Education, SDUSD senior leadership, and the SanDERA Board of Advisors.

2.4   External Researchers and Research Partners

SanDERA may partner with other universities or consortia to conduct research consistent with its research agenda. In every case, projects undertaken will first be approved by the SDUSD Research Project Review Panel (RPRP). All data access and security provisions outlined in this document apply to any project undertaken jointly by SanDERA and a research partner.

3.0   SanDERA Operations

3.1   Memorandum of Agreement (MOA)

The MOA between UCSD and SDUSD established SanDERA for the purpose of informing, supporting, and sustaining quality education in SDUSD and sharing information between parties in a manner consistent with the Family Educational Rights and Privacy Act of 1974 (FERPA) and SDUSD Administrative Procedures 6525, 6527, and 4930. The MOA describes the structure, function, and benefits of SanDERA, names the parties to the agreement, and binds those parties to agreements related to compliance with FERPA, costs of research, administrative and outreach activities, research methodology, data request and use, and research products. The current MOA expires on June 30, 2020. At that time, and every five years thereafter, the MOA must be renewed for an additional five-year period. A copy of the MOA is attached.

3.2   SanDERA Research Agenda

The SanDERA Executive Committee, in consultation with district leadership, develops a formal research agenda aligned with the district's mission, goals, and strategic plan. The research agenda is shared with the SDUSD Board of Education and the SanDERA Board of Advisors and reviewed and/or updated annually.

3.2.1   Research Approval Process

All SanDERA research activities based in SDUSD are approved by the SDUSD Research Proposal Review Panel (RPRP). Information about RPRP timelines and submission requirements can obtained from the

Director of SDUSD's Office of Research and Development or found at http://www.sandi.net/page/1586.

3.3   Funding and Fundraising

SanDERA, not SDUSD, assumes responsibility for securing funding to support SanDERA's operational expenses, research activities, and outreach.

3.4   Data Access and Security

3.4.1 SanDERA keeps all research files secure and maintains signed data confidentiality agreements for all individuals with access to data. All data received from SDUSD are maintained at a single workstation in a restricted access laboratory; other workstations hold extracts of the master datasets for specific research projects, with identities of individuals concealed. Data do not leave that laboratory and file sharing is not enabled or permitted. Data collected in the conduct of SanDERA research are similarly protected; research materials (e.g., interview tapes and transcripts, survey responses) are kept in locked file cabinets and all computers containing research materials are password protected.

3.4.2 SanDERA complies with all provisions of the Family Educational Rights and Privacy Act of 1974 (FERPA) and SDUSD Administrative Procedures 6525, 6527, and 4930.

3.4.3 The ability to access or maintain data will not be transferred from SanDERA to any other institution or entity without the written consent of SDUSD.

3.4.4 SanDERA requires all employees, contractors, and agents of any kind to comply with all applicable provisions of FERPA and other federal laws with respect to shared data. SanDERA requires each employee, contractor, or agent with access to data to sign an appropriate confidentiality agreement and maintains copies of agreements for periodic review.

3.5   Products and Publications

3.5.1   SDUSD Review of Findings, Draft/Final Reports, and Manuscripts

SanDERA has a strict "no surprises" agreement with SDUSD, and the district is always aware of the content of SanDERA reports prior to public release. This is accomplished via SDUSD's membership on the Executive Committee and Board of Advisors, and through specially arranged briefings for SDUSD senior leadership. SanDERA regularly consults with SDUSD leadership and staff to ensure that research data and products are accurate. Final decisions about research methodology and content are made by the SanDERA Executive Committee.

3.5.2   Dissemination of Research Findings

SanDERA research findings are shared with SDUSD leadership, the Board of Education, the SanDERA Board of Advisors, the San Diego community, the broader research community, and funders via briefings and presentations, public forums, a range of publications, and the SanDERA website.

3.6   Communication with SDUSD Senior Leadership and Board of Education

The SDUSD Director of the Office of Research and Development regularly communicates with the district Superintendent, the Superintendent's Cabinet, and other district staff to ensure that they are knowledgeable about SanDERA's research agenda and ongoing research activities. The SDUSD Board of Education is kept informed about SanDERA research via memoranda; at the Board's request, additional information and/or briefings about research findings are provided.

3.7   Relationships with Other Research Entities (Universities, Consortia, Research Groups)

SanDERA may undertake collaborative research projects with other universities, consortia, or research groups (e.g., regional education laboratories) if research topics are consistent with SanDERA's mission and research agenda. All activities associated with joint research projects will be approved by the SDUSD Research Proposal Review Panel (RPRP) and conform to these operating guidelines.

4.0   Benefits of SanDERA

The benefits of SanDERA include:

- A collaboratively developed and focused research agenda aligned with district goals/strategic plan, resulting in findings that inform ongoing work and district reform efforts;
- Support from external funders to conduct comprehensive research, supplementing district resources so that other key work can be accomplished. Strategic leveraging of new sustaining funding to initiate new projects;
- Facilitating focus during times of transition that are inevitable in any large urban district, allowing sustained effort to be directed to identified priorities;
- Development of links between research efforts centered at the UCSD Department of Economics (SanDERA) and other education research endeavors at UCSD, including but not limited to the Education Studies Department;

- With the help of regular public forums and the engagement of members of the Board of Advisors, enhanced outreach to and engagement with the San Diego community and increased relevance of research;
- Increased publication rate of independent, high-quality education research that is relevant to California education policy and San Diego in particular;
- Enhanced possibilities of collaborations with similar consortia in other districts, with the Public Policy Institute of California, with the University of California Educational Evaluation Center (UCEC), and with offices in campuses across the University of California.

Appendix C
Results of "Spend-a-Dot" Activity Designed to Elicit Board of Advisor Preferences for SanDERA Research

The numbers in the following table indicate the number of votes accruing to each research possibility the board had discussed at lead-up meetings. Each board member was given multiple adhesive red dots to attach to his or her ballot.

Spend-a-Dot Priorities

Topics Suggested by Board of Advisors ➜ SanDERA's Research Agenda

Spend-a-Dot	Suggested Research Topic
14	English Learners
12	What Works? Schools and Programs that Outperform Expectations
7	Technology and Student Outcomes
6	School Leadership
5	Parent Involvement
5	AAAE Blueprint: Accelerating Achievement?
5	What Skills Do Employers Expect in SDUSD Students/Graduates?
3	Relationship between 4X4 Scheduling and Student Outcomes
3	Connection between Education and Lifestyle
2	Small Schools/School Size
2	Student Voice
2	Charter Schools
2	Community-Based School Reform
2	Is Emphasis on Accountability Narrowing the Curriculum?
2	District's New UC "a–g" Policy
1	Special Education
1	Blended Learning
0	Class Size
0	Counseling and Student-Adult Connections

Appendix D

MASTER COOPERATIVE AGREEMENT BETWEEN THE COUNTY OF HENNEPIN AND THE UNIVERSITY OF MINNESOTA

THIS MASTER COOPERATIVE AGREEMENT, hereinafter referred to as "AGREEMENT" OR "Master Agreement", is between the County of Hennepin, a political subdivision of the State of Minnesota, located at A2303 Government Center, 300 South Sixth Street, Minneapolis, MN 55487, hereinafter referred to as "COUNTY" and the Regents of the University of Minnesota, a Minnesota constitutional corporation, located at 200 Oak Street SE, Suite 450, Minneapolis, MN 55455, hereinafter referred to as "UNIVERSITY".

WHEREAS, the COUNTY and the UNIVERSITY wish to work collaboratively in order to capture value for both organizations on a range of projects such as community-based research, sharing of academic and practitioner expertise, and providing students with field experience, and

WHEREAS, joint projects can be undertaken pursuant to approved Work Orders established under the terms and conditions of this AGREEMENT, and

WHEREAS, both parties wish to streamline the process for the COUNTY to contract with the UNIVERSITY for a wide variety of projects, work, and services, hereinafter referred to as "Work".

NOW, THEREFORE, in consideration of the mutual undertakings and agreements hereinafter set forth, the COUNTY and the UNIVERSITY agree as follows:

1. TERM, COST AND LIMITATION OF THE AGREEMENT.

1.1 This AGREEMENT shall be effective commencing July 1, 2010 and terminating June 30, 2015 unless terminated earlier pursuant to Section 5, except for the requirements specified in approved Work Orders under this AGREEMENT which contain completion dates that extend beyond the termination date specified in this sentence. This AGREEMENT may be extended by written agreement executed by both parties to this AGREEMENT.

1.2 The custody of all Work Orders with periods of performance extending beyond July 1, 2010 issued under Agreement No. A0712000 shall be automatically transferred to and subject to the terms of this successor AGREEMENT. A list of these Work Orders may be found in Attachment C. Future funding expanding or renewing those Work Orders shall be included in the funding ceiling listed in Section 1.3 below.

1.3 The cumulative dollar amount of all approved Work Orders issued under this AGREEMENT shall not exceed Seven Million Five Hundred Thousand Dollars and No Cents ($7,500,000).

1.4 This AGREEMENT shall not be utilized (a) for the licensing of pre-existing software or other intellectual property of the UNIVERSITY, (b) for creation and sale of new software, or (c) for the provision of services covered by other agreements.

2. WORK ORDERS.

2.1 The parties agree that the Work performed shall be accomplished by the execution of approved Work Orders (Attachment A). Each Work Order shall specifically reference this AGREEMENT, shall be deemed to be an attachment to this AGREEMENT, shall not, when aggregated with all other executed Work Orders, exceed the cumulative dollar amount set forth in Section 1.3 and shall be governed by the terms of this AGREEMENT. Each Work Order shall be executed by authorized signatories of both parties. The Work Order shall include, but not be limited to, the following:

    2.1.1 Project title and a description of the Work to be performed, including any deliverables,

    2.1.2 Identification of Departments and points of contact from the COUNTY and the UNIVERSITY,

    2.1.3 The cost of the Work performed, including a detailed project budget if required,

    2.1.4 The period of performance of the Work Order,

    2.1.5 Payment terms,

    2.1.6 Special terms and conditions, including reporting requirements, and,

    2.1.7 Whether UNIVERSITY will be provided with any data on individuals, vendors of services, licensees or registered persons from "a program for which authority is vested in a component of the welfare system" (within the meaning of Minnesota Statutes 13.46 Subd. 1(b)). Such data is referred to herein as "Welfare Data."

2.2 Any material alterations, variations, modifications, or waivers of provisions of an approved Work Order shall only be valid when they have been reduced to writing as a Change Order (Attachment B) executed by the authorized signatories of both parties.

2.3 Except as expressly provided as an exception to this provision in a Work Order, if there is any conflict between the terms of this AGREEMENT and a Work Order, the terms of this AGREEMENT shall prevail.

3. PAYMENT.

3.1 The UNIVERSITY shall submit invoices for services with the frequency stipulated in the Work Order. Payment shall be made within thirty-five (35) days from receipt of the invoice, unless in the opinion of COUNTY the invoice is incorrect, defective, or otherwise improper. If the COUNTY believes the invoice is incorrect, defective, or otherwise improper, the COUNTY will notify the UNIVERSITY in accordance with this AGREEMENT. UNIVERSITY must submit invoices to COUNTY within three hundred sixty-five (365) days of the date of service to be eligible for reimbursement.

3.2 Payment shall not constitute an acceptance of any Work or services not in accordance with the requirements of the Work Order.

4. DEFAULT AND CANCELLATION.

4.1. **Failure to Comply with the Terms of the Master Agreement.** If either party materially fails to fulfill its obligations or is believed to be in breach of the terms of the Master Agreement, the non-defaulting party may provide written notice specifying in sufficient detail the nature of the alleged default. If the defaulting party has not cured the default within thirty (30) days of receiving the written notice or described the reasons why it believes no default has occurred, the non-defaulting party may terminate the Master Agreement at its discretion, in accordance with the remaining provisions of this section.

4.2 Failure to Perform on a Work Order. If either party materially fails to fulfill its obligations under an approved Work Order, the non-defaulting party may provide written notice specifying in sufficient detail the nature of the default. Such detail shall include a description of what Work was not properly performed or what product was not properly delivered and what needs to be done to correct the nonconforming Work or deliverable. If the defaulting party has not cured the default within thirty (30) days of receiving the written notice or described the reasons why it believes no default has occurred, the non-defaulting party may terminate the approved Work Order in accordance with the remaining provisions of this section.

4.3. Delay of Payment for Default. Failure to comply with the terms of this AGREEMENT shall be just cause for the COUNTY to delay payment on those Work Orders adversely affected by the alleged failure. Before delaying payment, the COUNTY must furnish written notice to UNIVERSITY in accordance with Section 4.1 or 4.2 specifying the default and what Work Orders are involved in the alleged failure. Payment will be made promptly after resolution within thirty-five (35) days. Payments shall not be delayed on Work Orders not adversely impacted by the alleged failure.

4.4 Termination of the Master Agreement. Either party may cancel this AGREEMENT at any time, with or without cause, upon ninety (90) days' written notice by certified mail to the other party. The end of the ninety (90) day notice period shall be considered the "effective termination date." Termination costs will be governed by Section 4.6 below. The termination of the Master Agreement shall not impact active individual Work Order(s), which shall be completed as originally scheduled unless terminated in accordance with Section 4.5.

4.5. Termination of a Work Order. Either party may cancel a Work Order at anytime, with or without cause, upon thirty (30) days written notice to the other party. The end of the thirty (30) day notice period shall be considered the "effective termination date." The parties shall cooperate in good faith to wind down the Work. Termination costs will be governed by Section 4.6 below.

4.6 Termination Costs. In the event of expiration or termination of this AGREEMENT or an approved Work Order hereof for any reason, each Party agrees to reasonably cooperate with the other, and with any successor service provider to ensure an orderly transition and continuity of the Work.

Except as otherwise provided herein, in the event of expiration or termination of this AGREEMENT or an approved Work Order hereof for any reason, COUNTY shall pay UNIVERSITY for materials, supplies, equipment, unrefundable travel costs, and severance pay periods incurred prior to the effective termination date. The severance pay periods shall be for any contracted employee, that is not a tenured employee and the severance pay period amount shall be limited to an employee's approved remaining budgeted compensation on the Work Order. The UNIVERSITY must supply reasonable supporting documentaiton as requested by the COUNTY.

Except as otherwise provided herein, in the event of expiration or termination of this AGREEMENT or an approved Work Order hereof for any reason, COUNTY shall pay UNIVERSITY salaries, benefits, and tuition remission through the end of the current academic semester for students performing under a then current Work Order.

In the event of a student's malfeasance, misconduct, removal from the work order for cause, voluntary quits performing, or the UNIVERSITY cancels an approved Work Order for convenience, the COUNTY shall not be liable for the costs of students beyond those reasonable costs incurred as of the effective date of termination, or such lesser amount as the parties mutually agree to be appropriate.

In the event that the UNIVERSITY cancels this AGREEMENT or an assigned Work Order for convenience, the COUNTY shall pay only the costs incurred prior to the effective termination date.

Immediately following notice of termination, the UNIVERSITY shall stop further work on an approved Work Orders and to minimize all costs and uncancellable obligations, including promptly re-directing personnel paid by COUNTY to other projects, when possible.

5.   SUBCONTRACTING AND ASSIGNMENT.

5.1 The UNIVERSITY shall not assign, transfer, or subcontract any rights or obligations under this AGREEMENT without the prior written consent of the COUNTY and subject to such conditions and provisions as the COUNTY may deem necessary. The UNIVERSITY shall be responsible for the performance of all subcontractors. The written authorization of the County Administrator, or his/her designee, is required in order to effectuate an assignment or subcontract by the UNIVERSITY.

5.2 If the COUNTY approves the UNIVERSITY'S request to subcontract or assign a Work Order under this AGREEMENT, the UNIVERSITY shall incorporate all provisions of this AGREEMENT into all subcontracts and/or assignments and make copies of all subcontracts and/or assignments available to the COUNTY upon request. Permission to subcontract or assign, however, shall under no circumstances relieve UNIVERSITY of its liabilities and obligations under the AGREEMENT.

UNIVERSITY shall be fully responsible for the performance of the specified contractual services, notwithstanding that nonperformance may have been caused by the acts, omissions, and failure of its subcontractors and lower level contractors at all levels and/or such subcontractors' employees.

6.   AMENDMENTS AND MODIFICATION.

6.1 It is understood and agreed that the entire AGREEMENT between the parties is contained herein and that this AGREEMENT supersedes all oral agreements and negotiations between the parties relating to the subject matter hereof. It is further understood and agreed that each Work Order, together with this AGREEMENT, shall contain the entire AGREEMENT between the parties, and shall supersede all oral agreements and negotiations between the parties, relating to the subject matter of each Work Order. All items referred to in this AGREEMENT are incorporated or attached, or are to be incorporated and attached, in accordance with the express terms of this AGREEMENT and any Work Order, and are deemed to be part of this AGREEMENT.

6.2 This AGREEMENT may be amended or extended by written agreement executed by both parties to this AGREEMENT.

7.   LIABILITY AND SELF-INSURANCE.

7.1 Each party shall be responsible for its own actions and the results thereof to the extent authorized by law and shall not be responsible for the acts of the other party or the results thereof. The COUNTY'S liability shall be governed by the provisions of Minnesota Statutes Chapter 466 and other applicable law. The UNIVERSITY'S liability shall be governed by the provisions of the Minnesota Tort Claims Act, Minnesota Statutes, Section 3.736, and other applicable law. The UNIVERSITY maintains a program of self-insurance and shall provide COUNTY with a certificate evidencing such insurance upon request.

7.2 Nothing herein shall be construed as a waiver by either party of any of the immunities and limitations to which either party may be entitled pursuant to Minnesota Statutes, or pursuant to any other state or federal law, rule or regulation.

7.3 Each party agrees to promptly notify the other party if it becomes aware of any potential claims arising out of the Work or services to be provided hereunder.

8. NO UNIVERSITY ENDORSEMENTS.

8.1 In no event shall the COUNTY (or its successors, employees, agents and contractors) state or imply in any publication, advertisement, or other medium that the UNIVERSITY has approved, endorsed or tested any product or service. In no event shall the UNIVERSITY'S performance of the services described in Section 2 be considered a test of the effectiveness or the basis for any endorsement of a product or service. Notwithstanding the foregoing, the COUNTY may publicly release the Work, report, faculty names, research methodology, recommendations and other items that do not expressly state that the UNIVERSITY endorses the Work.

9. USE OF NAME OR LOGO.

9.1 Each party agrees not to use the name, logo, or any other marks (including, but not limited to, colors and music) owned by or associated with the other party or the name of any representative of the other party in any sales promotion work or advertising, or any form of publicity, without the prior written permission of the other party in each instance. Nothing in the foregoing restricts the COUNTY's right to publicly release the Work, including any name, logo, or other marks contained within the Work. The parties may amend the restrictions of this clause in an approved Work Order.

10. RECORDS – AVAILABILITY/ACCESS.

10.1 Subject to the requirements of Minnesota Statutes Section 16C.05, Subd. 5 (as may be amended), the UNIVERSITY agrees that the COUNTY, the State Auditor, the Legislative Auditor or any of their duly authorized representatives, at any time during normal business hours, and as often as they may reasonably deem necessary, shall have access to and the right to examine, audit, excerpt, and transcribe any books, documents, papers, records, etc., which are pertinent to the accounting practices and procedures of the UNIVERSITY and involve transactions relating to this AGREEMENT. Such materials shall be maintained and such access and rights shall be in force and effect during the period of the AGREEMENT and for six (6) years after its termination or cancellation. This clause does not require access to be provided to client/patient records.

10.2 UNIVERSITY agrees that it will provide access to its annual OMB A-133 audit to COUNTY, the State Auditor, the Legislative Auditor or any of their duly authorized representatives, at any time during normal business hours. A-133 audit reports are also available at any time on-line from the UNIVERSITY Controller's Office web site (see http://finsys.umn.edu/controller/controllerhome.html)

11. DATA PRACTICES.

11.1 The COUNTY and the UNIVERSITY, its officers, agents, owners, partners, employees, volunteers and subcontractors agree to abide by the provisions of the Minnesota Government Data Practices Act, Minnesota Statutes, Chapter 13, the Health Insurance Portability and Accountability Act and implementing regulations, if applicable, and all other applicable State and Federal laws, rules, regulations and orders relating to data privacy or confidentiality, and as any of the same may be amended. Each party shall be responsible for any claims resulting from its officers', agents', owners', partners', employees', volunteers', assignees' or subcontractors' unlawful disclosure and/or use of such protected data, or other noncompliance with the requirements of this section. The terms of this paragraph shall survive the cancellation or termination of this AGREEMENT.

11.2 Whenever UNIVERSITY will be provided any Welfare Data under a Work Order, this AGREEMENT and the Work Order constitute a contract under which UNIVERSITY becomes part of the welfare system in connection with performing services under the Work Order. All data received by UNIVERSITY under such a Work Order shall be presumed to be non-public, and UNIVERSITY agrees that neither the UNIVERSITY, nor any UNIVERSITY personnel, agents, employees, or subcontractors shall use, disclose or otherwise make available any such data during the term of this AGREEMENT or at any time thereafter except as required to perform services for COUNTY hereunder, including to perform research specified in the Work Order, or as required by law or with COUNTY's express written consent.

12. RIGHTS IN COPYRIGHTS AND PATENTS.

12.1 "Material" shall mean any and all work, product, deliverables, or ideas that UNIVERSITY may perform, create, prepare, conceive or originate either individually or jointly with others and which arise out of the performance of this AGREEMENT

Subject to the provisions herein, if any Material is copyrightable or patentable by UNIVERSITY, all copyrights and/or patents related to the Material will be the sole and exclusive property of UNIVERSITY. COUNTY agrees, upon request of the UNIVERSITY, to execute all papers and perform all other acts necessary to assist the UNIVERSITY to obtain and register copyrights and patents on the Materials.

UNIVERSITY grants COUNTY a perpetual, irrevocable, royalty-free, worldwide and nonexclusive license to use the copyrighted Material for any legal purpose including but not limited to using, disclosing, reproducing, modifying, preparing derivative works from, distributing, performing and displaying the copyrighted Material. UNIVERSITY also grants COUNTY a perpetual, irrevocable, royalty-free, worldwide and nonexclusive license to practice or have practiced on behalf of the COUNTY the inventions claimed in any patents arising from Work Orders.

UNIVERSITY shall acquire no right, title or interest in any Data collected, received, or acquired pursuant to this AGREEMENT. UNIVERSITY acknowledges and agrees that Data must be used, controlled and safeguarded in compliance with the terms of this AGREEMENT and applicable law including but not limited to the provisions of the Minnesota Government Data Practices Act and the Health Insurance Portability and Accountability Act. UNIVERSITY agrees that neither the UNIVERSITY, nor any UNIVERSITY personnel, agents, employees, or subcontractors shall use, disclose or otherwise make available any Data subject to controls under applicable law collected, received or acquired during the term of this AGREEMENT or at any time thereafter except as required to perform services for COUNTY hereunder or as required by law or with COUNTY's express written consent. For avoidance of doubt, subject to requirements and controls under applicable laws, UNIVERSITY may retain copies of Data collected, received or acquired pursuant to this Agreement for purposes of publication of methods and results pursuant to Section 14.

13. INTELLECTUAL PROPERTY INFRINGEMENT.

13.1 In the performance of this AGREEMENT and individual Work Orders, UNIVERSITY shall not knowingly infringe the intellectual property rights of any third party. Likewise, in the performance of this AGREEMENT and individual Work Orders, COUNTY shall not knowingly provide UNIVERSITY any materials or information or develop any material that infringes the intellectual property rights of any third party. In the event either the UNIVERSITY or COUNTY discovers either that any of the materials or information used or provided to it or by it, or that any of its other actions in the performance of this AGREEMENT and approved Work Orders, might infringe the intellectual property rights of any third party, or that any third party has claimed or may claim an infringement of its rights, the discovering party shall provide full and prompt notice to the other party of all the material facts and/or of the claim.

13.2 UNIVERSITY represents and certifies that materials produced or used under this AGREEMENT and all Work Orders, including but not limited to software, hardware, documentation, and/or any other item, do not and will not infringe upon any intellectual property rights of another, including without limitation patents, copyrights, trade secrets, trade names, and service marks and names. When legally required, UNIVERSITY shall either (a) obtain the written consent of both the owner and licensor to reproduce, publish, and/or use any such material supplied to the COUNTY hereunder, or (b) re-perform the Work in a manner that allows the COUNTY to use the revised material without violating the rights of any third party, or (c) return the amount paid under the applicable Work Order. Subject to the limitations of the Minnesota State Tort Claims Act, Minn. Stats. 3.736, UNIVERSITY shall defend, indemnify, and hold the COUNTY, its officials, officers, agents, volunteers, and employees harmless, at UNIVERSITY'S own expense, against any action or claim brought against the COUNTY to the extent that it is based on a claim that all or part of the materials infringes upon any patent, copyright, trademark, trade secret, or violates any other proprietary right of a third party, provided that COUNTY gives UNIVERSITY prompt notice of such claim and immediately ceases use of the allegedly infringing material upon direction from UNIVERSITY . UNIVERSITY shall be responsible for payment of any and all such claims, demands, obligations, liabilities, costs and damages including, but not limited to, reasonable attorney fees arising out of this AGREEMENT, Work Orders, amendments and supplements thereto, which are attributable to such claims or actions. The obligations of UNIVERSITY stated in this Section shall survive termination, expiration, non-renewal, or rescission of this AGREEMENT or Work Order.

13.3 COUNTY represents and certifies that materials produced by it or provided to UNIVERSITY for UNIVERSITY'S use under this AGREEMENT and all Work Orders, including but not limited to software, hardware, documentation, and/or any other item, do not and will not infringe upon any intellectual property rights of another, including without limitation patents, copyrights, trade secrets, trade names, and service marks and names. When legally required, COUNTY shall either (a) obtain the written consent of both the owner and licensor to reproduce, publish, and/or use any such material supplied to the UNIVERSITY hereunder, or (b) re-perform its work under the Work Order in a manner that allows the UNIVERSITY to use the revised material without violating the rights of any third party, or (c) pay the full contract price under the applicable Work Order. Subject to the limitations of the Minnesota Municipal Tort Claims Act, Minn. Stats. Chapter 466, COUNTY shall defend, indemnify, and hold the UNIVERSITY, its officials, officers, agents, volunteers, and employees harmless, at COUNTY'S own expense, against any action or claim brought against the UNIVERSITY to the extent that it is based on a claim that all or part of the information or materials infringes upon any patent, copyright, trademark, trade secret, or violates any other proprietary right of a third party, provided that UNIVERSITY gives COUNTY prompt notice of such claim and immediately ceases use of the allegedly infringing material upon direction from COUNTY . COUNTY shall be responsible for payment of any and all such claims, demands, obligations, liabilities, costs and damages including, but not limited to, reasonable attorney fees arising out of this AGREEMENT, Work Orders, amendments and supplements thereto, which are attributable to such claims or actions. The obligations of COUNTY stated in this Section shall survive termination, expiration, non-renewal, or rescission of this AGREEMENT or Work Order.

14. PUBLICATIONS AND DISTRIBUTIONS.

14.1 Publication of methods and results derived from this project in theses or academic or professional journals or their presentation at symposia or scholarly meetings is hereby authorized, provided they contain the required acknowledgement of COUNTY funding/support, and necessary steps have been taken to protect copyright and other intellectual property rights from the project. As appropriate, in the event that UNIVERSITY distributes any other Work Order deliverable in any format, UNIVERSITY shall include an acknowledgement of COUNTY funding/support.

15. NON-DISCRIMINATION.

15.1 In accordance with applicable law, both parties agree that they shall not exclude any person from full employment rights or participation in, or the benefit of, any program, service or activity on the grounds of race, color, creed, religion, age, disability, marital status, sexual orientation, public assistance status, or national origin, and no person who is protected by applicable federal or state laws against discrimination shall be otherwise subjected to discrimination.

15.2 AIDS Policy. UNIVERSITY agrees to adhere to Hennepin County's AIDS Policy which provides that no employee, applicant, or client shall be subjected to testing, removed from normal and customary status, or deprived of any rights, privileges, or freedoms because of his or her AIDS status except for clearly stated specific and compelling medical and/or public health reasons. UNIVERSITY shall establish the necessary policies concerning AIDS to assure that COUNTY clients in contracted programs and UNIVERSITY'S employees in COUNTY contracted programs are afforded the same treatment with regard to AIDS as persons directly employed or served by the COUNTY.

15.3 Culturally Appropriate Services. Consistent with applicable law, UNIVERSITY agrees that all services will be delivered in a manner which is respectful and culturally appropriate to the service recipients. Culturally appropriate is defined as services that are delivered to reflect the unique individual needs of the recipients such as language, racial/ethnic background, and social/religious background. UNIVERSITY agrees to make reasonable efforts both to provide staff for delivery of services who are effective in working with the diversity of the clients receiving those services, and to secure ongoing input from individuals who reflect the non-represented culture.

16. JURISDICTION AND VENUE.

16.1 The laws of the State of Minnesota thereto, shall govern this AGREEMENT, approved Work Orders and amendments. Venue for all legal proceedings arising out of this Agreement, or breach thereof, shall be in the state court with competent jurisdiction in Hennepin County, Minnesota.

17. INDEPENDENT CONTRACTOR.

17.1 Each party shall select the means, method, and manner of performing the services herein. Nothing is intended or should be construed in any manner as creating or establishing the relationship of co-partners between the parties hereto or as constituting one party as the agent, representative, or employee of the other party for any purpose or in any manner whatsoever. Each party is to be and shall remain an independent contractor with respect to all services performed under this AGREEMENT. Each party represents that it has or will secure at its own expense all personnel required in performing services under this AGREEMENT. Any and all personnel of a party or other persons while engaged in the performance of any Work or services required under this AGREEMENT shall have no contractual relationship with the other party, and shall not be considered employees of the other party. Any and all claims that may or might arise under the Minnesota Economic Security Law or the Workers' Compensation Act of the State of Minnesota on behalf of said personnel, arising out of employment or alleged employment, including, without limitation, claims of discrimination against a party, its officers, agents, contractors, or employees shall in no way be the responsibility of the other party. Such personnel or other persons shall neither require nor be entitled to any compensation, rights, or benefits of any kind whatsoever from the other party, including, without limitation, tenure rights, medical and hospital care, sick and vacation leave, Workers' Compensation, Re-employment Compensation, disability, severance pay, and retirement benefits.

18. NOTICES.

18.1. Duty to Notify. UNIVERSITY shall promptly notify the COUNTY of any claim, action, cause of action, or litigation brought against UNIVERSITY, its employees, officers, agents or subcontractors which arises out of the services contained in this Agreement. UNIVERSITY shall also notify the COUNTY whenever UNIVERSITY has a reasonable basis for believing that UNIVERSITY and/or its employees, officers, agents or subcontractors, and/or the COUNTY might become the subject of a claim, action, cause of action, criminal arrest, criminal charge, or litigation arising out of and/or related to the services contained in the Agreement. Failure to provide the notices required by this section is a material violation of the terms and conditions of this Agreement.

18.2 Any notice or demand which must be given or made by a party hereto under the terms of this AGREEMENT or any statute or ordinance shall be in writing, and shall be delivered personally or by certified mail or courier. Notices to the COUNTY shall be sent to the County Administrator with a copy to the originating COUNTY Department at the address given in the approved Work Order. Notice to UNIVERSITY shall be sent to the UNIVERSITY's Office of Sponsored Projects Administration and to the University Department at the address given in the approved Work Order.

19. SEVERABILITY AND NON-WAIVER.

19.1 In the event any provision of this AGREEMENT shall be held invalid or unenforceable by any court of competent jurisdiction, such holding shall not invalidate or render unenforceable any other provision of this AGREEMENT.

20. SURVIVING CLAUSES.

20.1 All provisions of this AGREEMENT which by their sense and content are intended to survive the performance, termination, or cancellation of this AGREEMENT shall survive, including, but not limited to, clauses 7 Liability and Self Insurance, 10 Records – Availability/Access, 11 Data Practices, 12 Rights in Copyrights and Patents, 13 Intellectual Property Infringement, 14 Publications and Distributions and 16 Jurisdiction and Venue.

21. CLINICAL SERVICES

If Work Orders involve clinical services, the following requirements shall also apply:

21.1. In the event that Contracted Services provided to Eligible Recipients that are defined in an approved Work Order may be reimbursed by private health insurance, Title XIX-Medical Assistance, Minnesota Care, or General Assistance Medical Care, the UNIVERSITY shall bill such third parties. COUNTY is responsible for informing the UNIVERSITY via the Work Order prior to the start of work if Contracted Services will be subject to this clause.

21.2. The UNIVERSITY agrees that every reasonable effort will be made to enroll individuals into private health insurance, Title XIX-Medical Assistance, Minnesota Care, or General Assistance Medical Care, prior to determining the eligibility of individuals to receive Contracted Services under the terms of the Work Order.

21.3. The UNIVERSITY agrees to notify the COUNTY if full or partial payment is received from any source other than this AGREEMENT for any Eligible Recipient also paid for by the COUNTY. In such cases, the UNIVERSITY shall return to the COUNTY any duplicate payment by the COUNTY for such eligible Recipients.

THIS PORTION OF PAGE INTENTIONALLY LEFT BLANK

SIGNATURE PAGE

The Regents of the University of Minnesota, by its Vice President for Research and by its Vice President for Budget and Finance, having duly approved this AGREEMENT on the 30 day of June, 2010, and the County of Hennepin having duly approved this AGREEMENT on the 30 day of June, 2010, and pursuant to such approval, the parties hereto agree to be bound by the provisions herein set forth.

COUNTY OF HENNEPIN

STATE OF MINNESOTA

By: _____

Co-Chair of Its County Board

Date: _6 - 3 o - 2 o 1 o_

Attest: _____

Deputy/Clerk of the Board

AND:

By: _____

County Administrator

Date: _6~30~10_

Reviewed by County

Attorney's Office:

Michael P Bernard

Assistant County Attorney

Date: _6/4/10_

REGENTS OF THE UNIVERSITY

OF MINNESOTA

By: _____

Vice President for Research

Date: _6 - 30 - 2010_

By: _____

Vice President and Chief

Financial Officer

Date: _6 - 30 - 10_

By: _____

Senior Vice President for

System Academic Administration

Date: _6 - 30 - 10_

Reviewed by Office of the General

Counsel:

Mark A. Bohnhorst

Associate General Counsel

Date: _May 28, 2010_

WORK ORDER # _____ (assigned by Hennepin County Purchasing and Contract Services)
FOR USE WITH MASTER COOPERATIVE AGREEMENT NO. A100460 BETWEEN THE COUNTY OF HENNEPIN AND
THE UNIVERSITY OF MINNESOTA
Developed through the Hennepin-University Partnership (www.umn.edu/hup)

All Work Orders start the approval process at Hennepin County and must be submitted electronically or by mail to
Mary Knickerbocker (mary.knickerbocker@co.hennepin.mn.us, Mail code 175, 612-348-6190)

University of MN staff with questions -- contact Kathie Doty, Hennepin-University Partnership Liaison (kdoty@umn.edu, 612-625-4383)

Work Order Type (to be completed by University of Minnesota Sponsored Projects Administration (SPA))

___ Sponsored Project
___ External Sale

SECTION A: PROJECT TITLE

Project title:

Start date:
End date:

SECTION B: WORK ORDER AMOUNT (attach detailed budget if required)

Work order amount (not to exceed amount) $

SECTION C: DESCRIPTION OF WORK AND DELIVERABLES (attach additional pages if needed)

SECTION D: CONTACT INFORMATION (please fill out as much information as possible)
Hennepin County Work Order lead contact
Name:
Mail code:
Telephone: Fax: Email:
Department:
Fund: Account: Center:

For HSPHD to fill out only:
Service area: Budget element: Taxonomy code:
HSPHD Contract Manager name:
Mail code:
Telephone: Fax: Email:

University of Minnesota Work Order administrative contact (for External Sales use dept. contact. All others, use SPA contact)
Name:
Address:
Telephone: Fax: Email:

Lead faculty/staff contact
Name: Academic department:
Address:
Telephone: Fax: Email:

SECTION E: PAYMENT TERMS

Invoice frequency (check one)

☐ Monthly
☐ Quarterly
☐ One time
☐ Other:

SECTION F: PROJECT SPECIFIC INFORMATION

Welfare Data
Will the University be provided with any Welfare Data under this Work Order? (Pursuant to the Master Agreement, Section 12.2, Welfare Data is defined as: "any data on individuals, vendors of services, licensees or registered persons from 'a program for which authority is vested in a component of the Welfare System' (within the meaning of Minnesota Statutes 13.46 Subd. 1(b))."

___ Yes

___ No

If so, pursuant to the Master Agreement, Section 12.2, the University becomes a part of the welfare system of the State of Minnesota in connection with performing services under this Work Order and any information received by the University is presumed to be non-public.

Does this Work Order involve clinical services?

___ Yes

___ No

Does this Work Order require a background check? If so, include pre-approved background check language in Section G below.

___ Yes

___ No

SECTION G: OTHER TERMS (optional; attach additional pages if necessary)

SECTION F: SIGNATURE PAGE

University of Minnesota
By:
_____
Authorized Signature
_____
Name and Title
_____
Date

County of Hennepin State of Minnesota
By:
_____
Chair of Its County Board
_____
Date
ATTEST:
_____
_____
Deputy Clerk of County Board

_____
Assistant/Deputy County Administrator
_____
Date

_____
Department Director
_____
Date
_____
Department

Reviewed by the County Attorney's Office
_____
Signature
_____
Date

CHANGE ORDER

For contract # _____ (attach first page of the Work Order to be changed and all previous Change Orders)

FOR USE WITH THE MASTER COOPERATIVE AGREEMENT NO. A100460 BETWEEN THE COUNTY OF HENNEPIN AND THE UNIVERSITY OF MINNESOTA

Questions regarding this form?

Hennepin County staff, contact Mary Knickerbocker (mary.knickerbocker@co.hennepin.mn.us, 612-348-6190)

U of MN staff, contact Kathie Doty, Hennepin-University Partnership Liaison (kdoty@umn.edu, 612-625-4383)

SECTION A: Administrative information

Change Order number (check one):

___ 1
___ 2
___ 3
___ 4
___ 5
___ Other _____

Project title:

Original start date:
Original end date:

Original Work Order amount: $

SECTION B: Details regarding applicable changes

Changes to scope of work to be performed:

Justification:

Changes to term:

Justification:

Changes to Work Order not-to-exceed amount:

Justification:

Other changes:

Justification:

254   *Appendix D*

SECTION C: Signature page

University of Minnesota

By:

_____
Authorized Signature

_____
Name and Title

_____
Date

County of Hennepin State of Minnesota

By:

_____
Chair of Its County Board

_____
Date

ATTEST:

_____

_____
Deputy Clerk of County Board

_____
Assistant/Deputy County Administrator

_____
Date

_____
Department Director

_____
Date

_____
Department

Reviewed by the County Attorney's Office

_____
Signature

_____
Date

Attachment C

Work Orders transferred from A0712000 to A100460

Work Order	Change Order	UMN PI	Funded Amount (Total)	Award Dates	Project Title	UMN CON #	Sponsored Projects or External Sale
UM1001		Pending approval	$ 86,991.00	1/18/2010-7/31/2011	Be @ School Program		
UM1003		Fan, Yingling	$ 25,000.00	5/15/2010-3/15/2011	Assessing Neighborhood and Social Influences of Transit Corridors	CON-24913	S
UM1004		Pending approval	$ 78,443.00	5/1/2010-8/31/2012	Co-parent court demonstration parent		
UM1005		Donath, Max	$ 15,000.00	5/1/2010-5/31/2011	Aggregating VMT within Predefined Geographic Zones Using a Cellular Network	CON-25775	S
UM1006		Hollister, David	$ 11,440.00	6/1/2010-9/1/2011	Homeless Refugees		S
UM7003	2	Mills, Deanna	$ 306,000.00	1/1/2008-12/31/2010	CUHCC-Child Mental Health Services	CON-4972	S
UM7005	5	Mills, Deanna	$ 1,939,381.00	1/1/2008-12/31/2010	Adult Mental Health Services (CUHCC) Community Clinic Program, MH Outpatient and Case Management	CON-4973	S
UM7010	2	Scott,Thomas Marshall & Doty, Kathie	$ 310,000.00	1/1/2008-12/31/2010	Hennepin County/ University of MN	CON-3621	S
UM8002		Wright, Kristine	$ 25,000.00	4/1/2008-12/31/2012	Tuition Prepayment Agreement - Hennepin County Service Corp		E
UM8003	1	Ritenour, E. Russell	$ 4,000.00	1/1/2008-12/31/2011	Medical Physics Services		E
UM8008		Winters,Ken C	$ 138,612.00	6/1/2008-9/30/2011	Clinical Supervision of Brief Intervention Specialists	CON-13961	S
UM9004		Fan,Yingling	$ 20,000.00	5/1/2009-6/30/2010	Impact of Twin Cities Transitways on Regional Labor Mark	CON-18873	S
UM9006		Fan,Yingling	$ 8,019.00	6/1/2009-6/30/2010	Impact of Twin Cities Transitways on Regional Labor Mark	CON-18874	S
UM9010		Ehlinger, Edward	$ 132,383.72	8/1/2009-6/30/2011	Smoke-free Policies and Cessation Services at Post-Secondary Institutions	CON-22108	S
UM9012	1	Cao,Xinyu	$ 26,974.00	7/1/2009-6/30/2011	Value-Added: Impacts of the Proximity to Transitway Stat	CON-21985	S
UM9016		LaLiberte, Traci	$ 8,400.00	11/23/2009-7/31/2010	Analysis of Literature and Evidence-based Interversions	CON-24095	S
UM9017		Doherty, William	$ 50,000.00	1/1/2010-12/31/2010	Citizen Professional Demonstration Project		E
UM9021		Stein,Jerome	$ 34,000.00	1/1/2010-6/30/2010	Learning Dreams		S

Appendix E

Steps for Completing Hennepin-University Work Orders
(Under Master Agreement: Hennepin County Agreement No. A100460)

1) **Work Together:** The primary contacts from Hennepin County (HC) and the University of Minnesota (UMN) should work together to draft a Work Order, including creating:
   a) a scope of work
   b) a budget
   c) other inputs for the Work Order

   For each Work Order, the division of tasks in preparing the Work Order can be different, depending on what makes most sense and who agrees to do what. If there are questions about how to work this out, contact the HUP office for assistance.

2) **Get a Work Order Number:** The HC contact should call or email Mary Knickerbocker, HC Purchasing, to have a Work Order number assigned. Mary will ask for 3 pieces of information:
   - the title of the Work Order,
   - the start and end date for the project, and
   - the budget amount. Mary's phone #: 612-348-6190 and email: Mary.Knickerbocker@hennepin.us

3) **Send the Completed Work Order to HC Purchasing:** The HC contact should:
   a) If required, get a signature from her/his department to approve submittal of the Work Order to the UMN (e.g. HSPHD requires a signature; other departments may as well)
   b) Deliver the completed Work Order to the HC Purchasing Department:
      - via Mail Code 175, OR
      - via email to Mary Knickerbocker at Mary.Knickerbocker@hennepin.us

4) **HC Purchasing Sends Work Order to the UMN:** HC Purchasing will send the Work Order to UMN Sponsored Projects Administration (SPA) for processing/signature.

5) **UMN Gets Appropriate Signatures:** UMN SPA determines whether the Work Order will be signed by SPA, or forwarded to External Sales, or to Extension. Once determined, it will be routed as follows:

   a) **If a Sponsored Project:** After a Proposal Routing Form (PRF) is submitted to SPA for a Work Order, SPA will sign and return the Work Order to HC.
   b) **If an External Sale:** After External Sales review the Work Order, they will notify the UMN department that it is approved for signature. The UMN department will sign, based on their delegation of authority, and return the Work Order to HC.
   c) **If Extension:** UMN Department will sign and return the Work Order to HC after following Extension's internal review process.

6) **UMN Sends Signed Copy to HC:** After signatures are obtained from UMN, SPA or the responsible UMN Department (as explained in # 5) will send two copies of the signed Work Order to HC via U.S. Mail to:

Mary Knickerbocker
Purchasing and Contract Services Department
A-1730 Government Center
300 South 6th Street
Minneapolis, MN 55487-0175

7) **Determine Final County Signature(s) Required:** HC Purchasing will determine what County signatures are required using County guidelines, as summarized below (these may change; refer to current County policy):
    a. If Under $15,000 Department Director may sign
    b. If Under $25,000 Asst. County Administrator signs
    c. If Under $50,000 County Administrator signs
    d. If Over $50,000 Board Action Requested (BAR) must be completed

8) **Obtain County Signatures:** HC Purchasing will send copies of the Work Order to appropriate individuals for signature (including the County Attorney for HSPHD only).

9) **Final Copy of Signed Work Order to the UMN:** HC Purchasing will mail one (1) **original** work order to the UMN SPA, keep one (1) **original**, and send one (1) copy to the HC contact. UMN SPA will distribute Work Order copies to the appropriate UMN department.

10) **Internal HC accounting:** HC Purchasing will enter Work Order in APEX and create a Purchase Order (PO). The HC Department will receive the PO in APEX.

FOR QUESTIONS, PLEASE CONTACT:

Hennepin: Mary Knickerbocker, Mary.Knickerbocker@hennepin.us, 612-348-6190.

University: Andrea Marshall, pete1518@umn.edu , 612.626.7634

HUP: Kathie Doty, kdoty@umn.edu, 612-625-4383

Appendix F

FALL 2011

SESIQ2 is the Supplementary Educational Services Integrated Quantitative and Qualitative Study of Implementation and Impact. Find out more at: www.**sesiq2**.wceruw.org

SESIQ²

Understanding Supplementary Educational Services (SES): A Guide for Parents and Guardians

What are Supplementary Educational Services?

Supplementary Educational Services (SES) is a free tutoring program available to students in schools identified by your state as in need of improvement. Eligible students will be notified by their schools on how to enroll for additional help in academic areas such as reading, writing and math. Parents and guardians can choose a tutoring program that best fits their students' needs. A school becomes eligible for these services when they have not met the state's set of annual academic performance goals for two or more consecutive years. SES is a program under the Federal No Child Left Behind Act.

SESIQ2 is a joint project of the Center for Health and Social Policy at Lyndon B. Johnson School of Public Affairs, University of Texas at Austin, the Rossier School of Education at the University of Southern California, and the Wisconsin Center for Education Research and Value-Added Research Center at the University of Wisconsin-Madison. We thank our funder, the Institute of Education Sciences (PR/Award number: R305A090301). For more information please visit www.sesiq2.wceruw.org. Contact the project at sesiq2@gmail.com or 1-855-471-1700

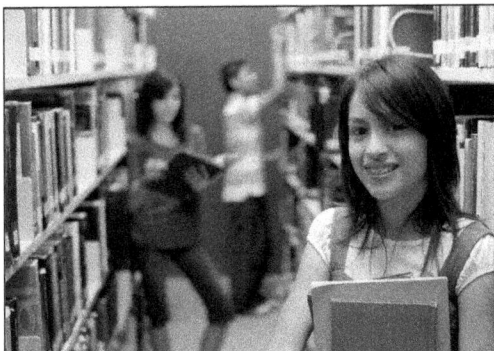

SES**IQ**²   Understanding Supplemental Educational Services

An Overview of Our Research

Our study, the Multisite Evaluation of Supplementary Educational Services, is an ongoing project that focuses on the following questions:

1. How does SES affect student achievement?
2. What are the different types of tutoring? Do these differences affect student achievement?
3. What specific parts of SES improve student outcomes?
4. What can lawmakers do to improve the program so that it has benefits for students?

This study examines supplemental educational services in five school districts: Austin, Chicago, Dallas, Milwaukee, and Minneapolis. It is a mixed-methods study where we conduct program observations, interview people involved in the program at different levels, and evaluate statistical data. The data we are gathering consists of: test scores, attendance records, student demographics, tutoring observations, interviews, parent focus groups, and other pertinent documents.

Our focus groups with over 150 parents and guardians across five school districts suggest that many parents do not have enough information about SES services, or about the process as a whole. Parents noted that they did not get the necessary follow-up information about tutoring services in the enrollment process and further voiced their concerns about the implementation of the tutoring programs.

In response, this guide is meant to summarize the information from our study's results and answer basic questions about SES policy. Our goal is that parents are able to use results from the study and make a more informed choice for their students when selecting SES providers. Even though the information in this guide is based on the results from five districts, it is our hope that parents from other districts also may find the data useful when making decisions to participate and select an SES provider.

Q & A: What is SES?

What does AYP mean?

Adequate Yearly Progress (AYP) is a set of annual academic testing goals that schools must meet if they receive federal funding.

Why is my student eligible for SES?

Schools that do not meet their AYP goals for two years in a row are identified as "In Program Improvement" and are considered to be underperforming. Only schools that have failed to meet AYP for two years in a row are eligible for SES. Students in these schools who receive free or reduced-price lunch are eligible for SES.

Who provides these tutoring services?

SES providers can be any of the following:

- For-profit companies
- Non-profit groups
- Local community programs
- Colleges or universities
- Other national organizations
- Faith-based groups
- Public schools and districts

Some providers will offer services through in-person, small or large group instruction. Others will offer online instruction that students may access via a computer.

Which students participate in SES?

- All students from low-income families who attend Title I public schools in their second year of school improvement, in corrective action, or in restructuring may apply to participate. This includes elementary, middle, and high school students. Title I students at a private school may not participate in SES.
- The lowest achieving eligible students must be given priority if funds are not available to serve all of the students who are eligible to receive SES. For example, a district in our study mandated schools to open up services to 3rd grade and high school students first. Then the district opened up services for students with the lowest reading achievement scores.
- Students may not be denied services based on language, race, ethnicity, nationality, or learning difference.

Q & A: Finding the Right SES Program

What does SES instruction look like?

Instruction must take place outside of school hours, and in our research, most are in one to one or small group settings. Reading, writing and math are emphasized. From our study's observations, very little time is spent on homework help, whereas the majority

of instruction focuses on skill-building and/or preparing students for what is required on state tests.

Where does this tutoring take place?

Tutoring takes place at school, home, libraries, or community centers. It is up to the specific provider to establish where services will take place.

How much tutoring should my student receive?

Providers offer a range of hours of services based on how much they charge the district per hour. To ensure that your student makes the best use of SES, review the information and ask district staff and/or providers about the amount of hours your student can get based on how much the district provides and providers charge. The more hours your student receives, the higher their chance of raising test scores, especially if the provider offers 40 hours or more of tutoring in a school year.

How important is attendance?

Our study suggests that test scores improve based on the amount of hours students attended SES. In general, the more your student attends and takes advantage of SES, the higher her or his chances are of improving their standardized test scores.

How do other parents and guardians feel about SES?

In our study, parents generally appreciate the additional assistance that their children received in math, reading, and writing. However, parents and guardians voiced the need for more accessible information. Parents have also been frustrated with the enrollment procedures from both providers and districts. Parents would also like to see improvements in the implementation of services in the areas of scheduling, behavior management, and technical support, especially for online tutoring. Finally, they would like improvement in the communication between school districts, providers, and schools.

What if my student has special needs?

All eligible students, regardless of disability status, have access to tutoring through SES. SES providers

SESIQ² Understanding Supplemental Educational Services

often advertise they can provide services for students with special needs and disabilities. However, from our research, SES instruction is not always adequate for students with special needs or disabilities. A major obstacle for providers, tutors, and researchers was identifying students with documented special education needs. The majority of tutors we observed and interviewed did not have access to Individual Education Plans (IEPs). If your student has an IEP, you can decide to share this document with your student's tutor if you think it would improve the tutoring experience. Ask providers about the level of training or information their tutors have for effective instruction of students with disabilities. You may want to talk to the district SES staff for options on choosing a provider for your student with a special need.

What if my student is an English learner?

Similar to students with special needs, there are SES providers advertising that they can provide services for English learners. Our research has indicated that SES instruction is not always adequate for the particular learning needs of English learners. Ask providers about the level of training or information their tutors have for effective instruction of English language learners. You may want to talk to the district SES staff for recommendations on choosing a provider for your English-learning student.

What are characteristics of a quality program?

There are a variety of types of SES services offered. Look for SES providers that offer smaller student to tutor ratios. Ask providers for the maximum amount of instructional hours your student can receive through them: the more the better and over 40 hours is most effective. Make sure your student's tutor provides the full amount of hours that were advertised.

Characteristics of Quality SES Programs

- Small group instruction
- Comfortable and quiet places to learn
- SES curriculum is connected to students' day school instruction
- Tutors are knowledgeable and experienced in subject areas and student learning needs
- Majority of tutoring session is spent on instruction
- Instruction is active and engaging
- There is frequent and positive communication between tutors, families, and schools
- Tutoring companies are responsive to families from registration through the end of tutoring
- Positive and engaging relationships are established between students and tutors
- Tutoring companies provide information about services in languages other than English

SES**IQ**② Understanding Supplemental Educational Services

Other considerations include: supportive tutors, tutors that can answer your student's questions, regular and positive communication between tutors and student's regular teachers, and whether the location is conducive to engaged learning.

If your student has a learning disability or is an English language learner, make sure that the provider's tutoring staff is adequately trained in that area. Ask the provider for examples of how their staff has accommodated special needs and English learners in the past.

Where can I get more information?

Schools must provide information about SES eligibility. If you are unsure whether your student qualifies for services, ask their teacher, the school's main office, or the parent liaison.

If you have access to the internet, district websites have information regarding which schools qualify for SES, as well as information on providers. Districts also have specific personnel that handle SES related questions. Your school's main office can give you this phone number. You can also look at our study's website at www.sesiq2.wceruw.org. In it you will find various studies and policy briefs with a more detailed analysis of SES. Feel free to contact us at sesiq2@gmail.com or toll-free at 1-855-471-1700.

Authors: Rodolfo Acosta, Patricia Burch, Annalee Good, Mary Stewart, Carolyn Heinrich & Christi Kirshbaum

Appendix G

MEMORANDUM

TO: [MPS staff], Milwaukee Public Schools

FROM: [Research team members]

SUBJECT: Research of Online Tutoring and Credit Recovery Providers

DATE: 10-29-2015

In response to your request for additional information on online tutoring (K-8) and credit recovery (9-12) vendors, our team has been searching for unbiased, high-quality evaluations of various programs. Unfortunately, very little research exists in this field; most studies that address these topics state that more research should be done to evaluate efficacy of online providers. Some reports address how districts should select and work with vendors, and others describe characteristics that are effective in online learning. We looked for the most recent reports possible, given the pace of change in digital learning, but found very little information published in recent years.

One of the difficulties with credit recovery vendors is that most providers we found offer online high school courses for a variety of purposes – advanced placement, full-time virtual students, and credit recovery. Reports on these providers tend to address full-time students more than credit recovery. The providers that are mentioned most frequently in the literature are Apex Learning, PLATO, K12 Inc, Aventa Learning (now Edmentum), and the Florida Virtual School.

Online Tutorial and Virtual Credit Recovery Providers	Additional Information	K-8 Online Tutoring	9-12 Virtual School/Credit Recovery
Apex Learning	Geared towards 6th-12th grades	x	x
Fuel Education (formerly Aventa Learning)	Students who are behind grade level	x	x
K12, Inc	Largest private education organization that provides services for public school students; has received public criticisms for ineffectiveness.	x	x
Connections Academy			x
Dreambox Learning	PreK-8th grade math	x	
e2020 (Edgenuity)		x	x
Edison Learning		x	x
Florida Virtual School		x	x
Michigan Virtual School			x
PLATO (Edmentum)	2004 Report showed positive effects in rural Puerto Rico schools.	x	x
SmartThinking (Pearson)			x
Tutor.com		x	
tutorvista.com (owned by Pearson)	Outsourced to India	x	

Additional resources may be helpful in understanding the overall efficacy of blended/online learning:

Other Reports/Sites of Interest	Additional Information
The Learning Accelerator	Non-profit that helps districts set up blended learning; provides multiple resources for school districts.
Department of Ed Meta-Analysis of Online Learning (2008)	Find positive effects for blended learning, but struggled to find evaluations of K-12 providers.
Hanover Research Report (2011)	Provides an overview of the current status of blended and online learning, describes the major considerations that a district or school wishing to implement a blended program should take into account, and profiles successful blended learning programs that operate on different basic models.
Gates/Rand Report on Personalized Learning in Public Charter Schools (2014)	Shows positive effect sizes, but doesn't name specific providers.
Christiansen Institute	Provides case studies of schools who have implemented blended learning.
International Association for K-12 Online Learning (iNACOL)	Provides research and resources on various forms of online learning.
Center on Online Learning and Students with Disabilities	Provides information about adaptable capabilities of various digital tools and programs.

The research we found on online tutoring is compiled here:

Company/Product	Subject	Grades	Effects	Researcher
MathWhizz	Math	Ages 5-13	Positive	Academic - Journal of Educational Research
G-Math (Google)	Math	all ages	Positive	Academic - Computers & Education (Journal)
Khan Academy	Math	Grades 5-12	Positive correlation between time on Khan and increase in expected test scores	SRI, funded by Gates Foundation
Cognitive Tutor Algebra I	Algebra	Grades 8-12	Positive effect size of .20 SD	Rand Corporation
Intelligent Tutoring for Structure Strategy	Reading	4th grade	Positive	Institute of Education Sciences (IES)
LeapTrack	Math & Reading	1st-8th	Positive effect of .09 SD	Institute of Education Sciences (IES)
ICanLearn	Algebra	Grades 8-12	Positive effect of .17 SD	Institute of Education Sciences (IES)
ST Math	Math	Elementary	Positive effects of .40-.47 SD	WestEd
Teach to One	Math	Grades 5-8	Effect size of .35 in 2nd year of implementation	Self-funded, completed by Columbia Teachers College

Appendix H

SPRING 2012

SESIQ² is the Supplemental
Educational Services Integrated
Quantitative and Qualitative
Study of Implementation and
Impact. Find out more at:
www.sesiq2.wceruw.org or call
toll-free at 1-855-471-1700.

SESIQ²

Policy and Program Recommendations for Redesigning Supplemental Educational Services

Patricia Burch and Carolyn Heinrich

What are Supplemental Educational Services?

Under No Child Left Behind (NCLB), schools that have not made adequate yearly progress in increasing student academic achievement for three or more years are required to offer parents of children in low-income families the opportunity to receive free after school tutoring, or supplemental educational services (SES). Districts must use a portion of their Title I federal funding to pay for SES. Tutoring providers complete a state application and district contract process, and can take a variety of forms (public, private, not for profit, for profit, faith-based, online, in person, national, local, etc.).

We suggest the following recommendations to district and state administrators faced with the opportunity to redesign SES, or similar out-of-school-time programs. We base these recommendations on findings from our multi-site, mixed method and longitudinal study of SES.

Policy and Program Recommendations

Resource Allocation

- Dedicate portions of SES fund towards the costs of managing performance-based contracts, as well as the rigorous assessment of provider effectiveness and instructional quality
- Redirect SES resources from high school level to lower grades, where SES tends to have a greater impact on student achievement

SESIQ² is a joint project of the Center for Health and Social Policy at Lyndon B. Johnson School of Public Affairs, University of Texas at Austin, the Center on Educational Governance and Rossier School of Education at the University of Southern California, and the Wisconsin Center for Education Research and Value-Added Research Center at the University of Wisconsin-Madison. We thank our funder, the Institute of Education Sciences (PR/Award number: R305A090301). For more information and the research behind these recommendations, please visit www.sesiq2.wceruw.org.

SESIQ² Policy and Program Recommendations for SES

SESIQ²: Research Design

Our integrated mixed-method, longitudinal study examines SES in five school districts: Austin, TX; Chicago, IL; Dallas, TX; Milwaukee, WI; and Minneapolis, MN.

Qualitative analysis draws upon observations of full tutoring sessions; interviews with provider administrators and tutoring staff; interviews with state and district staff, and parent focus groups.

Quantitative analysis employs an interrupted time series design with internal comparison groups and multiple non-experimental approaches to estimate SES impacts on student academic achievement.

- Prioritize SES resources towards greater attendance and better programming for students with disabilities and English Language Learners (ELLs)

Role of Districts and States

- Establish performance-based contracts, where tutoring providers must fulfill established criteria (e.g. minimum hours, evidence of student progress, minimum tutor to student ratio, etc.) before payment can occur
- Build in expectations that students attend at least 40 hours of tutoring per school year
- Set a maximum hourly rate based on an assessment of the elements impacting providers' process for setting rates (e.g. facility use fees, insurance requirements, wage levels for local labor market, transportation, etc.)
- Establish minimum criteria (beyond simply referring to state standards) for aligning the tutoring curriculum to that of the day school (e.g. both providers and day school use Six Trait Writing for developing writing skills)
- Assess instructional quality (e.g. through observation tools) that encourage enrichment and differentiation
- Require providers receiving public funds to offer services to all eligible students, including those with disabilities and ELLs
- Require tutors to have minimum qualifications (e.g. bachelor's degree, teaching experience, etc.)
- Require providers have tutors on staff with demonstrated knowledge about diagnosing and addressing the educational needs of student with disabilities and ELLs

Communication Between Stakeholders

- Frequently disseminate rigorous, concrete, accessible and up to date findings on SES provider effectiveness to parents and other stakeholders (i.e. community organizations, taxpayers, state agencies)
- Increase level and frequency of communication between providers, parents and day school teachers regarding students' needs
- Develop systematic ways to communicate the particular needs of ELLs and students with disabilities to providers during all stages of the tutoring process (e.g. enrollment, assessment, instruction)
- Develop processes to insure the tutoring plans for students with disabilities are aligned with their individualized education programs (IEPs)

Please contact Patricia Burch (pburch@usc.edu) or Carolyn Heinrich (cheinrich@austin.utexas.edu) with inquiries.

Appendix I

MEMORANDUM OF UNDERSTANDING
BETWEEN
THE NEW MEXICO CORRECTIONS DEPARTMENT
AND
THE NEW MEXICO SENTENCING COMMISSION
AND
THE NEW MEXICO LEGISLATIVE FINANCE COMMITTEE

THIS MEMORANDUM OF UNDERSTANDING ("Memorandum") is made by and between the New Mexico Corrections Department ("NMCD"), the New Mexico Sentencing Commission ("NMSC") and the New Mexico Legislative Finance Committee ("LFC").

RECITALS

WHEREAS, the New Mexico Results First model is a cost-benefit analysis approach that provides estimated monetary benefits, costs, return on investment, and measures of risk of investment based on the application of meta-analyses of national studies and thousands of New Mexico specific data points.

WHEREAS, the New Mexico Legislative Finance Committee (LFC), with technical assistance from the Pew-MacArthur Results First Initiative, has developed the New Mexico Results First model;

WHEREAS, the LFC requests information on program costs, agency operational costs, program participation, resource use information, recidivism data, victimization data and other relevant data points in order to populate the New Mexico Results First model;

WHEREAS, agencies using the New Mexico Results First model would benefit from annual updates in data used to populate the model;

WHEREAS, the New Mexico Corrections Department (NMCD) and the New Mexico Sentencing Commission (NMSC) could find results of the New Mexico Results First model informative in programming decisions and in conducting research;

WHEREAS, the purpose of this Memorandum is to establish roles and responsibilities in regards to housing, use and updating of the New Mexico Results First model;

NOW, THEREFORE, IT IS AGREED as follows:

I. TERM OF MEMORANDUM

This Memorandum shall take effect upon signature by the authorized representatives of NMCD, NMSC, and LFC, and shall remain in effect unless terminated by NMCD, NMSC, or LFC, upon fourteen days written notice pursuant to Paragraph VI herein.

II.　DEFINITIONS AND ABBREVIATIONS

a)　Consensus process refers to meetings to occur quarterly with representatives from the three agencies for the purposes of agreeing on the data to be used in the criminal justice portion of the New Mexico Results First model with the intent that all agencies use the same version of the model for analyses.

III.　REQUIRED TASKS UNDER THE MEMORANDUM

a)　**Joint Responsibilities**

1. NMCD, NMSC, and LFC shall identify at least one authorized representative from their respective agencies who shall be the point of contact for New Mexico Results First related activities among identified agencies, and shall be responsible for participating in consensus processes.

2. NMCD, NMSC, and LFC shall populate the model with the same data and only update or change data within the criminal justice sections of the New Mexico Results First model through a consensus process to be established by representatives from each agency.

b)　**Responsibilities of NMCD**

1. NMCD shall share the information detailed in Exhibit A with LFC through NMSC, for purposes of population of the New Mexico Results First model on an annual basis with a target date of December 31 each year for the previous fiscal year ending July 31.

2. The NMCD agrees to develop and share with LFC and NMSC a comprehensive list of programs offered to adults involved in the NMCD criminal justice system including program costs and participation rates by December 31 each year for the previous fiscal year ending July 31.

3. NMCD agrees to participate in a consensus process to determine data used in the criminal justice sections of the New Mexico Results First model.

c)　**Responsibilities of NMSC**

1. NMSC agrees to assist with and coordinate data collection from the NMCD, the Administrative Offices of the Courts (AOC), the Children, Youth, and Families Department (CYFD), Department of Public Safety (DPS) and other agencies to provide data for the New Mexico Results First Model.

2. NMSC agrees to assist the LFC and the NMCD with data analysis for the purposes of the New Mexico Results First Model.

3. NMSC agrees to participate in a consensus process to determine data used in

the criminal justice sections of the New Mexico Results First model.

d) Responsibilities of LFC

1. LFC agrees to share a current copy of the populated criminal justice sections of the New Mexico Results First model with NMCD and NMSC and provide background for the data currently in the model.

2. LFC agrees to participate in a consensus process to determine data used in the criminal justice sections of the New Mexico Results First model.

3. LFC agrees to share results of LFC New Mexico Results First dedicated criminal justice reports with NMCD and NMSC 7 days prior to publication for the purposes of receiving comments and suggested edits.

IV.   ADDITIONAL RESOURCES REGARDING RESPONSIBILITIES

The Pew-MacArthur Results First Initiative provides the following resources at no cost to the State of New Mexico.

1. The cost-benefit analysis model software and periodic updates that incorporate new research and enhancements identified through their work in participating states/counties.

2. Orientations and educational briefings for state policymakers and staff to explain their approach to cost-benefit analysis and how the model can help inform policy and budget deliberations.

3. Ongoing technical assistance including periodic site visits by staff and technical assistance contractors as well as regular communication via virtual meetings, conference calls, and email.

4. Community of practice of states participating in the Pew-MacArthur Results First Initiative; this includes an annual convening and ongoing opportunities for communicating with other states through conference calls, webinars, and a robust information sharing platform.

V.   SCOPE OF MEMORANDUM

This Memorandum incorporates all the understandings between NMCD, NMSC, and LFC concerning the subject matter hereof.   No prior Memorandum, verbal representations, or understandings shall be valid or enforceable unless embodied in this Memorandum.

VI.   TERMINATION OF MEMORANDUM

This Memorandum may be terminated by the NMCD, NMSC, or LFC, upon written notice delivered to the other not less than fourteen (14) days prior to the intended termination date. By such termination notice, none of the agencies shall negate obligations already incurred or required to be performed prior to the effective date of termination.

IN WITNESS WHEREOF, the parties have caused this Memorandum to be executed on the year and date indicated, with the effective date being the most recent signature.

NEW MEXICO CORRECTIONS DEPARTMENT

By   Date:

Secretary, New Mexico Corrections Department

NEW MEXICO SENTENCING COMMISSION

By   Date:

Director, New Mexico Sentencing Commission

NEW MEXICO LEGISLATIVE FINANCE COMMITTEE

By   Date:

Deputy Director, Legislative Finance Committee

EXHIBIT A: LIST OF ITEMS TO BE UPDATED ANNUALLY

A. Marginal operating costs (per unit costs) of adult state prison, probation, parole, and community corrections.

B. Probability of resource use (prison, probation, parole) likelihood by crime type as designated in the New Mexico Results First Model.

C. Number of years of use or length of stay per resource (prison, probation, parole) by crime type as designated in the New Mexico Results First Model.

D. Change in the length of stay (in years) for each subsequent sentence.

E. Cohort data for supervision and prison for the 6 year cohort previously provided. If possible include recidivism risk data (e.g. COMPAS score), convictions, and length of stay for each offender.

F. Prison and supervision program information including number of participants, graduates, cost per participant, average age of participant, length of program, any performance data available (e.g. recidivism rates for participants and graduates).

Appendix J
Additional Tools and Toolkits for Partnerships

The following is a list of additional tools available online that support the work of the types of partnerships described in this book. We do not endorse any specific tools, but feel these and others like them are worthwhile to consult when engaging in partnership work.

Partners	Information	Link[1]
City of Los Angeles, UCLA, Los Angeles Regional Collaborative for Climate Action and Sustainability (LARC)	**Engage and build partnerships with local universities** Through a case study on a climate change projections partnership, this kit provides steps and materials for building an effective partnership that should apply to any collaboration between a local entity and university researchers.	http://www.arccacalifornia.org/toolkit/element9/
Universities and local child welfare agencies	**Fostering Accountability: Using Evidence to Guide and Improve Child Welfare Policy** Chapter 11 in this book highlights the history of child welfare–researcher partnerships and the importance of cultivating and sustaining them.	http://www.oxfordscholarship.com/view/10.1093/acprof:oso/9780195321302.001.0001/acprof-9780195321302-chapter-11

Partners	Information	Link[1]
National Legal Aid & Defender Association (NLADA) and North Carolina Office of Indigent Defense Services (NCIDS)	**Toolkit Building In-House Research Capacity** This toolkit offers insights and recommendations for agencies interested in building internal research and measurement capacity. It is discussed in a legal aid framework, but many points apply to other agency types.	http://www.nlada100years. org/sites/default/files/ NLADA%20Toolkit%20-% 20Research%20Capacity.pdf
The Center for Construction Research and Training, National Institute for Occupational Safety and Health	**Construction Research to Practice [r2p] Partnership Toolkit** This toolkit describes multiple aspects of building and sustaining effective partnerships in the health, construction and occupational safety sectors. Lessons and recommendations should apply to other fields as well.	http://www.cpwr.com/sites/ default/files/Complete%20 r2p%20Partnership%20 Toolkit%202–10–15.pdf
Research and Policy in Development program, researchers, think tanks, policymakers	**Tools for Policy Impact: A Handbook for Researchers** This toolkit offers suggestions for communicating effectively about research with policymakers and other elected leaders. Although written for think tanks, lobbyists and civil society organizations, many lessons should apply to researcher–policymaker partnerships as well.	http://www.odi.org/sites/ odi.org.uk/files/odi-assets/ publications-opinion-files/ 194.pdf

(Continued)

Partners	Information	Link[1]
Any sectors partnering across sectors	**National Implementation Research Network's "Organization Drivers" tool** This tool has been built to support implementation of new initiatives in education settings. The information can also be useful for researcher–policymaker partnerships.	http://implementation.fpg. unc.edu/sites/implementation. fpg.unc.edu/files/NIRN-Imple mentationDriversAssessingBest Practices.pdf

Note

1 Please note that some web links may change over time. Readers are encouraged to search specific project names and affiliations if web links are broken.

Index

Note: Page numbers in *italics* denote references to Figures and Tables.

For Product Safety Concerns and Information please contact our EU
representative GPSR@taylorandfrancis.com
Taylor & Francis Verlag GmbH, Kaufingerstraße 24, 80331 München, Germany

www.ingramcontent.com/pod-product-compliance
Lightning Source LLC
Chambersburg PA
CBHW070601270326
41926CB00013B/2381